THUNDER
AT TWILIGHT

PREVIOUS BOOKS BY FREDERIC MORTON

FICTION

The Hound
The Darkness Below
Asphalt and Desire
The Witching Ship
The Schatten Affair
Snow Gods
An Unknown Woman
The Forever Street

NONFICTION

The Rothschilds
A Nervous Splendor: Vienna 1888/1889
Crosstown Sabbath: A Street Journey Through History

DA CAPO PRESS
A Member of the Perseus Books Group

The James Joyce quote in the epigraph is from *James Joyce* by Herbert Gorman (New York: Rinehart & Co., 1938).

Cataloging-in-Publication data for this book is available from the Library of Congress.

First Da Capo Press edition 2001
Reprinted by arrangement with the author.

ISBN 0–306–81021–2

Published by Da Capo Press
A Member of the Perseus Books Group
http://www.dacapopress.com

10 9 8 7 6 5 4 3

TO M. C. M.

TO MY TWO DEAREST VIENNESE:
MY PARENTS,
FRANK AND ROSE MORTON

AND TO ELISABETH AND LESTER COLEMAN,
FOR SO MUCH

CONTENTS

PREFACE

In July 1916, Fritz Mandelbaum, a junior officer in Austria's Seventh Army on the Russian front, near the river Dnjestr, was shot in the abdomen and died shortly thereafter. Twenty-four years later the name suffered erasure again. This time it was borne by a refugee boy arriving in New York in 1940. His father changed the family's name. Fritz Mandelbaum became Frederic Morton.

In a way this book is a memorial to the first Fritz Mandelbaum—my uncle—and to the more than ten million who died with him in the Great War. But since much of this book is set in Vienna, it is also an exploration of history backstage. The baroque died in Vienna with flamboyant afterquivers while at the same time some peculiar force here generated energies that would shake the new century. Here were streets uniquely charged with both nostalgia and prophecy. Three of my recent books have tried to penetrate the phenomenon.

My novel *The Forever Street* centered on a family of Jewish manufacturers in Austria, from fin de siècle to Anschluss; it is based on the real-life Mandelbaum factory whose machines stamped out Habsburg military decorations, then political badges for the successor republic; then, suddenly and just as smoothly, Wehrmacht medals after the Nazis took it over in 1938.

My nonfiction work *A Nervous Splendor: Vienna 1888/1889* is an account of the months before and after the suicide of Crown Prince Rudolf. The story ends on the Saturday of the Easter weekend of 1889, when Rudolf's sarcophagus was consecrated at the hour of Adolf Hitler's birth.

The present book deals with the events, ideas, unpredictabilities and inevitabilities surrounding the death of the next Crown Prince, Archduke Franz Ferdinand. The bullet that tore into his jugular sounded the initial shot in the most devastating slaughter mankind had known so far. It set off the dynamics leading to World War II. In other words, it galvanized a Zeitgeist whose consequences live today in the international news, on the street corner, in encounter sessions, on the canvases of Soho galleries. Many of the threads of the scene all around us were first spun along the Danube in the year and a half preceding the thrust of that pistol at the Archduke's head.

Imperial Austria has become a byword for melodious decay. It also stoked—crucially—the ferment that is the idiom of modernity. Why did that happen just then and just there? And how? In what twists of the labyrinth did the world of the first Fritz Mandelbaum fragment into the world of the second? Is there a pattern to the maze? The pages that follow attempt an answer.

—F.M.

I cannot begin to tell you the flavor of the Austro-Hungarian Empire. It was a ramshackle affair but it was charming, gay and I experienced more kindness [here]. . . . than ever before or since in my life. Times past can't return, but I wish they were back.

—James Joyce, to a friend

And when we were children, staying at the arch-duke's,
My cousin's, he took me out on a sled,
And I was frightened. He said, Marie,
Marie, hold on tight. And down we went.

—T. S. Eliot,
The Waste Land

THUNDER AT TWILIGHT

1

ON THE EVENING OF JANUARY 13, 1913, VIENNA'S BANK EMPLOYEES' Club gave a Bankruptcy Ball. It was the height of pre-Lenten carnival—in mid-winter at its meanest. Ice floes shivered down the Danube, galas sparkled inside baroque portals, and the bankruptcy gambol really warmed the Viennese imagination.

A number of ladies appeared as balance sheets, displaying voluptuous debits curving from slender credits. Others came as collateral. Their assets, ready to be garnisheed, were accented sometimes with a décolletage, sometimes with a bustle. Thin men were costumed as deposits, fat men as withdrawals. Sooner or later everybody ended up at Debtors' Prison—the restaurant of the Blumensaal where the festivity was held. Here mortgage certificates served as doilies for Sachertortes. Ornamented with the bailiff's seal, eviction notices made colorful centerpieces; each was topped by a bowl of whipped cream. If you wrote your waiter an I.O.U., he would pour you a goblet of champagne.

The merriment increased steadily until 5 A.M. when the orchestra leader stopped his men, suddenly, in the middle of the Emperor Waltz. To great laughter he announced that since the musicians still hadn't been paid, there would be no more music.

The next day parliament voted on the flotation of a bond issue; its proceeds would subsidize the installation of plumbing into apartments that had none. In working class districts like Hernals and Favoriten most families must use outside toilets and corridor sinks. The bill was killed. Such news would anger the toiling poor when they read about it later. It did not affect their carnival routine. Many trudged to work with their ball clothes in a paper bag. Changing at home would have meant an extra streetcar ride beyond their means. Therefore they went directly from wee-hours waltz to morning shift. Before the lunch bell sounded, soot had grayed the confetti in their hair.

That week glacial winds punished the streets. But—rare for Vienna in the winter—the sun shone. In the center of town the Ringstrasse, a palatial wreath of a boulevard, glowed like a mirage. The snow capping its hundreds of rooftop statues looked more marmoreal than the imitation marble of the figures. During carnival everything Viennese seemed to revel in being what it was not.

On the night of January 18, for example, Prince Auersperg

gave a "Bucolic Lark" at his *palais*. The Duke of Teck made an entrance in the homespun of a shepherd. Prince zu Windischgrätz honed his sickle with a weariness as peasant-y as his leather-shorts. Princess Festetics and Countess Potocka, milkmaids, in dirndls authentic down to the grease stains on their bodices, swung pails.

The greengrocer Mataschek, on the other hand, threw a Fancy House Ball in his basement store. Turnips and potatoes had been cleared away to make a dance floor. Produce crates impersonated tables and chairs. For the price of a beer, Mataschek's uncle, though blind at eight-two, had agreed to scrape some three-quarter time out of a violin borrowed from the pawn shop around the corner. He struck up the first bars of the *Fledermaus* overture when—behold!—Alois, the cobbler's apprentice, sauntered over to Nandl, the chambermaid. A blue-blooded lieutenant of the hussars could not have improved his bow. She curtsied almost as impeccably. Together they swept into the waltz.

In the Vienna of January 1913, illusion and reality embraced elegantly, seamlessly. The smoothness of their mingling affected even the publisher of *The Truth*. He was a firebrand from Russia, in charge of a Vienna-based monthly that became a fortnightly whenever he could scrounge enough funds. He called his paper *Pravda*—that is, *The Truth* as seen by his cause, the revolution. Vienna was not an ideal place of exile, as he would write later in his autobiography: He would have preferred Berlin, but the police were more lethargic by the Danube.

Still, under that January's arctic sun, he entered wholeheartedly into the Viennese spirit of intimate contradiction.

With his wife and his two blond boys he began the day by freezing in style. During winter the family occupied a villa in the fashionable suburb of Huetteldorf—at a very low rent. It was not winterized. When it became too cold, he left the house to warm up the Viennese way, in a coffeehouse. On the street, this professional insurgent, nemesis of the upper classes, showed a touch of the lordly flaneur. His clothes were simple but well cut; his black hair handsomely combed. Even the pince-nez on his nose managed a certain dash. Under his arm he carried the latest French novel. He read it on the tram ride to the center of town.

A ceremonious welcome awaited him at the Café Central. "Oh, a very good morning, Herr Doktor Trotsky," the head-waiter said. "My compliments. Compliments also from Herr Doktor Adler who much regrets he will not be available for chess today as he has a psychoanalytic emergency. A mocha as usual? And the London *Times*? The Berlin *Vorwärts*?"

Dr. Trotsky nodded. He sipped his steaming mocha. His scrutiny of newspapers in various languages produced political jottings in his notebook. But he also played litterateur among the literati; argued rather charmingly with a neighbor about Stefan Zweig's feuilleton in the *Neue Freie Presse;* exchanged repartee here, kissed a hand there—in short, practiced the Viennese brand of courtliness, that is, the art of maintaining an entirely pleasant mask over a psyche of usually mixed emotions.

It was a courtliness he would preach nine years later from the Kremlin as co-ruler with Lenin over the Soviet Union. "Civility and politeness," his booklet *Problems of Life* would instruct the proletariat, "Civility and politeness and cultured speech are a necessary lubricant in daily relationships." In 1913 he was just a hand-to-mouth expatriate, but he lived in a city lavish with civilities (if short on a few other things), and he was a quick study. He read his French novel during the ride home, where he proceeded to edit a *Pravda* article (on the new strikes in Moscow) in his unheated mansion, freezing in style.

A rather different Russian revolutionary arrived in Vienna during that glacial January week. He was thirty-four, exactly the same age as Trotsky, and when he stepped out of the train from Cracow at the North Terminal, not even the most Viennese of headwaiters would have been tempted to call him "Herr Doktor Stalin."

In fact, the name "Stalin" had barely begun to exist. Only that week it had made its debut as a brand-new pseudonym in *The Social Democrat,* a legal Socialist periodical published in Russia. In its pages K. Stalin* attacked the editor of the Vienna *Pravda* as "Trotsky, a noisy champion with fake muscles, a man of beautiful uselessness . . ."

And indeed K. Stalin was not good at noising clever words or beautiful phrases like Trotsky. Felicity of attire, elegance of limb did not distinguish him. In Cracow (then capital of the Austrian province of Galicia) he had just spent some weeks with Vladimir Lenin, chief of Russian Socialists abroad. Lenin had tutored him in the politics of exile; but he had also tried to teach him biking. The result was a bruised knee. And now, as K. Stalin walked from the North Terminal toward his first Viennese tram ride, he still limped a bit in his peasant boots. The sleeve of his coarse overcoat hung over his somewhat withered left hand. In his good right hand he carried a wooden box with a handle—a peasant suitcase. A thick peasant mus-

* "K." stood for "Koba," Stalin's nickname among comrades.

tache covered much of his face, but not enough to hide the pockmarks.

Of the five weeks he lived in Vienna (much more time than he would ever spend in any other city outside Russia), K. Stalin did not waste one hour in any of the town's intellectual coffeehouses. Yet he might have been a sensation at the Café Central because he would have beaten both Dr. Trotsky and Dr. Adler at chess. In Cracow he had trounced Lenin seven times in a row, and Lenin had not been a bit surprised. It was probably one of the reasons why he had dispatched "our wonderful Georgian" to the Austrian capital.

The fact was that carnival-minded Vienna and this limping yokel shared a trait: a talent for disguise, for the cunning feint. Stalin's real name was Joseph Dzhugashvili. His passport read Stavros Papadopoulos. He had learned to give his Georgian gutturals a vaguely Greek cast. The tram he boarded by the North Terminal did not take him to any slum in which one might expect a Socialist to go undercover. No, K. Stalin rode toward the aristocratic district of Hietzing. He got off at Schönbrunner Schlossstrasse and walked toward No. 20. One of the most important missions of his prerevolutionary career began as he, his crude boots, and his wooden suitcase disappeared into a façade splendid with stucco garlands.

Just a few hundred yards away from Stalin's hide-out in the Schönbrunner Schlossstrasse loomed Schloss Schönbrunn, the vast Habsburg summer palace whose seclusion the Emperor Franz Joseph had begun to favor even in winter, now that he was eighty-three. Here a meeting took place the week of Stalin's arrival that also fit the carnival season. It was a sort of masquerade. But it was a masquerade that had gone on for years. The very opposite of merry make-believe, it involved the bitter summit level of political reality.

Its protagonist sat in a motorcar, as huge as it was hurried, which barely slowed for the opening of the palace gates. Abruptly, it crunched to a halt. Peremptorily, the Archduke Franz Ferdinand, Crown Prince of the realm, debarked. He scowled past the salutes of guards. To the clinking of the sabers of his entourage, to the blunt drumming of boots against parquet, he marched toward the emperor's study. His eyes were pale blue and glared. His black mustache was the fiercest south of Kaiser Wilhelm. His bruiser's shoulders, his wrestler's chest swelled the uniform of a general of the Imperial and Royal Army.

When he met Franz Joseph, the archduke's face glowered forward and swooped down as if to bite his sovereign's hand. Of course he only kissed it. But he kissed it unsmiling. Then he stood at grim attention, waiting for the Emperor's invitation to sit. It came. He sat. Instantly he hammered away at the Serbian Question.

A prickly matter; for Serbia, the feisty little kingdom, had become a thorn in the Empire's southeastern flank. Serbia was challenging Austria's predominance east of the Adriatic. Serbia subverted fellow-Slavs in the adjacent Habsburg province of Bosnia-Hercegovina; Serb-inspired radicals there smeared walls with slogans, threw stink bombs, plotted the assassination of Austrian governors. Most disturbing, only last year Serbia had destabilized the whole area in the Balkan War of 1912. With Bulgaria and Greece it had fought Turkey for the Sultan's European possessions. After victory, Serbia claimed much of Albania, hitherto under Ottoman rule but presently a strategic prize the Serbs could use against Habsburg. No wonder Serbia vexed Vienna even during Mardi Gras. Between toasts and tangos the question kept coming up: How severely must Serbia be disciplined? Or should it be utterly destroyed?

Serbia, then, was the inevitable subject of the All-Highest meeting at Schloss Schönbrunn. ("All-Highest" was Habsburg parlance for the Emperor.) The Crown Prince fulminated. But all the trappings of a fierceling—the booming basso, the vehement gestures, the trembling of medals on his chest—were deceptive. They disguised a fact to which very few were privy. The Crown Prince was a dove. A dove all the more ferocious because there was hardly any other in the Empire's highest council.

He utterly condemned, he said now, the thought behind the Chief of Staff's memorandum to the Emperor, the one dated January 20, a copy of which had just reached his chancellery. He loathed the lunacy of a preventive war against the Serbs. He detested all those trigger-happy fools who didn't realize that such rashness must provoke Russia as Serbia's great Slav protector. He couldn't emphasize too strongly to His Majesty that war between Russia and Austria would be a catastrophe for Habsburg and Romanov alike. Therefore, in view of recent tensions he must urge His Majesty to send a special emissary to St. Petersburg with a personal note for the Tsar stating Austria's peaceful intentions. Furthermore . . .

His Majesty listened. Franz Joseph had been on the throne for sixty-five years, but he still sat ramrod straight. His white sideburns, long become emblems of his empire, were just slightly turned away from all those "furthermore's." Not that he necessarily disagreed with them. But the man who thumped them out was so disagreeable. Franz Joseph followed the dictum of his forebear Franz I: A just ruler distributes discontent evenly. And this spouting nephew of his would never achieve any kind of evenness. Franz Ferdinand had a bully's temperament, and Franz

Joseph did not like being subjected to it for one second longer than protocol demanded.

He rose. So did his nephew. With his low, supreme voice the Emperor said: "I'll have it thought about." Silence. Franz Ferdinand's mustache quivered as the Archduke swooped down for the hand kiss. His heels thundered away, down the parquet. Behind him, the sabers of his retinue clinked. To fight frostbite, the guards outside presented arms with extra energy. The liveried chauffeur cranked the motor of the mountainous Gräf & Stift. The automobile roared through the palace gates, and His Imperial and Royal Highness, the heir apparent, was gone.

Most Viennese who saw the swerve of that automobile guessed who was riding in it. The darkness of the man's mood expressed itself in the brute speed of his driver. Onlookers shook their heads. The older ones remembered the Crown Prince before this one, the Archduke Rudolf. He, too, had been notorious for his rush, though his vehicle had been the two-horse fiacre. And where had these horses gotten him, too fast? To the hunting lodge in Mayerling where he had put a bullet through his temple. Now there was this newfangled motor-borne Prince with his booming golden-spiked chariot. What impatience, what sullenness powered *his* thrust? Toward what end was he receding?

Let others worry. Josip Broz did not. If, on his holidays in Vienna, he watched Franz Ferdinand sweep past, he was not one to frown at the Habsburg prince. The archducal car was much too enthralling. A twenty-year-old mechanic, Broz came from Croatia, another Slav province the Serbs were subverting against Austria. In his mind, though, automobiles outranked ideologies. He worked at the Daimler auto plant at Wiener Neustadt, very close to the capital. There, as he was to confess later, he got his first "whiff of glamor . . . from the big powerful cars with their heavy brasswork, rubber-bulb horns and outside handbrakes." The best thing about his job was the thrill of test-driving exciting new models. Decades later he would glide in even longer limousines, his chest aglitter with more medals than an archduke's. But in 1913 Josip Broz was not yet Marshal Tito. He didn't see the world as primarily a political arena. For him Vienna was a seductive metropolis where he spent much of his wages on dancing and fencing lessons and on any pretty girl whose eye he might catch from an adjoining café table. Many of his best young weekends were Viennese. Saturday night and all day Sunday he was a playboy by the Danube.

The Emperor received the Crown Prince on January 24, a Friday. Just on that Friday, Broz might have been in town. He had an excellent reason for coming to Vienna a day early, as soon as the factory let out, even if he had to take the milktrain back to Wiener Neustadt for the Saturday morning shift. He and other young bucks of his particular craft had a motive for taking some extra trouble: On the night of Friday, January 24, the Sophiensaal in Vienna gave an Automobile Mechanics Ball.

In Vienna almost every walk of life generated its own carnival festivity. Even the Insane Asylum at Steinhof held a Lunatics' Gala. But there was no fête for psychiatrists. Sigmund Freud, fifty-seven years old and becoming globally controversial as arch-analyst and founder of the psychoanalytic faith, stooped alone over his desk at Berggasse 19. He was filling page after page of a big lined notebook. Outside the windows of his study, the city was transmogrified into a masked ball. Inside, the master explored the origins of the mask—the primeval mask, the totem. In January 1913 he was finishing an essay called *Totem and Taboo.* It turned out to be a subject eerie not only in theme but in timing. For all carnival celebrations crest toward Lent; they all say "carne vale"—good-bye to the flesh—as penance for the death of the Lord. Freud's essay deduced from the anthropology of primitive man that the totem was an animal symbol of greatness slain, of the father-leader killed by his sons and followers. After his murder they donned a mask representing the sacred corpse. As their victim's worshippers, they banded together under his symbol in order to bear their guilt better in unison. They ate his flesh or assumed his face to partake of his power, to obtain his forgiveness.

Here was not only the dynamic of primeval myth. Here was the drama of the Eucharist and the plot of Easter, explored by a pen in the Berggasse, scratching on into the night. The ambivalence of carnival/Lent—so opulently celebrated in Vienna—pulsed around the once and future murder of the prince.

The brooder in the Berggasse was not the only man to stay aloof from the city's revels while being inwardly attuned to its darker currents. About nine tramway stops northeast of Freud's study, a twenty-three-year-old artist subsisted at Meldemannstrasse 25. This was the address of the Männerheim, in a desolate corner of the district of Brigittenau.

The municipal government had established this barrack to keep failures from becoming beggars. The Männerheim—"Home for Men"—gave shelter to the black-sheep baron who had drunk away his last remittance, the evicted peddler, the bit-actor too long between engagements, the free-lancer down on his luck, the day laborer always missing out on a steady job, the confused farm boy from the Alps, the flotsam from the Empire's Balkan fringes. They were men without anchor, without family, without sustaining women. All of them were lost in the merciless glitter of the metropolis. For three kronen* a week the Männerheim gave them a last chance. That small sum provided a clean cubicle with a bed, a communal kitchen, a library with penny dreadfuls, a writing room for composing letters of application unlikely to be answered.

Six years earlier, in 1907, the young artist had arrived in Vienna to hunt, like thousands of other ambitious provincials, for the greatness that must be waiting for him somewhere in the great city. Since 1910 he had done his vain striving at the Männerheim. Twice he had tried to pass the entrance examination at the Academy of Fine Arts. Twice he had been rejected. He had carried to every important architect's office in town his portfolio of architectural drawings; not even the lowliest assistant's job had been offered to him as a result. His watercolors—unusually conventional renderings of Biedermeier scenes—failed to draw the interest of any gallery. He painted watercolors of famous Vienna sights such as Parliament or City Hall. These, when hawked on street corners by a friend, did yield some occasional cash.

Actually he did not need to earn a penny. By 1913 his mother and his aunt had left him two fair-size legacies. He kept both

* A two-room apartment in a lower middle-class neighborhood rented for about 40 kronen a month. Each krone had 100 heller.

secret. Nobody in the Männerheim suspected him of an income that could have easily paid for quarters at a comfortable hotel.

But he felt more at ease with fellow losers. Here, among his Männerheim peers, he enjoyed a special niche. He quite literally occupied it. At the end of a long oaken table near the window of the Writing Room was "the Hitler Chair." It had the best light for painting postcards. Nobody but Adolf dared sit there. Everybody honored his obsession with the chair, partly out of gratitude: If a Männerheim tenant fell short of his week's rent, Hitler was amazingly fast in organizing a collection. Respect also played a role in obeying the man's wish: He was one of the very few in the house never to splurge or debauch. When the Court Opera played *Siegfried* he would indulge himself in a standing-room ticket. Once a week he might drop into a pastry shop for a chocolate square. But he always practiced sobriety.

And he was a worker. He would daub away with his brush even on carnival nights such as those in 1913 when the gas light outside gleamed on domino masks and décolletages. It didn't seem to bother him that he was excluded from a season so festive for the more fortunate.

Most of the others in the Männerheim were restless. Even the cheapest ball glittered at them from an impossible distance. They could only afford to drop by a local pub, hoist a lager, ogle prostitutes, leer about sending them to a Serbian bordello. They'd return home for the 11 P.M. curfew, not ready to be shut into their cubicles. So they lingered in the Writing Room to jaw about politics or to reminisce about hot women. And then, without warning or preamble, it would happen.

Hitler would straighten up in his chair. He had been working all along, hunched over. Now the brush would drop from his hand. He would push the palette aside. He would rise to his feet.

He began to speak, to shout, to orate. With hissing consonants and hall-filling vowels he launched into a harangue on morality, racial purity, the German mission and Slav treachery, on Jews, Jesuits, and Freemasons. His forelock would toss, his color-stained hands shred the air, his voice rise to an operatic pitch. Then, just as suddenly as he had started, he would stop. He would gather his things together with an imperious clatter, stalk off to his cubicle.

And the others would just stare after him. They had come to accept his fits along with his "chair." He was, after all, a good man otherwise. And he did give his Männerheim audience a good show, producing so dramatically the gesticulations of a clown and the screeching of a demon. In January 1913, it was the Männerheim's way of experiencing the Vienna carnival.

2

CHRONOLOGICALLY THE CARNIVAL OF 1913 CONFORMED WITH OTHER YEARS. It began shortly after New Year to end on Shrove Tuesday. This was the Merry Season as defined by the calendar. But carnival in the sense of opulent, ingenious, finely organized Viennese make-believe knew no such limit. In this city it had flourished continuously for over half a millennium.

Here the fairy tale of Habsburg splendor, with orb, scepter, and throne, with pomp of blazons and gonfalons, with the choreography of homage and precedence, of raised trumpets, white stallions, and bowed heads . . . here it had been enacted and re-enacted every day through endless generations.

The solemn, perpetual ball that was the Imperial court encompassed the entire town. London was other things besides the King's residence. Even in Bourbon days, Paris had been much more than a royal encampment. But Vienna meant Habsburg. Habsburg meant Vienna. Vienna and Habsburg kept inventing each other into a crowned, turreted, sunset-hued fable that floated above ordinary earth. Compared to other urban centers in Europe, Vienna had little commerce, less industry, and hardly any of the workaday grayness of common sense. Fact-ridden pursuits could not leave much of an imprint on a city busy with the embroidery of Christendom's foremost escutcheon. Factory and counting house were dwarfed by the magnificent shadow of the Palace. Century after century the Viennese devoted themselves to the housing and feeding and staging of their suzerains' legend.

Of course that legend needed a legal character through which the Habsburgs could exercise their dominion. From the fifteenth to the nineteenth century they were Holy Roman Emperors. They wore that dignity like a preternatural carnival mask—a mask whose illusion was obvious to all yet whose charisma no one could escape. This peculiarity has been a commonplace among historians: the Holy Roman Empire was hardly Roman. It was not holy (being a cauldron of profane ambitions). It was not an empire (being a mess of brawling princes beyond the emperor's control). The Habsburgs practical power issued from the patchwork of their own huge possessions. As executive instrument, the title of Holy Roman Emperor was vapor. As mask of Christ's paladin it wielded incalculable force.

Napoleon appreciated its resonance. In 1806 he forced the House of Austria to abandon it. Habsburg put the Viennese imagination to work. Other constitutional fictions were devised. By 1913 the latest of these had been in force for nearly fifty years. It was called the Empire of Austria-Hungary, and it was decked out in a legal framework as fanciful as any of its predecessors.

This creation combined quite marvelously the heraldic with the schizoid. Here was a monarchy ruled by one monarch whose subjects passed an official border as they traveled from Hungary, where Franz Joseph was King, to Austria, where his title became Emperor. The realm had two Prime Ministers who were really less premiers than governors of their respective imperial or royal sub-realms. On the other rather dizzying hand, there was only one Foreign Minister; in a number of ways his power and prestige exceeded that of the Prime Ministers because he formed the chief link between the monarch and the twin cabinets. A further incongruity distinguished him above all other panjandrums. In addition to the conduct of Exterior Affairs he was also charged with "participating in family celebrations of His Majesty's household," as if these duties were complementary.

Constitutional wonders did not end there. The two premiers shared between them one common Minister of Finance and one common Minister of War who commanded the common armed forces. The two men headed these departments as Imperial Excellencies in Vienna, as Royal Excellencies in Budapest. To endow Hungary with the dignity of being a separate country, all other, less essential, ministries were separately headed and staffed; so were the judiciaries and the civil services on both sides of the Austro-Hungarian hyphen.

As for the legislatures, their doubleness came with an extra dollop of paradox. In Budapest, the Parliament of the Kingdom of Hungary convened. But in Vienna there was no such thing as an Austrian Parliament. Officially speaking, there was no such thing as "Austria." Yes, Habsburg was known as the House of Austria. Yes, the world knew Franz Joseph as the Austrian Emperor. Yet nowhere in the constitution of his empire did an entity named "Austria" appear. "Austria" seemed to be a grandiose ghost whose radiance must not be bounded by definition. The non-Hungarian portion of the Austro-Hungarian Empire was not called Austria. The constitution referred to it obliquely and indirectly as "the lands and provinces represented in the Imperial Council."

The Imperial Council was the Parliament sitting in Vienna. And the Parliament in Vienna was at least in part another feat of illusion. It was not very parliamentary. Electoral districting and balloting procedures gave Austria's German-speaking citizens proportionally more representation than Slav voters. What's more, one stroke of the Imperial pen could dissolve the Imperial Council at any time. Until the next elections (whose date the Emperor determined), the Emperor could rule and legislate by decree. Usually he refrained. The option always loomed. The Vienna parliament was a masterpiece of that famous Austrian speciality, latent absolutism.

In physical terms, too, it was an interesting deception. On a Ringstrasse rampant with architectural heroics, Parliament looked like a temple of calm. Its granite ramps, huge but gently angled, led up to the serenity of a colonnade. It was guarded by the monumental poise of a statue of Pallas Athene. The façade breathed neoclassic serenity.

Inside seethed a witches' sabbath of nationalisms. Here the ethnic groups of the Empire's non-Hungarian part went at each other through their representatives. Six million Czechs attacked ten million Germans for under-financing Czech schools in Bohemia and Moravia. Five million Galician Poles banged desks to demand greater administrative independence. Three and a half million Ukrainians stamped feet for a Russian-language university to counteract the Poles' cultural domination. Deputies from the South Slav area contributed to the multinational brawl. Through their representatives' throats, over a million Slovenes and three-quarters of a million Serbo-Croats shouted their grievances. German-speaking deputies split bitterly into Socialist and Conservative movements, the latter divided still further into the anti-Semitic Christian Socialist and pan-German parties. Such schisms inspired similar front lines within other ethnic factions. Occasionally all groups joined to excoriate Hungarian politics as practiced by the sister parliament in Budapest.

It was less a legislature than a cacophony. But since it was a Viennese cacophony it shrilled and jangled with a certain flair. Polemics were delivered through clenched teeth. Yet the vitriol came with whipped-cream rhetoric: *"If Your Ministerial Excellency would finally condescend to reason!"* Friction ran red hot without becoming altogether raw. Instead of exploding the Empire, nationalist fury spent itself in theater. Representatives bristled so histrionically against each other that often they had little energy left to use against the Emperor's Double Eagle under whose wings they were allowed to stage their confrontation.

Vladimir Lenin, resident in the Austrian province of Galicia, followed parliamentary performances in Vienna through the Cracow papers. The way Habsburg survived the ethnic imbroglio impressed him. In an article he sent to the St. Petersburg *Pravda* he declared that "Austria handles the national problem far better than the Tsar."

As a matter of fact, Lenin admitted that he himself, as the leader of a revolutionary movement composed of different Slavic as well as non-Slavic elements, had things to learn about handling the ethnic problem. "As to nationalism," he wrote Maxim Gorki in February 1913, "I am fully in agreement that it is necessary to pay more serious attention to it. We have here a wonderful Georgian who is writing a long article for *Prosveshchenye,* for which he has gathered all the Austrian and other material."

The "wonderful Georgian"—Stalin—had been entrusted with a task in Vienna that was vital to the Party. To Stalin himself it was a breakthrough opportunity. True, by 1913 he had already become something of a Bolshevist journalist through his contributions to the legally published *Pravda* in St. Petersburg. But his initial and still primary reputation among comrades was quite different. He had made his mark as a rough-and-ready activist, a fomenter of strikes, an organizer of bank robberies on behalf of the party's treasury—in brief, a red buccaneer who did not shrink from gun or bomb. His challenge in Vienna involved much subtler aspects of the cause. Socialism was international and supra-national by its very motto: *"Workers of All Countries, Unite!"* Yet in 1913 Europe's workers were subject to divisive nationalisms. Even the proletariat longed for national identity. How could that need be fulfilled without setting the oppressed of one land against the oppressed of another? This was the question worrying Lenin. During his Austrian mission, Stalin was to answer it by way of an essay in *Prosveshchenye,* the Party's sociological journal.

The Wonderful Georgian had to address a complex issue in a foreign city under unfamiliar circumstances. Especially unfamiliar were Stalin's hosts in Vienna. They didn't resemble the underground comrades he had known in Georgia or the tough pamphleteers of St. Petersburg or the better educated but blunt and hard-eyed pragmatists around Lenin in Cracow. The Troyanovskys who took in Stalin at Schönbrunner Schlossstrasse 20 were *élégants.* Alexander Troyanovsky, a son of a high Tsarist officer, graduate of Voronezh Cadet School, destined to be Soviet Ambassador to Washington, spoke an aristocratic Russian and played a brilliant game of bridge when partnered with his wife Elena, who was a lawyer born of a noble family. "They have money," Lenin said in a letter describing the couple. Of course they also had impeccable party credentials including some years in Siberia, a region not known for its bridge tournaments. At any rate, the Troyanovskys were the most *comme il faut* comrades in Vienna. Quite possibly Lenin sent the Wonderful Georgian to them as to a finishing school. They were to polish this diamond in the rough.

It proved unpolishable. The Troyanovskys failed to civilize their guest. He ignored Vienna's cafés, its suavities, frivolities, balls—even those given by trade unions. With a surly, even pace he kept tramping through the city's gayest month in pursuit of nothing but his mission.

"I was in conversation over tea with a comrade," Trotsky would recall of a very cold day in Vienna, "when suddenly, without knocking at the door, there entered from another room a man of middle height, haggard, with a swarthy grayish face showing marks of smallpox. The stranger, as if surprised by my presence, stopped a moment at the door and gave a guttural grunt which might have been taken for a greeting. Then, with an empty glass in his hand, he went to the samovar, filled his glass with tea, and went out without saying a word."

Not that Stalin meant to be rude to Trotsky specifically. The two men had clashed in print before; within ten years they would begin the world-famous duel destined to split Communism on all continents. But on that January afternoon of 1913, when they first came face to face in Vienna, each did not know who the other one was. Stalin took in that dainty comrade with the French novel under his arm and proceeded to behave—like Stalin.

Frills or manners were not for him. Nor did he bother with pleasantries when talking about his own work. "Greetings, friend," he said early in February 1913 in a letter to a fellow Bolshevik in St. Petersburg, "I am still sitting in Vienna and writing all sorts of rubbish."

"Rubbish" turned out to be a strategic milestone. In Vienna, Stalin was researching and composing a treatise calculated to enrich his party image. His *Marxism and the National Question* examined (for its relevance to Russia) the position of prominent Austrian Socialist thinkers like Karl Renner and Otto Bauer. They favored cultural autonomy for minorities under a federalist charter. But Stalin marshalled evidence to conclude that a Socialist commonwealth must go further—far enough to grant nationalities the right to secession.

This argument had to please Lenin because it suited an imperative he'd often discussed with his disciples: the need to entice more non-Slavic Socialists within the Tsarist empire into the Bolshevist camp, that is, into Lenin's wing of the Party. Stalin's essay thus further increased the wonderfulness of the Georgian (non-Slavic himself) in the eyes of the master.

And the Vienna essay did more. It established Stalin as a theoretician eligible to participate in ideological leadership. Four years later it helped catapult him to the top echelon of the Soviet revolutionary government as Commissar of Nationalities. (In fact, Stalin's Vienna experience had still further, rather ironic, consequences. When he seized supreme power after Lenin's death, he resorted to the "Austrian" solution after all. In other words, he dealt with the nationalities problem by giving them only cultural—not political—independence.)

All in all, Stalin had a great deal of fine-tuning work to do during the Vienna carnival of 1913. He managed impressively, considering his lack of German. Though some comrades helped him with interviews and library sleuthing, he mastered most difficulties himself. At the same time he expedited other chores in the teeth of a pleasure-mad season of a city strange to him. He set up a better coordination system between various international Bolshevist centers, using Vienna as the hub. He devised a mail-forwarding mechanism from Cracow to Vienna and from Vienna to Paris. He located a cheap, serviceable print shop for putting out Party pamphlets and circulars.

And that done, with the first draft of his essay locked into his wooden suitcase, still impervious to the city's charm and the Troyanovskys' chic, he tramped in his boots to Vienna's Northwest Railroad Terminal on February 16th. In a third-class carriage he rolled away from the Vienna carnival, a grim virtuoso wearing the mask of a clod.

3

On the morning of February 11, 1913, Franz Schuhmeier arrived in Vienna at the same station by which Stalin would leave it five days later. Schuhmeier was returning from a brief overnight trip to the suburbs, but before he could walk out into the streets he must submit to a ritual unknown in any other modern capital. At the Northwest Terminal, as at every principal entrance point, Vienna exacted a consumer's tax on goods purchased outside the city—a levy going back to the Middle Ages.

Schuhmeier let a green-capped customs official search his briefcase. He was waved on. A moment later a slight figure in a torn raincoat stepped behind him. *"My revenge!"* said the little man, drew a Browning from his pocket, and fired a bullet through the back of Schuhmeier's skull.

It was no ordinary homicide. Every newspaper roared out the news. Both slayer and slain bore front-page names. Schuhmeier had been a very prominent and vastly popular deputy of the Social Democratic Party. Paul Kunschak, his killer, turned out to be the brother of Leopold Kunschak, one of the most dynamic leaders of the opposing conservative party, the Christian Socialists.

Police interrogation established Paul Kunschak as a mumbling paranoiac convinced that Schuhmeier had been persecuting him personally. He had planned the killing without his brother's knowledge.

The significance of the tragedy lay less in its politics than in its timing. The shot in the Northwest Terminal rang out six days after Ash Wednesday, one week after the end of Fasching, Vienna's carnival. It brought home to a reluctant Vienna that the levity and therapy of Fasching make-believe were over. The Viennese could no longer play-act actuality away. They were stuck with the thing. It stung Paul Kunschak into murder. But it also aggravated many stabler citizens.

Among the victims of the process may have been Arnold Schönberg. Early in February the avant-garde composer had had his first success by the Danube with a performance of his *Gurrelieder* in the Golden Hall of the Musikverein. But that had been during Mardis Gras. A few weeks later, Schönberg found himself facing something of a lynch mob in the same Golden Hall. This time he conducted his *Chamber Symphony* as well as Anton von Webern's Orchestral Pieces Op. 6 and Alban Berg's "Songs with Orchestra after Picture Postcard Texts by Peter Altenberg." Berg and Webern were atonalists—musical heretics. Peter Altenberg wrote novel fragments somehow powered by their very incompletion; he also wore sandals in snow storms. While in its carnival mood, the city tolerated such modernists as piquant harlequins. However, Schönberg's second Musikverein appearance took place in the depths of Lent. In more sober air, Schönberg and Company neither titillated nor amused.

"Nihilism!" the shouts went up. *"Anarchists!"* Catcalls multiplied. The concert stopped, but not the commotion. Program booklets became missiles. Hands became fists. Oscar Straus, the famous composer of the operetta *Waltz Dream,* punched the president of the avant-garde Society for Literature and Music. A physician who had witnessed the imbroglio testified that the effect of the music had been "for a certain segment of the public so nerve-racking and therefore so harmful to the nervous system that many present . . . showed obvious signs of severe neurosis."

During Lent the very sound or sight of otherness had become taxing. Yet Vienna teemed with "other" people. The police blotter of the University Precinct suddenly filled up with incidents of beer steins flung in student *kellers,* usually at "individuals of Hebrew descent" whom the flingers accused of "staring."

Some of the "others" offended by doing even less. On February 28 a Negro with a top hat strolled down the Praterstrasse. He was attacked by a man in a dinner jacket who shouted "Impostor!" before snatching the black's headgear, throwing it to the pavement, stamping on it.

At the subsequent court case, the Negro identified himself as Benson Harrington Adams, a professor of English from Baltimore, Maryland. The dinner jacket, a waiter, said that he "had just felt like having some fun before going to work." He was sentenced to making a one-sentence apology to the professor.

The point, of course, was that outside of carnival, a Negro in a top hat was not fun. Nor was excessively original music nor Hebrews in student *kellers.* They were "nerve-racking."

The city, never a haven of tranquillity, had increasing trouble with its nerves. Its traditional trick had begun to fail. No longer could it so easily turn the stress of life into baroque caprice. Not that Vienna's talent was fading. No, the problem lay with life. Life had become too beset by reality. Fin de siècle Vienna had managed to cover the bleakness of workaday life with scrollwork and grace note. But by 1913 life seemed to tolerate less and less of anything but the rawly real.

Franz Schuhmeier's final journey signaled a change. The funeral of the murdered Socialist was the biggest in Vienna's history, bigger even than Karl Lueger's, all-time favorite among Viennese mayors, three years earlier.

Now over a quarter of a million men and women accompanied the coffin to the grave. Housemaids by the many hundreds swelled the procession. The law entitled them to only seven hours off every other Sunday; yet they gave up *this* Sunday to escort Schuhmeier on his way. Workers, shut in their factories eleven hours daily during the week, sacrificed their weekend rest as they trudged in the cortege. Slowly it moved along the Ottakringerstrasse; whole families streamed out of tenements to join the flow.

Ottakring constituted the largest workers' district. It was the district Schuhmeier had represented in Parliament and whose wretched statistics he had often shouted from the rostrum. *Why?* he had demanded. Why did only 5 percent of all people in Ottakring have a room of their own? Why were nearly half the houses in this borough-wide slum without running water? Why, more than a third of the staircases without gas light, let alone electricity? Why was the mortality rate of Ottakring more than twice as high as that of the upper class

Inner City district? Why, in the name of the Twentieth Century?

And why, somebody else had to ask now, was Franz Schuhmeier dead? Why had he not even reached the age of fifty? Why must good men die too soon and by such senseless violence?

An old bafflement. Yet at the same time Franz Schuhmeier's funeral produced something new; something not seen before in the demeanor of mourning crowds. That Sunday they broke with Vienna's tradition of the *"Schöne Leiche"*—the Beautiful Corpse. For generations, death by the Danube had been cultivated as a good show. A funeral aimed to be like a *Singspiel,* from the aria of the eulogy to the mobile stage of the hearse, to the chorusing of the wine-happy wake at the end. A funeral was often the only opera a proletarian could afford. While alive he displayed connoisseurship as spectator or as member of its supporting cast. When dead, he was its star.

The Schuhmeier burial broke with all that. There was no pomp festooned in sable; no black-ribboned horses, no opulence of wreaths, no black-clad band that trumpeted a majestic succession of dirges. Here there was a simple hearse and the oceanlike crowd tiding behind it under frayed caps and wrinkled babushkas, tiding and tiding, sometimes pushing prams, sometimes thumping along on crutches, tiding slowly, tiding in silence, tiding and tiding with the awesome, ominous, unrelenting rhythm of great waves.

In the late winter of 1913 Vienna woke up to discover that perhaps its poor were not what they used to be.

Nor were the rich—even the paradigmatic rich: the Austrian aristocrats. No elite in Europe had a more venerable pedigree. Supremacy came to its members as naturally and casually as yawning. They looked (as Consuelo Vanderbilt put it) "... like greyhounds, with their long lean bodies and small heads." They could impress even a star-spangled bucko like Teddy Roosevelt. When asked what type of person had appealed to him the most in all his European travels he said unhesitatingly, "The Austrian gentleman." In 1913 the Austrian aristocrat could still ring superlatives from the most hard-eyed Americans by simply being himself.

There were some two thousand of him, grouped into eighty families. Not one had been founded by a hard-working, clever nineteenth-century tycoon whose son was only the second generation to sport a baronial escutcheon in his Ringstrasse *palais*. For Austria's "First Society" the Ringstrasse was parvenu; Baron was a title denoting a Jew. The princes and counts constituting major nobility usually had as their Vienna seats mansions of dusty rococo raised centuries ago on the cobbles of the Inner City.

A number of the founders of these clans—the Schwarzenbergs, the Auerspergs, the Wilczeks, the Palffys, et al.—had been medieval bullies of the first water. Sometimes Habsburg had recruited their prowess by bettering their blazons with a lion rampant or two, sometimes by investing them with a fief that would make them *zu* as well as *von*.

Many of their descendants ignored the twentieth century. They kept on leading lives exquisitely detached from middle-class reason. Their elegance seemed heedless, spontaneous, barbaric, anachronistic, enviable. During sojourns in their country castles, they would often still use the *chaise percée;* a small portable neo-Gothic cathedral, it would be borne into the bedroom by footmen whenever the need arose. Highness would enter it as if to make a sacrament of nature's call.

Highness would emerge again; footmen would bear away the temple of digestion.

It was all still a normal part of country life. In the capital it seemed almost as normal that the First Society would claim as their inalienable estates the twenty-six Parquet Circle boxes of the Court Theater and the Court Opera. Nary a diva dared complain if a blue-blooded latecomer scraped back a chair during a performance. Since the noise came from one of *their* boxes, it expressed not rudeness but a world that wafted a marvelous distance away from irritabilities lower down.

On the other hand, Austrian aristocrats were most sensitively subject to what the outside eye did not even recognize as the done thing. They knew it wouldn't do to dance a left-turn waltz with an archduchess; that it was gauche to take the reins of a one-horse coach; that it was all right to order caviar for a ballet girl at the Sacher bar or to treat her to a chocolate éclair at Demel's—establishments devoted to princes and their peccadilloes; that it was not all right to do the same at restaurants like the Bristol Hotel's, designed for the gawking monocle of the arriviste. They knew what worn lederhosen to don for the chase and what game to hunt when: the stag in the fall; the black chamois in the winter; the woodcock, heathcock, and capercaillie in the spring; the red roebuck in the summer. They knew how to greet each other the right way by the right name. They didn't say: *"Guten Tag, Nicholas."* They said: *"Servus, Niki."* It was Niki and Kari and Koni and Turli—a code of rarefied diminutives.

In the late winter of 1913 the Nikis and Konis still met and joked and kissed hands (more often ironically than ardently) at the right At Homes at the right times of the week. On Sundays at the Princess Croy. Mondays at the Countess Haugwitz. Tuesdays at the Countess von Berchtold in the Ballhausplatz Palais, the office of her husband, the Foreign Minister.

Wednesdays at the Countess Buquoy . . . and so on to the Saturdays of Countess Ferenczy, lady-in-waiting to the late Empress Elizabeth.

But there was a "but." By 1913 most such gatherings had become afternoon receptions, grayed by the winter sun. Where was the dash of nightly galas that once continued into spring? What had happened to the post-Lent soirées of yesteryear?

Money was blamed: Soirées demanded extra footmen, who nowadays demanded higher pay; so did midnight musicians. Therefore one made do with one's in-house staff serving Doboschtorte at 4 P.M. The mobility of modern times was blamed: Vienna emptied after the carnival; too many of the Nikis and Konis suspected that they might be missing something at St. Moritz, at Biarritz, or on the Riviera. Do-Somethingness was blamed: gossiping over champagne was no longer enough; one had to *do something* like join the bridge tournaments at Countess Larisch's or the weekend ski outings to the Semmering Alp organized by Countess Sternberg.

But all this compulsive busyness smelled of a wholesale grocer sweating his way toward a bankruptcy. It did not become a Niki or a Koni. The top was still the top—but did it still have its instinct for the *au fait*?

Many thought that the First Society needed, urgently, one paramount and centering social leader. Once upon a time, of course, the Emperor had played that role. Now he had become too old, too reclusive. Pauline Princess Metternich, daughter-in-law of the great chancellor, was almost as ancient and still quite robust. But though her parties enjoyed a good press, they were so full of waltzing Jewish bankers that she had acquired the title of *Notre Dame de Zion.*

Who else could be the center? Crown Prince Rudolf with his ingratiating wit, his fascinating quirks, had shot himself a quarter of a century ago in the Vienna Woods. The new lodestar should have been his successor, the Archduke Franz Ferdinand. His Imperial and Royal Highness, however, displayed none of the grace of Rudolf; none of the bonhomie of Edward, Queen Victoria's Prince of Wales, whose visits had set aglow so many Viennese salons. By contrast, Vienna's own heir apparent did nothing but disquiet the town—with his absences, for one thing.

Of course his principal seat was here, the magnificent Belvedere. Not one but two palaces defined this domain within the city; they were joined by a French garden splashing with fountains, perfumed by rose beds, mazed with yew. Franz Ferdinand's shadow cabinet worked on both sides of the maze, ready to take over a moment after the old Emperor's last heartbeat.

As for the Crown Prince himself, he seldom stayed at his official residence—less than ever as the icicled March of 1913 thawed reluctantly toward Easter. The weeks were raw and squall-wracked. The rumors were evil. They whispered that Franz Ferdinand was quarantined in his Bohemian castle at Konopiste. His fits had passed beyond sanity. Sober observers like Wickford Steed, correspondent of the London *Times*, heard alarming reports: The Crown Prince lay all day on the floor of his children's playroom at Konopiste, busy with their toys; anybody entering was commanded to lie down, too, to help hook up electric trains. Other accounts had the Archduke using his clock collection as a pistol range where any moving second hand became his target. One persistent story claimed that half the lackeys in Konopiste were really psychiatrists dressed in footmen's breeches.

And, in truth, Franz Ferdinand was mad. But he was mad

at a number of things. Apart from many lesser angers, he had two major ones. Both tended to keep him away from Vienna during the frosty pre-Easter weeks of 1913.

Anger animated his war with Alfred Prince Montenuovo, First Lord Chamberlain of his Majesty. A vintage feud, it went back thirteen years to 1900 when the Archduke had proposed marriage to Sophie von Chotek. The Chotek escutcheon brimmed with the full sixteen quarterings of major nobility but still fell far short of prerequisites for a Habsburg bride. The woman lacked royal blood. She was "only" a countess, as Montenuovo kept reminding the monarch who had to rule on the permissibility of the match; Franz Ferdinand had met her in the household of his cousin where she served as lady-in-waiting to the Archduchess Isabella.

Montenuovo himself descended from a lopsided union, namely the marriage of the Archduchess Marie Louise, Napoleon's widow, to "only" an officer of her guard, Major Adam Neipperg (German for New Mountain, or Montenuovo, in Italian). Perhaps for that reason he orchestrated an all the more insidious anti-Chotek campaign. At thirty-four, the Countess was four years younger than the Archduke; but Montenuovo thought nothing of circulating a photograph of her to which retouched wrinkles had been added. It was the portrait of an aging wanton who had seduced the Crown Prince into a scandal.

Out of sheer spite—at which the Crown Prince was very good—the very scandal seduced the Crown Prince all the more. His anger incandesced his ardor. He let everybody know, from the Emperor down: It was Sophie Chotek or no one; it was Sophie, or he would remain a bachelor forever—unthinkable for a Habsburg heir.

The Emperor had to give in. But he gave in with a crushing proviso, formulated by Montenuovo. Franz Ferdinand must perform a permanent and irrevocable renunciation for his wife as well as for any children issuing from their marriage of all rights to succession as well as all archducal privileges. This solemn humbling took place in the Imperial Palace before the Emperor, the Cardinal, the principal ministers of His Majesty's Government, and every adult male Habsburg, on June 28, 1900. Neither the Emperor nor the Cardinal nor any minister nor any archduke (not even Franz Ferdinand's two brothers) attended the Crown Prince's wedding three days later at Reichstadt, an out-of-the-way castle in Bohemia. A common parish priest officiated.

The couple spent their honeymoon at the groom's estate in Konopiste. Here he bitterly named their favorite garden walk "Oberer Kreuzweg"—the Upper Stations of the Cross. It was to remind them that the road to fulfillment had been paved with sufferings.

But the sufferings continued into an otherwise happy marriage. By way of a wedding gift, Franz Joseph had raised Sophie from Countess Chotek to Princess Hohenberg (Hohenberg being one of the seventy-two ancillary Habsburg titles). But she was still an abysmally morganatic wife, unable to share the perquisites and precedence not just of her husband but of a number of his inferiors. At all court functions the Crown Prince entered immediately after the Emperor—wifeless, alone. The Princess Hohenberg must lead the backstairs existence of a nonperson while her husband, who doted on her doubly, must nurse his fury amidst pomp.

The fury did not dissipate with time. Years later, after the last of three Hohenberg children had been born, Franz Joseph advanced Sophie's rank to *Duchess* of Hohenberg. No longer merely "Your Princely Grace," she was addressed henceforth as "Your Most Serene Highness." Yet the limitations imposed on her even now, in 1913, must have taxed anybody's serenity, high or low. Sophie's husband still entered events of state alone, immediately after the Emperor; other members of the Imperial family followed. At last, behind the most junior archduchess, the wife of the Crown Prince was permitted to set foot on the parquet of the Court.

Nor was that all. Prince Montenuovo's jealous, zealous eye saw to it that Sophie continued to suffer other indignities of protocol. She could not sit with her husband in the Habsburg boxes at the Court Opera and the Court Theater. When riding by herself in Vienna, she must not use any of the Court carriages with their gold-threaded spokes. If she stayed in Franz Ferdinand's Vienna residence after he had left, all sentries were promptly withdrawn as if nobody worth guarding were left behind. And whenever Franz Ferdinand entertained a visiting sovereign there, she must remain invisible; Prince Montenuovo, the First Lord Chamberlain, decreed that on such occasions the existence of a hostess could be acknowledged—as a ghost: An extra place setting would be laid which would remain unoccupied.

The Crown Prince's first major anger, then, burned at the inflictor of high-altitude humiliations, far above the common ruck. His second major anger, however, involved an issue so down to earth that it would bloody fields across the continent.

The issue, of course, was Serbia. And the target of the Archduke's second major anger, the great foe of all Serbians, occupied the enormous desk of the Chief of Staff in Vienna's Ministry of War. General Franz Conrad von Hötzendorf stood out in the Austrian officer corps as its ablest military technician, unmatched in his flair for organizing and deploying army units. Franz Ferdinand stood out as the keenest mind by far among archdukes. An affinity linked the two men, cordial at first, livid in the end.

The Crown Prince had quickly discerned the General's talent. As early as 1906 he had persuaded the Emperor to leapfrog Baron Conrad beyond the seniority of other generals. That year His Majesty appointed Conrad head of the General Staff at the relatively tender age of fifty-three. Slim, blond, strikingly mustached, he had a facial tic flavoring his handsomeness. He also had a personality as hard-edged as Franz Ferdinand's. In 1911 a clash with the then Foreign Minister led to his dismissal. Again the Crown Prince championed him. After the advent of the new Foreign Minister, Count von Berchtold, the Crown Prince had Conrad reappointed. Almost simultaneously, toward the end of 1912, friendship changed to conflict. To the degree that the Archduke had once supported the General, the General now vexed, disturbed, outraged the Archduke.

The General kept writing position paper after position paper about Serb aggression against Albania and Serb agitators in Habsburg Bosnia. Every other day he urged a massive preventive strike at Serbia as the one way of restoring Austrian security in the Balkans. The Archduke, on the other hand, knew that only conciliation would serve the Empire in the end.

The General lobbied for war at the ultimate level of decision through his audiences with Franz Joseph in Vienna's Imperial Palace. It was a venue uncongenial to the Archduke. He did not like the capital because he did not like seeing his wife humbled there; furthermore he could not trust his temper even in an All-Highest confrontation. Therefore much of his peace-pleading was done by letters to Franz Joseph.

By the start of 1913 the contest appeared to tilt in the General's favor. Conrad produced new intelligence of Serb infiltrations into Albanian territory. Though the Emperor still refused to unleash his divisions, he did authorize the strengthening of garrisons along Russian as well as Serb borders with reservists called up for that purpose. Russia, Serbia's protector, countered in kind. Mobilization seemed to replace diplomacy. In early February Franz Ferdinand determined that he'd better go to Vienna after all.

He went without his Sophie (so that the Court would not have the pleasure of punishing her with etiquette). He also refrained from requesting an audience (to circumvent a very possible, very personal collision with the Emperor). However, he did attend a dinner for his brother-in-law, Duke Albrecht of Wurtemberg. It was a gathering of the crested great during which the Crown Prince dashed the hopes of the haut monde again. At this rare appearance, too, he did not so much enliven Vienna socially as irritate it politically. At the height of the gala he raised his glass to his cause: "To peace! What would we get out of war with Serbia? We'd lose the lives of young men and we'd spend money better used elsewhere. And what would we gain, for heaven's sake? Some plum trees and goat pastures full of droppings, and a bunch of rebellious killers. Long live restraint!"

Dutiful applause around the table. A headshake on the part of the Emperor after he was informed of his nephew's exclamations. They coincided with news from the Chief of Staff of more misdeeds by Belgrade. Franz Joseph had to agree with his general: Restraint vis-à vis Serbia would look like weakness. Army reserves kept entraining for the borders.

Returned to Konopiste, Franz Ferdinand tried to sway his uncle via the Foreign Minister. In mid-February he wrote Count von Berchtold, ". . . God forbid that we annex Serbia.

We'd spend millions on keeping these people down and would still have a horrendous insurgent movement. As for the irredentists within our frontiers, the ones to whom hotheads in our government are pointing—all that would stop the moment we give our Slavs something of a comfortable, just and good existence."

In his letter of reply the Foreign Minister bowed and scraped, and did nothing that might countervail Hothead No. 1, the Chief of Staff.

The third week of February began with snow and rumors of further mobilization, all swirling thickly. Franz Ferdinand dispatched the head of his Military Chancellery to General Conrad's office in Vienna. "His Imperial Highness," the aide said with the proper stiffness, "wishes Your Excellency to understand that neither he nor any Austrian patriot covets a square meter of Serbian ground. His Imperial Highness is convinced that if we march on Serbia, Russia will march on us. His Imperial Highness is further convinced that war between Austria and Russia would encourage revolution in both countries and thereby cause the Emperor and the Tsar to push each other off their thrones. For these reasons His Imperial Highness considers war lunacy. He considers preludes to war, like constant requests for mobilization, preludes to lunacy. His Imperial Highness trusts that Your Excellency will ponder these thoughts with the care they deserve."

The Chief of Staff, handsome blond mustache a-twitch, answered that he humbly and duly noted the Highest sentiments thus conveyed to him. Within twenty-four hours, at an All-Highest audience, he recommended calling more reserves to the colors.

* * *

Now Franz Ferdinand had no recourse but Franz Joseph's great ally, Germany's Kaiser Wilhelm II. It was a desperate move, and the Crown Prince executed it cunningly. What made it a bit easier was his habit of clothing anti-war arguments in vehement rhetoric. It suited his temperament, but in addressing the fustian Wilhelm it was also part of a strategy well calculated in advance. His message to Berlin resounded with carefully crafted bluster. The Crown Prince intoned the mightiness of great realms like Germany, Austria, and Russia; he hurled contempt at scummy little bandits like Serbia who tried to foment trouble between the giants; he vowed to wipe away the poison sprayed by these pygmies by insisting on troop reductions along the Russian-Austrian borders, and to continue insisting regardless of political risks but hopeful of the backing of his powerful great cousin and friend, the German suzerain. . . .

Seldom has pacifism bristled with such militancy. Europe's foremost swaggerer was quite beguiled. "Dear Franzi," Kaiser Wilhelm answered, "Bravo! It can't be easy, that sort of thing. It takes stubbornness and stamina. But success will earn you the enormous credit to have freed Europe from such pressures. Millions of grateful hearts will remember you in their prayers . . . Even the Tsar will be grateful when he can order some of his divisions back from the border . . ."

Franz Ferdinand called the Chief of Staff to Konopiste, thrust at him Wilhelm's words, dismissed him in triumph. At the same time a copy of the Kaiser's letter reached Franz Joseph. It happened that shortly before, the special emissary to the Tsar, sent by Franz Joseph at the Crown Prince's request, returned with a message of "most friendly and fraternal feelings" from Nicholas II. Shortly afterward, Franz Joseph came to a decision. He instructed his diplomats to moderate their anti-Serb stance. And he ordered General Conrad to demobilize some reserves. Recent reinforcements along the Russian border were withdrawn again.

The problem didn't end there—but February did: a cold and difficult month in which the Crown Prince had done some good work. As March began he was ready to relax for a while in gentler climes.

His First Lord Chamberlain summoned his private train. With his wife, his daughter, and two sons, he traveled southward to Merano, in the semitropical foothills of the Dolomites, making a detour around Vienna, of course.

"Schani, trag den Garten ausse!"

It was a command often heard after winter's end in Vienna. Headwaiters shouted it at busboys: *"Johnny, carry the garden outside!"* All over town Johnnys carried onto the sidewalk foliage made of green-lacquered cloth leaves, then added tables and chairs to complete "the garden terrace." Spring had come to Vienna's restaurants as it did to the rest of this most theatrical of all cities: It came in the form of a stage set.

By April most props were in place. Only the mood music seemed still a bit wrong. Perhaps the weather had something to do with it. Not that the temperatures remained wintry; usually the sun drove away the night's chill. But there had been no rain for weeks, and the drought had delayed budding.

Only restaurant gardens displayed some leafy green. It was fake and dusty. Dust, sooty, grainy proletarian dust, drifted from the proletarian districts in the West where the sanitation department did not trouble to send many brooms. Uncouth dust mottled the breasts of goddesses whose marmoreal charms supported balconies of the Imperial Palace. But dust could not stop Vienna from play-acting like Vienna. The city kept furbishing the decor and the costumes of Maytime.

Tailors cut and stitched deep into the night. Now was the moment for the city's fashionables to start fittings for their summer wardrobe, which this year featured slimmer single-breasted suits. Fiacre drivers used their lunch hour to wield the paint brush; time to refresh the gray-black design of their carriages. On the gothic elegance of the menu card of Demel's, the ultimate patisserie, a herald of the warmer season appeared—iced coffee with a tiara of whipped cream.

Still, the trees in the Vienna Woods were less than verdant; so, underneath the busyness, was the feeling in town. Even on the day of the Resurrection, a sense of Ash Wednesday weighed on the roofs. Over the Easter weekend, Sunday, March 23 and Monday, March 24, twenty-three people tried to kill themselves, a majority of them in that unswept slum to the West; seventeen of these drank concentrated lye. It was the cheapest poison and therefore the most cost-effective means of suicide. Over six thousand crammed nightly into the municipal *Wärmestuben.* These were "warming rooms" where the capital's homeless could sleep sitting up on wooden benches.

The somberness of Lent, stubborn past its season, extended to the upper reaches. True, the rich could afford to ease their spirit at chic new entertainments like the cinema. A film of Dante's *Inferno* was the dernier cri in the genre. You could see it at the Graben Kino, a theater with seats of plush and walls of silk and an orchestra of two pianos and three violins to make musical the shadows on the screen. No wonder that the jeunesse dorée elected the Graben Kino as a favorite courtship rendez-vous. Perhaps it was no wonder, too, that in the early spring of 1913 one went a-Maying to the *Inferno*.

Dust thickened as the rains held off. Fires increased. Cinders sprinkled the time of rejuvenation. A touch of hell at the edge of heaven: that seemed to be the motto of the weather, of politics, and of the social scene as exemplified by the dinner party of Herr Hermann von Passavant, Consul General of the German Reich in Vienna.

On Monday, March 31, his table saw a cross-section of the powerful: Baron Conrad, the Chief of Staff; Hermann von Reininghaus, the beer magnate of the Habsburg Empire, with his lush, dusky-eyed wife; Baron Leo von Chlumetzky, influential publisher of the *Öesterreichische Rundschau;* and Joseph Redlich, a key member of Parliament as well as a political scientist and assiduous journal keeper who often recorded in detail his experiences as intellectual-in-residence of the Vienna establishment.

Delicious was the Tafelspitz that evening; delicate, the juxtaposition of personalities. Everyone in the know (and everyone here was) knew of the capital's foremost triangle: Herr von Reininghaus, Frau von Reininghaus, and the Chief of Staff. The last two were seated next to each other.

Alas, the piquancy could not be fully savored. Just as the General looked deeply into his neighbor's eyes, history interrupted him with a knock at the door. It was his adjutant with a bulletin concerning the latest Serb aggression. During the last few weeks the Serbs and their Montenegrin henchmen had reopened hostilities with Turkey, driving the Sultan's troops south on Albanian territory until they reached a critical zone, the town of Scutari, near the coast. Vienna had stated publicly that extension of Serb control into Scutari would jeopardize Austria's security and undermine all hope of Balkan stability. The news which had just reached the General indicated that Scutari might fall at any moment.

The General's facial tic had accelerated. His irritation dominated what was left of dinner. He should get up right now, he said, and walk to the telephone and call the Military Chancellery at the Imperial Palace and request permission through the Duty Officer to bring the Adriatic fleet into action. Before dawn he could dispatch a battleship and two cruisers with marines ready to land. They would make short work of Belgrade's provocations in that area. It would be the logical thing to do. But there was no point calling the Palace. Lately he was not allowed to apply logic when it came to Serbia. Never! Not once. Each time he tried, the Palace said No, pressured by the Crown Prince. It was always the bugbear of Russian intervention. Why, just recently His Majesty had said that war with Russia would be the end of His monarchy. Actually it would be the end of the Tsar. Conrad himself, with his own hands, had placed on the Emperor's desk intelligence that proved the illogic of any Russia-panic. This intelligence came from a source so high he could name its identity only to the Emperor (it was Count Sergius Witte, former Prime Minister at St. Petersburg), and the information proved that thirty million non-Russians would revolt against the Tsar—including Finland and Poland. The time to strike Serbia was now, before Russia could get organized. But that was out of the question—just because it would be the logical thing!

An excellent chocolate mousse could not mellow the General's frustration. Nor did mocha end it. The dinner party was eventful, though not as personally piquant as one had hoped.

Before the night was out, however, Frau von Reininghaus took our diarist, Herr Redlich, aside. It was so valorous of the General, she breathed in Redlich's ear, to press for action, since the General had three sons of military age; in fact, he had confided to her his premonition that his eldest, Herbert, would fall before the enemy. . . .

As April ended, rain came to Vienna at last. Then the sun broke through, and the flowers burst forth. Suddenly spring swept through the streets like a galloping pageant. Suddenly the Vienna Woods interlaced so closely with the pavement that cobbles became fragrant. In the West and the South where the vineyards touched the sidewalks, they touched them with the pearly blossoms of the grapevine. The hills looming so closely above the roofs—those "house mountains" beloved of the Viennese like Kahlenberg, Cobenzl, Leopoldsberg—turned into waves of vivid hue: crocuses, cyclamens, primroses, daisies, lilacs, all blessed with the songs of blackbird and thrush. Along the banks of the Danube cherry orchards flamed into color.

In the city itself blossoms swamped bricks. Violet vendors surrounded the Opera and scented the piazzas. In parks like the Stadtpark and Volksgarten peacocks jaunted under festive trees. White roses garlanded the fiacres that brought children to their First Communion: the girls like buds unfolding in their snowy lace, the boys with white carnations glowing from their buttonholes.

Elsewhere in Europe spring happened to other cities as well. But here it burgeoned as a gala that was intimately Viennese. It affected someone so no-nonsense as Trotsky's wife. "From our windows we could see the mountains," she wrote. "One could get into the open country through a backgate without going to the street . . . In April the scent of violets filled our rooms from the open windows . . ."

In Vienna spring belonged to culture more than to nature. Here spring merged its green arts into the town's architecture, whose seasons bloomed from romanesque to rococo, sprouted as gargoyles, fountains, statues. With its vernal rose windows, its tendrilled friezes, its sculpted bowers and garden amorettos, the Maytime city conjured the poetry of the West. Now it exuberated in the same vein with leaf and petal. Vienna experienced spring as yet another urban fancy, opulent and stylish, moving through its dream of history.

Here, against this time and this place, against this backdrop, Leon Trotsky wrote some somber lines. In an essay for *Kievan Thought* he shuddered at the barrenness of his country's past. It seemed so tundra-dreary compared to the occidental succulence surrounding him in Vienna. "We are poor," he said of Russia, "with the accumulated poverty of over a thousand years . . . The Russian peoples were as oppressed by nobility or by the church as the peoples of the West. But that complex and rounded-off way of life, which on the basis of feudal rule grew up in Europe—that gothic lacework of feudalism—has not grown on our soil . . . A thousand years we have lived in a humble log cabin and stuffed its crevices with moss. Did it become us to dream of vaulting arcs and gothic spires? . . . How miserable was our gentry! Where were its castles? Where were its tournaments? Its crusades, its shield bearers, its minstrels and pages? . . . Its fêtes and processions? . . . Its chivalrous love?"

Asking such questions in Vienna amid the prodigalities of an elegant tradition, Trotsky laments that its absence in Russia impoverished all classes, including Russia's radical intelligentsia of the new century, to which he himself belonged:

Russia was too far away "... from the sunlit zone of European ideology ... We have been shaken by history into a severe environment and scattered thinly over a vast plain." And there, isolated from the very people it wanted to liberate, the intelligentsia "... found itself in a terrible moral tension, in concentrated asceticism." Psychologically its members could maintain their strength only by a "fanaticism of ideas, ruthless self-limitation and self-demarcation, distrust and suspicion and vigilant watching over their own purity ..."

Some twenty years later Trotsky's freedom from such paranoia and puritanism prepared his downfall, as did his Viennese sense of the uses and pleasures of style: felicities that earned him the anger of a ruder rival in the Kremlin; because of them he fell all the more easily victim to the superior "distrust and suspicion and vigilant watching" of the non-Western Stalin.

This same Stalin was shipped in the spring of 1913 to one of the world's most un-Austrian regions—Siberia. After his stay in Vienna, and as if by way of a bizarre postscript to the Viennese carnival, he had been arrested wearing a woman's clothes, on February 23, in St. Petersburg. That evening the legally published *Pravda* held in the Russian capital a musical benefit which some "illegals" attended. When the police raided the show, one of them tried to escape in an actress's coat and wig. The police ripped away the disguise and identified the pockmarked insurrectionist. Before long Stalin was exiled to the village of Turkhansk in the Arctic Circle. For more than three years he lived in just the log cabin—its crevices stuffed with moss—where Trotsky, from his Austrian vantage point, had seen Russian backwardness linger for ten centuries.

* * *

Meanwhile Trotsky basked in "the sun-lit zone"—in the sumptuousness of the Viennese spring. Accompanied by his art-minded wife Natalya, he visited the great classic collections of the Kunsthistorisches Museum. But he did not neglect newer painters shown at the *Sezession* building or the avant-garde galleries scandalizing civic virtue with Kokoschka and Schiele. All these he included in the cultural chronicles he contributed along with his political reportage to *Kievskaya Mysl* (*Kievan Thought*), to the Berlin *Vorwärts* and *Le Peuple* in Brussels.

In Vienna he developed more fully his sensitivity to new esthetic directions. And with his smooth German (his children had already mastered Viennese dialect), his gift for pamphleteering not only with the pen but with the tongue, he savored the intellectual voltage of the coffeehouse, where repartee flashed from spoonful to spoonful of whipped cream.

Years later, from the perspective of a revolutionary leader, he would sniff at the smug, overly patriotic mocha-Marxists of Vienna and their weak-kneed reformism. Yet while in the city he remained a zestful partaker of the Viennese scene and of the cakes, cigars, conversation of its café life. Even the Socialist intellectuals with whose chauvinist ways he disagreed impressed him: "They were well-educated people, and their knowledge of various subjects was superior to mine. I listened to them with intense and, one might almost say, respectful interest in the Café Central."

To the Central Trotsky brought some fellow Russians, not least A. A. Joffe, chief contributor to his Vienna *Pravda* (later to be the Soviet Ambassador to Germany). It was at the Central that Trotsky wanted Joffe to chat and sip away the nervous tension that plagued his friend. It was here that Trotsky introduced Joffe to Alfred Adler. It was through this introduction that Joffe became Adler's patient. And it was Joffe's experience with Adlerian therapy that acquainted Trotsky (as he states in his autobiography) "with the problems of psychoanalysis, which fascinated me."

In 1913 the chief problem of psychoanalysis, and therefore of its founder, continued to be its own internal rifts. The one between Sigmund Freud and Alfred Adler kept Freud away from Adler's Café Central, and therefore Trotsky (himself predestined to become one of the century's great schismatics) never met Freud.

Yet the two had a good deal in common. Both Trotsky and Freud were full-blooded subverters of burgher pieties, both liked to play chess, and both relaxed by reading novels not in their mother tongue (Freud's English, as against Trotsky's French). Trotsky's love-hate relationship with Russia matched Freud's with Austria. Furthermore, the Trotsky of the year 1913 was no less than Freud an autocrat in command of an embattled sect, one that did not hesitate to lacerate its own allies. For example, Trotsky's Vienna *Pravda* often attacked the *Pravda* of St. Petersburg for its "disruptive 'egocentralism,' " which undercut all original and independent Socialist initiatives.

At the same time Freud started a purge within his own movement. Two years earlier he had gotten rid of Alfred Adler, until then one of his principal disciples among psychiatrists; Adler and his coterie had become un-Freudian by tracing neuroses not to sexual maladjustment but to general inferiority feelings. Now in 1914, a Swiss group of psychoanalysts led by Dr. Carl Jung was straying toward heresy; they no longer viewed the libido as Freud's erotically centered concept; to them it was the vehicle of a more multi-faceted psychic energy. In other words, they were undermining an article of faith.

On occasion the master of the Berggasse seemed capable of tolerating dissent. But this patience was a stratagem. His instinct was to show no mercy to antagonists in his fold—a trait he openly discussed. Only someone seeing so deeply into others could, when he wished, unmask himself so well. "I am by temperament nothing but a conquistador," he wrote to a friend, ". . . with all the inquisitiveness, daring and tenacity of such a man." And with just such a man's ruthlessness he referred to Adler as "a loathesome individual . . . that Jew-boy out of a Viennese backwater." This was contempt as stinging as any in Trotsky's polemics. Trotsky would have understood why Freud never patronized the Jew Boy's favorite establishment, the Café Central.

In 1913 Freud had his own favorite coffee house, the Café Landtmann, a fifteen-minute walk from his house. Though close to the University, it was of an upper bourgeois, not of a literary persuasion. The Landtmann featured softer upholstery, cleaner spittoons, more financial journals and fewer avant-garde magazines than the Central: a pleasant place for Freud, who had come to accept, almost with a gloat, his insulation from the city's mainstream intellectuals.

He visited the Landtmann most often on Wednesday nights, after the weekly meeting of his Psycho-Analytical Society (from which Alfred Adler had been forced to resign two years earlier in 1911). Here he would pick a table at the café's Ringstrasse terrace overlooking the Gothic tracery of City Hall and the Renaissance loggias of the Court Theater; he would order *einen kleinen Braunen,* light a cigar, exchange Jewish jokes with favorite followers, and exhale smoke rings into the mellowness of the evening air. In May of 1913 they were leisured hedonist's smoke rings: He had just finished *Totem and Taboo.* "When my work is over," he had confessed in a letter, "I live like a pleasure-loving philistine."

He took care to add that these pleasures were limited and that he was "vegetating harmlessly." However, his character was too robust, the Viennese ambiance too seductive, and the doctor's own view of human nature too libidinal to keep mean-eyed observers from speculating. Just a few months earlier, in 1912, the American psychiatrist Moses Allen Starr had gone beyond speculation in remarks to the New York Academy of Medicine's Section on Neurology. "Vienna is not a particularly moral city," Dr. Starr had said, "and working side by side with Freud . . . I learned that he enjoyed Viennese life thoroughly. Freud is not a man who lives on a particularly high plane. He is not self-repressed. He is not an ascetic. I think his scientific theory is largely the result of his environment and the peculiar life he leads."

Later, faced with this charge, Freud would sigh a rather Freudian sigh: "If it were only true!" Jung insisted it *was* true on the basis of, to him, unmistakable clues. While still friendly (Jung told an interviewer) the two doctors had often analyzed each other's dreams, and Freud's had exhibited evidence of his carnal relationship with Minna Bernays, his wife's younger, very attractive sister, who lived with the Freuds in their Berggasse apartment. "If Freud had tried to understand consciously the triangle," Jung said, "he would have been much better off."

Of course that statement was made after Jung had broken with his mentor. And of course the picture of Freud as a Viennese libertine fits the polemic of an enemy, not authenticated fact. It is a picture that conflicts with Freud's digs at his city for combining the frivolous with the narrow-minded. But during the spring of 1913 all this didn't keep him from tasting the joys of the season with Viennese gusto.

Every Sunday, every holiday, Freud acted like any of the capital's countless hiking enthusiasts. His children were ordered to "get ready for the meadows!" This meant getting into the dirndls and gallused shorts of peasant lasses and lads. He himself threw on leather knickers, a green jacket, a loden cape, and a Tyrolean hat with chamois brush. Off they went all together, to the Vienna Woods or beyond—off on one of the mushroom hunts he delighted in leading. The zest he showed on such occasion was—to borrow from his self-description—almost conquistadorial. He had an indomitable thirst for booty. It was always Papa Freud himself (his son Martin would recall) who spotted the prize specimen. "He would run to it and fling his hat over it before giving a piercing signal on the silver whistle he carried in his waist pocket to summon the platoon. We would all rush toward the sound of the whistle, and only when all of our concentration was complete, would father remove the hat and allow us to inspect and admire the spoil."

In the town itself, Freud led the 1913 spring outing of the Vienna Psycho-Analytical Society. The event took place after dark and involved the doctor's professional rather than personal family. Members of Freud's flock (some passing near Hitler's lodgings in the adjacent district) converged on the Prater. This was Vienna's favorite pleasance—a huge, exuberant park combined with a midway. Having met at the main entrance, the psychiatrists trooped in the twilight up the incline of a jasmine-laced path to a terrace. A huge table, lavishly set, awaited them.

So did an ex-patient of Freud's; he paid homage to the master by presenting him with a figurine from ancient Egypt. A witness records that Freud placed the gift in front of his plate, at the head of the table, "as a totem." Then two dozen bearded soul-doctors began to feast the night away under the moon, the stars, and the multicolored glow of Chinese lanterns.

The restaurant providing the banquet was called "Constantinhügel" after the man-made hill ("hügel") whose top it occupied; and the hill received its name from Prince Constantine von Hohenlohe, late First Lord Chamberlain to His Majesty; under his aegis the hill had been created at the opening of the Vienna World Exhibition of 1873. Now, in 1913, the perfumes of real blossoms brimmed from an artificial slope and mingled with the bouquet of Gewürztraminer from the psychoanalysts' goblets.

The moon waned but not the doctors' gemütlichkeit. Their chief kept lifting his "totem" to their toasts. All along a ballet of fireflies danced through a vernal nocturne quintessentially Viennese: nature and culture in ceremonious fusion.

On a night like this, who would suspect civilization of discontent?

5

The Vienna Psycho-Analytical Society was not the only group holding a spring fête. Much bigger and therefore more widely controversial was the workers' procession on May 1.

It played no part in the life of a nonpolitical man like Sigmund Freud—except as an impediment to his high-speed walks along the Ringstrasse after lunch. Yet this Socialist rite had been charted, of all places, at Berggasse 19, under the very roof where Freud had conceived psychoanalysis.

A quarter of a century earlier, Dr. Viktor Adler had lived here in the house then owned by his father. Viktor was no relation of Alfred Adler. But like Alfred, Viktor was a trained psychiatrist. Like Alfred, young Viktor developed Socialist sympathies. And with Viktor Adler, these sympathies became his life's engulfing mission. Very soon he abandoned medicine for politics to lead the new Social Democratic Party. In 1889, in the apartment soon to be Freud's, he initiated and choreographed what the world came to know as the May Day Parade.

And in 1913 the parade gave, as always, gorgeous hints of its Viennese lineage. May 1, the international proletarian festival, was a descendant of the society corso in the Prater. Every May 1 the Austrian aristocracy in full panoply of escutcheoned carriages, liveried drivers, passengers in princely capes and floral hats used to promenade through the Prater, followed by caparisoned parvenus.

Sic transit primavera. Since 1890 Viktor Adler had the working class celebrate spring with equal pride and comparable showmanship. On May 1 of 1913 the parade was particularly splendid. Every category of labor—from foundry stoker to papermill hand to shoemaker to tanner—assembled at a different inn or coffeehouse early in the morning. At 10 A.M. sharp they sallied forth, phalanx by phalanx, each group in the garb of its craft, be it apron or overalls or smock. But red carnations shone in all their buttonholes; they all wore black armbands to commemorate the recent murder of their deputy Schuhmeier; all their arms were linked into comradely chains. Chanting against war, chanting for livable wages, chanting for bearable housing, the groups merged on the Ringstrasse where the chants united into a hundred-thousand-throated boom. The weather chimed in with sunshine, crisp air, and just enough breeze to make the banners come alive. Chanting, marching, waving their banners in the same cadence, the mass moved toward the meeting ground in the Prater.

* * *

By 1913, May Day had become familiar. But it still exhilarated the proletarian soul. It still terrified the prosperous. In "better districts" like Hietzing or Doebling, maids were instructed to hoard food in advance of the critical weekend. Stefan Zweig recalls that well-to-do parents like his had the doors locked so that their children might not stray into the streets "on this day of terror which might see Vienna in flames."

The spectacle also shook up at least one man who was not a member of the upper classes, twenty-four-year-old Adolf Hitler.

In *Mein Kampf* he reports his awe

> at the endless rows of Viennese workers marching four abreast in this demonstration. I stood almost two hours with bated breath observing this immense human snake as it rolled by. In fearful depression I finally left the place and wandered homeward.

But why so fearfully depressed? Because these workers

> rejected everything: the nation as an invention of the "capitalists"; the Fatherland as an instrument of the bourgeoisie to exploit the working class; the authority of the law as a means to repress the proletariat; school as an institution for breeding slave material, but also for the training of slavedrivers; religion as a means to stupefy the people intended for exploitation; morality as a sign of stupid, sheeplike patience . . . There was absolutely nothing that was not dragged through the mire of horrible depths.

Spring is the visceral season, felt deep down. The man appalled by these "horrible depths" was puritan, celibate, and volcanic at once. Eventually he would forge an empire out of the ambivalence. Meanwhile he abhorred the elemental mire. Yet he also watched it "for almost two hours with bated breath." The money he'd inherited could have bought him shelter more elevated than the Männerheim. Yet he lingered for years amidst its primitivities. He rejected the new elemental artists—Egon Schiele, Oskar Kokoschka—who had begun to excite Vienna with their expressionist eruptions; they were so different from the dainty banality of Hitler's own paintings; their "fleshly" work, he would sneer later in *Mein Kampf,* might as well have been "the smears of a tribe of Negroes." Yet his contempt for "fleshliness" was also engrossment: He accompanied a friend to the Spittelberggasse where prostitutes drew on black stockings in lit windows. Hitler never touched them—just lashed out at "the iniquity"—and came back to look and lash out again.

A similar revulsion-obsession made him shiver, at length, at the proletariat thrusting up from below. Since he could not deal with the primal physically or esthetically, he went at it politically—sniffed it, imagined it, fantasized it, developed a mania to tap it, manipulate it, tame it, control it. "At this time," he says in *Mein Kampf* of his Vienna years, "I formed a view of life which became the granite foundation of my actions."

His horror of May Day on the Ringstrasse became a permanent inspiration. The elemental obedience of so many thousands to their Socialist chiefs leads him to conclusions prophetically detailed in *Mein Kampf:*

> The masses love a commander more than a petitioner and feel inwardly more satisfied by a doc-

> trine tolerating none other besides itself . . . They are unaware of their shameless spiritual terrorization or the hideous abuse of human freedom, for they absolutely fail to suspect the inner insanity of the whole doctrine. All they see is the ruthless force and brutality of its calculated manifestation, to which they always submit in the end . . . *If Social Democracy is opposed by a doctrine of greater truth but equal brutality of methods, the latter will conquer.*

The italics are Hitler's. An unitalicized sentence two pages later begins and ends with the word summarizing the central lesson he drew from May Day: "Terror in the workshop, in the factory, in the assembly hall, and on occasion in mass demonstrations, will always be accompanied by success as long as it is not met by an equally great force of terror."

But terror did not enforce the workers' May Day. It was a voluntary procession and, in the radiant weather, joyous. To Hitler, the sight was apocalyptic.

The apocalypse is the cataclysm through which death convulses into birth. Some day Hitler would summon apocalyptic emotions before a global audience. Meanwhile May of 1913 marked for him, on a modest scale, an end that introduced a beginning. This was the month in which he left Vienna for Germany, ". . . that country for which my heart had been secretly yearning since the days of my youth." And though he still lived in the Männerheim during those final weeks, he spent most of his time at the other end of the city, in the streets and cafés close to the West Terminal: his original port of arrival whose precinct had been the haunts of his early years in Vienna from 1907 to 1909. He seemed to be revisiting the ambitions that had driven him to the city in the first place. They had been dashed; yet they were still fermenting, as fierce as ever. Now he would fulfill them in a worthier land. On Saturday, May 24, 1913, he rose for the last time from his seat in the Writing Room of the Männerheim. He went to pack the few belongings that cluttered his cubicle. Then he took the streetcar to the West Terminal to board a Third Class compartment on the train to Munich.

May 1913 promised Hitler hope and change. It also brought him safety. His passport recorded his birth date: April 20, 1889. At twenty-four he had just passed the age of conscription, having failed to register for service since 1909. The man who turned into the century's most thunderous war lord no longer needed to fear that some border guard would hold him as a draft evader.

The Honorable Joseph Redlich, diary-keeper, centrist member of Parliament, and Christian convert born into the Jewish haute bourgeoisie, did not watch the May Day march of 1913. However, two days earlier, on April 29, 1913, he observed another movement on the Ringstrasse, a sight that on the surface seemed unremarkable. A gentleman, all by himself, gray-haired, dapper under a bowler, was sauntering in the balm of noon. He had come out of Ballhausplatz 1, the Foreign Minister's residence, and was heading for the Ministry of War. As Redlich's diary attests, the buoyancy of this single stroller turned out to be more momentous—in the short run—than the resolute tramp of a hundred thousand proletarians forty-eight hours later.

"Good morning, Excellency," Redlich greeted Alexander Baron Krobatin. "How are you today?"

"I am well," said the Minister of War of Austria-Hungary. "Very well. Very well—at last."

From one knowledgeable insider to another, no more needed to be said. It was a bad day for pacifists like Crown Prince Franz Ferdinand. It was a fine day, at last, for hard-nosed patriots like General Conrad, the Chief of Staff, or like the two men now smiling at each other on the Ringstrasse: His Majesty had just authorized the drafting of an ultimatum. It was to be sent off today, Tuesday, and it gave the bandit government of the kingdom of Montenegro—ally of the bandit government of Serbia—until Thursday to pull its troops out of the Albanian town of Scutari. Failure to respond would prompt instant Austrian military moves to restore stability in the Balkans—regardless of Serbian or even Russian repercussions.

The ultimatum delivered this message in more diplomatic but no less unequivocal language. The two gentlemen could bask in its forcefulness as they sauntered together along the sunny boulevard. At last the Emperor had made a stand that would re-establish Austria's credibility as a major power.

By the morning of May Day, Thursday, Montenegro had not budged. But that afternoon its King wired Franz Joseph that he "was reviewing the situation." On Sunday, May 4, Montenegrin troops began to withdraw. Happy rumors began to animate coffeehouses like the Landtmann. Monday morning, May 5, hours before the news was officially announced, the Vienna stock market rose as it hadn't risen in years. For the first time in a long time (thought Krobatin, Redlich, Conrad, et al.), the old monarchy had taken a firm young step. Neither Serbia nor Russia did more than a bit of diplomatic mumbling.

Even Crown Prince Franz Ferdinand, who had cautioned in vain against the ultimatum, could not deny its success. It had improved the international standing of the realm that was his inheritance. Yet at the same time he kept advising against any further bravura displays, and he assiduously documented his admonitions. From Austria's most brilliant intelligence specialist, Colonel Alfred Redl, the Archduke had obtained an assessment of the Montenegrin army; it showed how potent that small force was and, therefore, how costly a potential showdown. Also from Redl came an analysis of a growing undercover movement in Bohemia directed against Habsburg. Franz Ferdinand used it all in his long-distance exclamations to the Imperial Palace. He was still staying in the Empire's South, at Fiume on the Adriatic shore. From there he worked the Imperial Courier Service and burned the telephone wire to the Emperor's chancellery. He still avoided audiences whenever possible. He was still afraid his temper might overpower his manners. But in messages he could drape the vehemence of his alarm in formulas of deference: those reckless, short-sighted circles that wanted to push the Empire into exterior adventures before the interior was pacified—would His Majesty graciously deign to bring them to reason?

His uncle's responses from the Palace were immovably noncommittal. They were also unfailingly courteous. Furthermore, "reason," or an approximation thereof, appeared to be in vogue again, at least for a while. Montenegro's retreat before Vienna's ultimatum appeased war-happy circles; it removed some of the rationale for "exterior adventures." As the world calmed and greened around the Crown Prince, he let the amenities of May enfold him.

With Sophie and the children he returned to his beloved estate at Konopiste. This was the finest time to stalk woodcock, snipe, and capercaillie. Mornings were for hunting, afternoons for flowers, all hours for his family. He whispered with his children as they watched for game. He crowded them into the pony trap to range through the vasts of his rose garden; the Dark Archduke, who never smiled in public, laughed freely as they invented names for the flowers they didn't know.

A certain prospect enhanced his mood. On May 24, Kaiser Wilhelm's daughter, Princess Marie Luise, was to marry Prince Ernst August von Braunschweig und Lueneburg. Attending would be two of the Kaiser's cousins, Tsar Nicholas II and King George V of England—also called "the twins" because of their resemblance. Confident of an invitation, Austria's Crown Prince looked forward to using on the Tsar the big-teddy-bear charm he could surprisingly produce when the occasion warranted it. And this was the moment—after the Montenegro set-to—to warm Russia into trusting Austria.

The Berlin wedding held still another promise. Away from the Austrian capital, beyond the reach of the Hofburg camarilla, yet against a backdrop august and imperial, Franz Ferdinand's Sophie would not be treated as some inflated concubine. In Berlin she would emerge as the Crown Prince's full-fledged, fully honored consort. Side by side with All-Highest wives, Sophie would shine in photographs of the reviewing stand, would be featured in Court *Gazette* accounts of the state dinner table and in newspaper reports of the pew seating in church.

With such trophies he would then come to Vienna with his family to enjoy the Derby the first week of June. It was, or should have been, a very pleasant spring.

6

May lost some warmth toward its end; the twenty-fourth dawned as the coolest day of the month. It was a nippy Saturday, yet sunny and clear—and very exciting for at least three people in Vienna. In different ways it brought them the elation of a payoff long delayed.

That morning Adolf Hitler left for Germany, having sweated out seven sour years in the Austrian capital. That afternoon the chance to pounce finally came to Detective Sergeant Ebinger and Detective Sergeant Steidl, both attached to the Intelligence Bureau of the Imperial and Royal Army.

They had been on a stake-out for six long weeks. Their mission was the climax of a hunt that was secret and urgent and international. Under an agreement set up in 1911 by Colonel

Alfred Redl, then in charge of Austrian Counter-Intelligence and its most capable leader in decades, the counter-espionage agencies of Austria and Germany exchanged mutually relevant information. Early in April 1913 Berlin directed Vienna's attention to a letter addressed to Herr Nikon Nizetas, c/o General Delivery, Vienna. Unclaimed, it had been returned to Berlin, the place of its postmark. There its bulk attracted the curiosity of the Secret Police who opened it. Inside were 6,000 kronen together with two addresses, one in Paris, one in Geneva, both known to be used by Russian spies.

An exciting discovery. It might help solve a problem of considerable concern in recent years: the leak of vital Austrian military secrets to Russia. The German office handed the letter to its Viennese colleagues. They re-sealed it carefully, returned it to the General Post Office on Fleischmarkt Square. In a room of the building opposite, Detectives Ebinger and Steidl took up position. Here they waited through all hours during which the General Delivery window was open. They waited for a certain sound—the ringing of an electric bell whose wire ran from their hide-out to a button under the desk of the General Delivery clerk.

Ebinger and Steidl waited for days and days. Nothing happened but the arrival of two more letters addressed to Herr Nizetas. Austrian intelligence opened them to find two more bland little notes together with cash sums totalling 14,000 crowns. These letters, too, were re-sealed and returned to General Delivery in the hope that their addressee would call.

Many more days passed. Herr Nizetas did not appear to claim his money. The detectives kept vigil by the bell that would not ring. Their chief, Colonel Redl, had by then been transferred to head the General Staff of the Eighth Army Corps in Prague. But he still retained wide intelligence responsibilities in view of his forthcoming appointment as Chief of Intelligence for all the Empire's armed forces. Still present in the Vienna bureau were the skills and habits Redl had implanted, and principal among them was patience, patience. Patiently, detectives Ebinger and Steidl were waiting, day after day, week after week, waiting and waiting in their little room opposite the General Post Office, waiting for the ringing of the bell.

Suddenly, at 5:55 P.M. on Saturday, May 24, it rang. It rang in an empty room. Sergeant Steidl had gone to the privy down the corridor. Sergeant Ebinger was having a cup of coffee in the canteen on the ground floor. Both men were good, Redl-trained agents. At the same time they were also two Viennese in May, a season that tuned up the body's needs. The bell was ringing when both men, returning along the corridor, heard it through the door. The sound swivelled them into an about-face. Together they raced down the one flight of stairs and across the square.

Too late, almost.

Behind the General Delivery window, the clerk could only shrug his shoulders. Yes, Herr Nizetas had come at last to claim his mail. Yes, just now, he'd signed for it in such a hurry, he might still be outside. Ebinger and Steidl rushed to the street—in time to see a cab pull away and vanish around the corner. Ebinger (who had better vision) had barely time to note its license number: A 3313.

The cool May evening must have felt even colder on the perspiring forehead of those two. To identify a cab by number would be slow; the driver, cruising all over Vienna, might not be found for hours. And Herr Nizetas had just shown how fast he could manage a disappearance.

The two sergeants ran back to General Delivery. What did Herr Nizetas look like? Again the clerk could only shrug: the face had been just about invisible since the hat had been pulled so far down. What kind of hat, what brim, what color? Oh, medium brim width, sort of gray. The man's height? Oh, medium, perhaps a little on the small side. His voice? Well, a normal male voice with the usual Austrian accent. Anything distinctive at all? Not really—no, nothing.

Nothing. Six weeks of waiting for nothing. Dazed by that "nothing" Ebinger and Steidl walked out of the General Post Office to the street once more. And there they saw, with unbelieving eyes, a cab rolling toward them with the license number A 3313. It was the very one that had escaped them ten minutes earlier. They screamed it to a halt. They thrust their badges at the driver's face. Astounded by the hysteria, the driver said he'd just taken his fare to the Café Kaiserhof a few blocks down, a gentleman in such a fearful hurry he'd forgotten the sheath of the penknife he'd used to open some mail. There it still was, the sheath, on the back seat.

At the Café Kaiserhof minutes later, the head waiter said that nobody with a pulled-down hat, in fact, nobody at all had entered the café in the last fifteen minutes.

Stymied again. But at least Ebinger and Steidl had Herr Nizetas's knife sheath. And, querying the cab drivers outside the café, they had another bit of luck. The cabbie next in line said, oh yes, the gentleman with the hat down over his face, he'd gotten out of the taxi fast to take another, now what was the name he'd heard him call out? . . . Oh yes, the Klomser, the Hotel Klomser, that was it.

At the Hotel Klomser the concierge was sorry. He did not recognize the knife sheath. There was no Herr Nizetas registered at the hotel—he knew the names of all guests. No Herr

Nizetas had come to visit either, he knew that because he always announced visitors by name. He was very sorry.

Ebinger and Steidl kept hissing more questions. Who had come into the hotel recently? Name? Description? At exactly what time? Anybody and everybody during the last half hour!

The concierge furrowed a flustered brow. Well, there had been a number of people, though he didn't constantly look at his watch. But during the last half hour, well, there had been Mr. Felsen, and then the two ladies, that was Mrs. Kleinemann, the wife of Bank President Kleinemann, with her friend Mrs. Luechow, the wife of Director Luechow, and who else, yes, the new guest, Dr. Widener, they'd all asked for their keys, and Colonel Redl and Professor Zank—

"Colonel Redl!"

The two detectives stared at each other. They couldn't believe they'd heard that name.

"Colonel Alfred Redl?"

"Oh yes, he always stays with us when he arrives from Prague. Always Room Number One."

"My God!" Detective Steidl said. "What a coincidence! Let's consult him—"

"We're not supposed to consult anybody," Detective Ebinger said, "except Control."

Again the two stared at each other.

"When the Colonel came in just now," Ebinger asked the room clerk, "how was he dressed?"

"Oh, civilian clothes. He's always dressed very smart."

"Did he wear a gray hat?"

"Well, he always takes it off when he comes in. He is such a gentleman."

"All right, but what was the color of the hat?"

"Well—yes, gray. It was gray."

"What time did he come in?"

"What time? About ten, fifteen minutes ago."

"Did he go to his room?"

"Why, yes, of course. He took his key."

"Did he say he'll come down again soon?"

"No, but he always goes out at night. He likes to dine out."

"When he comes down, ask if he has lost this knife sheath."

The six weeks Ebinger and Steidl had waited in the room of the nonringing bell were as nothing compared to the eternity they spent hidden behind a potted palm in the lobby of the Hotel Klomser. It lasted about an hour.

Shortly after 7 P.M. a man in his forties, slight, slim, with a well-brushed blond mustache, stepped down the red carpet of the stairs that led from the second floor of the Hotel Klomser to the lobby. He did not wear a hat but carried under his arm his officer's kepi. The gold choke-collar of his blue General Staff blouse gleamed with the three stars of his rank.

"Good evening, Colonel Redl," said the concierge. "Pardon me, sir, but did you happen to misplace this knife sheath?"

"Why, yes," the Colonel said. He extended his hand. He retracted it fast. Too late.

Shortly after 9 P.M. on that same night, another colonel, August von Urbanski, darted through the neo-Renaissance portals of the Grand Hotel. It was one of the most imposing entrances on the Ringstrasse. In the dining room the gypsy orchestra had finished playing the waltz "Wiener Blut." The Chief of Staff, General Conrad, flushed from a turn around the dance floor with Frau von Reininghaus, had just sat down and cupped his hand around a glass of champagne. He would never drink it.

Colonel von Urbanski, his Intelligence Chief, stood over him, bending down, whispering even before he had finished his salute. Within seconds the General's face turned gray, grayer than the gray streaks in his blond hair. His hand dropped from the goblet. He called to his adjutant at the next table. He had to call twice because most of his voice had abandoned his throat. The adjutant jumped up to alert the General's chauffeur.

Four hours later, at one o'clock in the morning of Sunday, May 25, 1913, four officers walked from the staircase of the Hotel Klomser past the dozing night clerk to the street. One of the four carried folded in his breast pocket a white sheet covered with gothic script. It was a statement signed by the occupant of Room One. In exchange for the signature the occupant had received a loaded pistol.

In Room One the occupant sat, motionless, in the gold choke-collar of the General Staff uniform. The mahogany table before him was bare except for three sealed letters and the pistol.

On the day following, Monday, May 26, Vienna's foremost newspaper, the *Neue Freie Presse,* discussed at length the tension between Serbia and Bulgaria, only recently fellow-victors over Turkey in the Balkan War of 1912. There was also detailed coverage of the nuptials of Kaiser Wilhelm's daughter Marie Luise to Prince Ernst August von Braunschweig—the sermon of the officiating bishop, the titles, uniforms, and dresses adorning the ceremony and its social significance. A much smaller story began:

> VIENNA, May 26. One of the best known and most able officers in the General Staff, Colonel Alfred Redl, General Staff Chief of the Eighth Army Corps in Prague, committed suicide Sunday night in a hotel in the Inner City. The highly gifted officer, who was on the verge of a great career, killed himself with a shot in the mouth, an act prompted, it is believed, by mental overexertion resulting from severe neurasthenia. Colonel Redl, who served for a long time in a military capacity in Vienna, and who was equally popular in military and civilian circles, had only arrived from Prague on Saturday night and had taken quarters at the hotel . . .

On the same day the Army announced that Colonel Redl would be buried with full military honors.

A respectable illusion was thus clapped over an evil reality. It might have shut out the truth forever if, on the Sunday of the suicide, an underdog soccer team had not upset the favorite; that is, if, a hundred and thirty miles northwest of Vienna, in the Prague Amateur League, the Club Union-Holleschowitz had not unexpectedly beaten the Club Sturm by a score of seven to five; and if the Sturm captain, Egon Erwin Kisch, had not been so furious with his star halfback Hans Wagner for not showing up at the game and thus causing the debacle; and if Wagner, coming to Kisch's office the next day to explain, had not produced such peculiarly lame excuses that they fanned Kisch's rage still further—until Wagner finally blurted out the truth.

Wagner was a locksmith by profession and Kisch was a journalist. When he'd been about to leave for the game on Sunday, Wagner said, a detail of soldiers had come down on him. He'd been virtually thrown into a military car, driven at top speed to his shop, ordered to collect his tools, driven at top speed to corps headquarters where he'd been commanded to break open the door to a private apartment.

And then, voice lowered, Wagner told about the queer sights behind the door, the perfumed drapes, the pink whips hanging from the walls, the photographs in snakeskin frames . . .

His football captain, listening, was no longer a football captain. He was a reporter whose investigative instincts had been alerted. His pencil was racing across a note pad. And then he himself began to run.

Within twenty-four hours Kisch not only did all the right leg work, ferreted out all the right people whom he asked all the right questions, but also managed to outmaneuver the usually inexorable arm of Habsburg censorship.

His trick worked because it was as Austrian as the authorities he must circumvent. A straight exposé would have been instantly suppressed. But Kisch, knowing that the official Redl account was a masquerade, produced a counterillusion. In the newspaper that employed him, the *Bohemia,* he planted a "reverse disclosure":

> We have been requested by official sources to deny the rumors particularly current in military circles that the General Staff Chief of the Prague Corps, Colonel Alfred Redl, who the day before yesterday committed suicide in Vienna, has betrayed military secrets and has spied for Russia. The Commission sent from Vienna to Prague, which was accompanied by a Colonel and which

> this past Sunday broke open the apartment and the drawers and closets of Colonel Redl and undertook a three-hour search, was investigating irregularities of a quite different nature.

Prague censors thought that Vienna had authorized the item; they let it pass. Kisch had smuggled a bombshell through their very fingers. But he had done more. He'd sent the real Redl story to a Berlin paper. And the moment the truth was printed in Germany, it swept across the border into Austria to combine bizarrely with a thousand rumors started by the report in *Bohemia*. Some of the vilest speculation involved the Imperial family itself. The only way to disperse the miasma was to stop the government lie. On Thursday, May 29, the War Ministry's *Military Review* published an official statement:

> The existence of Colonel Alfred Redl has ended through suicide. Redl committed this act as he was about to be accused of the following severe misdeeds:
>
> 1. Homosexual affairs which caused financial difficulties.
>
> 2. Sale of secret official information to agents of a foreign power.

This jolt was followed by shock waves. A clamor rose up in the press, in parliament, in the public, demanding more facts from the Ministry of War. The facts came, and they sent Vienna reeling through the beginning of June.

Colonel Alfred Redl, honored with the Order of the Iron Cross Third Class for his outstanding service in Counter-Intelligence; Colonel Redl who had been privileged to personally brief the Emperor; whom the Emperor had awarded, in a face-to-face ceremony, a medal signifying "Expression of Supreme Satisfaction"; Colonel Redl, decorated by the German General Staff with the Royal Prussian Order of the Crown, Second Class, an honor seldom bestowed on ranks lower than general; Colonel Redl, for whom the Chief of Staff Baron Conrad had already proposed the award of the important Military Service Medal; Colonel Redl, the exemplary light and hope among younger officers of the General Staff; Colonel Redl, known for his uprightness, discipline, good humor, and camaraderie, who wore the sky-blue of the Austrian officer's uniform with as trim and slim a grace as any of his colleagues; whose fitness report on the part of his superiors judged him to be "... strong, honorable, open ... highly gifted and highly intelligent ... and brilliantly demonstrating these qualities in espionage cases ... "; who was characterized during his off-duty hours as "... very companionable with excellent manners and frequenting only elegant society ..."—this same Colonel Redl now stood unmasked as a serpent, as a grotesque, as a criminal, as a treasonous fraud. He had been a secret homosexual debauchee. He had spent a small fortune on hair dyes, scents, cosmetics. He had filled his closets with women's dresses. He had bought his male paramour, a young cavalry officer named Stefan Hromodka, the most expensive automobile and gifted him with an apartment. He had financed his excesses by selling to Russia data on Austrian mobilization plans, army codes, border fortifications, military transport facilities, and supply structures.

Like a riptide the disaster churned through the Empire. Some it raised to the crest. Many others were swept under.

Egon Erwin Kisch, the young reporter that had brought to light a whole world of darkness, became owner of the most famous byline in Central European journalism for the next quarter of a century; henceforward the best table at the Café Central waited for him on all his visits to Vienna. On the other hand, Redl's lieutenant-lover, Stefan Hromodka, was tried, found guilty of unnatural prostitution, sentenced to loss of commission as well as to three months of hard labor. (He later married, had children, and lived another fifty years.) Baron Giesl von Gieslingen, Redl's Commanding General in Prague, was pensioned off. Colonel von Urbanski, chief of the Intelligence Bureau, would be suffering early retirement within the year. Baron Conrad as Chief of Staff offered his resignation. The Emperor refused it. With the Balkans still seething, this was no time for high-level changes. Conrad continued in an office that now faced very heavy weather.

He found himself summoned to the Castle Belvedere. At the Crown Prince's Vienna residence the air was sulfurous. It was an infuriating week for Franz Ferdinand even without a spy scandal. He had *not* been invited, after all, to the wedding of Kaiser Wilhelm's daughter—the pretext being that "this was a family affair." Behind the slight he detected the hand of his old foe Prince Montenuovo, Franz Joseph's First Lord Chamberlain. On top of this affront, for which there was no ready retaliation, came the Redl disgrace. But at least here the Archduke need not hold back. He received General Conrad with a wrath that was almost joyful.

It had been the General, had it not, who had sent instructions to this wretch Redl to kill himself? And thrusting a suicide pistol at the wretch—that had not been exactly a very religious act, had it? Not exactly the act of a good Catholic? Nor an act observing the chain of command, since the General had not troubled to obtain permission from His Majesty or the

Heir Apparent—or had he? Nor a prudent act either! By having the wretch blow his brains out, one eliminated along with his skull all possibility of useful interrogation, didn't one? But perhaps it was an act consistent with the act of raising such a wretch to a position of responsibility? And leaving such considerations aside—how did the General feel now about his saber-rattling vis-à-vis Serbia and all the Slavs? How much did the General crave a war with Russia now—now that one of his key officers had peddled military secrets to the Tsar? Would the General have the kindness of an answer?

The General, rigidly at attention, went through the litany of his defense. He had tried to contain the scandal by eliminating its source, Redl. Since it had to be done very fast, there'd been no time to inform the Palace. As to a war with the East, Russia had not gained any really crucial information.

The Crown Prince waved away such feeble arguments. The General saluted, retreated. The same day he renewed his offer of resignation to the Emperor who refused it once more.

Less rude than the Crown Prince but equally disturbed was the Chief of Staff of the German Army, General von Moltke, with whom Redl had sometimes conferred in person. Here General Conrad must reassure his ally that Redl had no access to German secrets; that the damage in Austria was limited and remediable; that in fact he, Conrad, had already ordered the devising of new codes, new mobilization plans, and new supply and transport procedures—all of which would make the information now in Russian hands useless.

Berlin's response was a mixture of unease and courtesy. More complex still was another man's attitude—the most important man of all—Franz Joseph. His adjutant reported that on the night after the news broke, the old gentleman could not sleep. But after he rose, as was his custom, at 4 A.M., he strode to his desk and said calmly to his adjutant, Count Paar, "So this is the new era? And that kind of creature comes out of it? In our old days something like that would not even have been conceivable."

7

The Redl monstrosity made the upright splendor of Franz Joseph's "old days" seem so distant. Yet only forty-eight hours before Redl's unmasking, the ancient Emperor himself had animated an occasion that made those "old days" young again in Vienna. At the age of eighty-three, the monarch, bareheaded under the morning sun, had walked for two hours at the center of the Corpus Christi procession.

This spectacle was the Church's counterpoint to the workers' May Day, as consummately Viennese in its pagentry and many centuries older. On May 22, 1913, the procession had flowed again like a river cascading with costumes and colors. All the bells in all the city's towers tolled as it started at St. Stephen's Square, swirled past the fountains, gargoyles, loggias of the Inner Precinct, poured on under the eyes of thousands of saints (for all apartment dwellers placed their holy pictures on their window sills) until it reached St. Michael's Square where it stopped for an open-air Mass before flowing back to St. Stephen's Cathedral.

At the head billowed the massed senior clergy in long gilt-embroidered vestments, bishops and prelates holding aloft ancient gonfalons of the Fifteen Mysteries of the Faith; then came the Lord Mayor of Vienna with his Great Chain of Office; then the Dean of the University and the faculty in their richly hued gowns with their swords in silvered sheaths; then officers of the great orders, first and foremost among them the Knights of the Golden Fleece, their collars wrought of firestone and steel; then the white-gold canopy under which the Cardinal strode in undulations of his scarlet cape, holding the monstrance that was shrouded in incense and heralded by the acolytes' tinkling of sanctus bells and flanked by medieval guards with halberd and cuirass; then, all by himself, surrounded by awed, empty space, walked His Majesty, Franz Joseph I, white-fringed head bare to the sky, a white general's uniform snug on his slightly stooped, still slender frame, green-plumed hat under his left arm, his right holding a candle; he was followed by his First Lord Chamberlain and then by the high members of his Court, the Crown Prince, the Archdukes according to seniority, followed by the Archduchesses down to the most junior, followed in turn by the Crown Prince's wife, followed by the imperial and ducal equerries and ladies-in-waiting—all in full-dress robes, epaulettes, sashes, and decorations . . .

Though it began early in the morning, the procession did not escape the strong May sun. Newspaper accounts emphasized "the Emperor's youthful step"—how well he'd taken the strain. Would he have taken it so well had he known that he was marching toward Redl?

The Vienna Derby of 1913 was run on Sunday, June 8, but since it came within two weeks of the Redl revelation, it turned out to be a waste of good weather. Bright was the sun, but not the mood. The Crown Prince smoldered in Konopiste. The Imperial Box at the Freudenau track remained empty. But few missed his frown, and anyway, it would have been the frown of someone almost fifty: The Derby, being a very sporty affair, belonged to the new generation. For Vienna's young bloods it was an annual watershed of fashion: One wore derbies only until the Derby—afterward, summer boaters. The Derby also made a fetching stage for young officers; for their white glacé gloves, their casual cigarettes, the ladies on their arms.

This year, instead of shining in their uniforms, many seemed to cringe. There was much less flaunting by lieutenants of the guard, less flirting, and hardly any dining afterward, in the Sacher Garten of the Prater. Colonel Redl had dishonored the tunic they wore.

That sunny day on the race track lit up yet further dimensions of damage. It wasn't just the Imperial and Royal Army that had been soiled. It was a whole class of comers; a class that was about to earn by merit what earlier could only be inherited by birth; a class that advertised its advent through occasions like the Derby and whose most brilliant representatives included Alfred Redl—until now.

Weaned on cabbage soup as the ninth son of a lowly railway clerk, the Colonel had been well on his way to a field marshal's baton. A rising star of comely ascent, he'd been described by the Army's character report mentioned earlier as "very companionable with excellent manners and frequenting only elegant society . . ." Yes, the horses of June ran for the Redls of the realm. The Derby was the one social ritual in Austria where the very talented, very ambitious, very presentable arrivés could mingle and chat with those who had arrived many generations ago. Now such mingling had proved calamitous. Redl, the only commoner among the Counts and Barons of the General Staff, had turned out to be its only traitor.

An unmistakable contrast: Corpus Christi and the Derby. The Corpus Christi procession, two days before Redl's suicide, had displayed Old Austria's continued virtuosity in dramatizing its own myth. But the Derby, after Redl, disclosed a loss of image and of nerve among the dynamic young. Now the new generation could not enact "honor" or "dash" with the élan expected of them in Vienna. The case had shown up the hollowness of Redl's parvenu mask as well as the hollowness of General Conrad's attempt to cover horror with yet another masking. The art of illusion itself had been compromised—the future of its practice in the twentieth century. A Viennese essence was in jeopardy.

And so the very word "Redl" spelled poison to the town. Alfred Redl's two surviving brothers, Oskar and Heinrich, received permission to change their names to Oskar and Heinrich Rhoden. Stefan Zweig, one of Austria's belletrists, ordinarily heedless of matters military or political, felt, after the first Redl bulletin, "a noose of terror tightening around my throat." There was no end to the toxicity of the affair. The Colonel had been among the Army's most up-to-date careerists, enlisting telegraph and wireless for the transmission of intelligence. Now this demon of forward-mindedness had crashed. It was as if in Vienna any attempt at modernity was doomed. "Redl" affected the city's dealings with the shape of things to come.

* * *

On June 9, 1913, an avatar of the twentieth century rose from the Black Forest into the air and flew toward the Austrian capital. Longer than the tower of St. Stephen's Cathedral, it darkened the heavens as the world's largest dirigible and, by far, the most gigantic aircraft. At a record speed of 101 kilometers per hour, it needed only eight and a half hours to traverse the distance from Baden-Baden to Vienna.

Vienna's progressive newspaper, the *Arbeiter Zeitung,* called on the populace to hail the skyborne arrival of a great secular archangel "for that is how one prays in the twentieth century."

Indeed the Zeppelin appeared over Vienna in angelic perfection, without mishap or delay or even omission of protocol. Passing Schönbrunn Palace, it circled and dipped respectfully while the hoary Emperor on the terrace saluted, for the first time in his life, up instead of down. Many of his subjects, though, could not match his aplomb. Hundreds of children fled indoors from the gargantuan shadow overhead. Grown men flinched, women swooned. A few days later the *Arbeiter Zeitung* noted drily that at a mass celebration of the twenty-fifth anniversary of Kaiser Wilhelm's reign, twenty-six ladies had keeled over, prostrate with either heat or awe. "In Berlin, it seems, people faint out of reverence for the past; in Vienna, out of fear of the future."

The future had never been a great favorite along this bend of the Danube. Now it was less popular then ever. Even a futurist bauble like the cinema—and there were several dozen of them in Vienna now—developed warts. Those phantoms on the screen could burn very real flesh. The extreme flammability of film—a danger hitherto unnoticed—killed three people in a theater fire on June 18. At nearly the same time, a medical journal reported headaches in adult cinema addicts and, in children, a regression of speech patterns by limiting their vocabulary to the primitive phrases of the explanatory titles. When it was reported that an American film producer had come to town to explore the Redl story as a basis for a motion picture, it was like the closing of a viciously modern circle: turning the life of a corrupt young luminary into a corrupting new entertainment. At the center of the circle sat, like a spider, the future.

"Redl" became an emblem of decay; of the inevitability of degeneration in a monarchy so ancient. Would the Habsburgs, for centuries suzerains of the Holy Roman Empire, ever be able to develop their realm into a great modern power? Serbia, its adversary, was small, defiant, and pulsing with the young passion of nationalism. Until now it had yielded, however reluctantly and belatedly, before Austria's warnings against its Balkan presumptions. But it never yielded for long. Toward the end of June, Serbia inveigled Greece and Montenegro, its partners in last year's victory over Turkey, to join her in demanding a re-division of the Turkish spoils at the expense of the fourth partner, Bulgaria. Since Bulgaria was a Habsburg ally, Vienna protested to Belgrade. In vain. Belgrade politely acknowledged the protest and promptly ignored it. Serbia's troops and those of its cohorts—which Rumania had joined for good measure—massed along the Bulgarian borders. In Vienna, General Conrad once more managed to defeat the Crown Prince's cautions. The Chief of Staff obtained authorization for an Army Alert. Reservists were called up. The capital's railroad terminals teemed with mothers hugging their sons who looked like strangers in their sudden uniforms.

The weather turned queasy. It was still spring, but a breath of humid mid-summer came down on the city. Policemen sweated, in part thanks to Redl. To counteract the Redl malaise, the Police Commissioner devised an Austrian remedy. He decided to fortify the morale of his men with the glitter of their headgear. Instead of light summer caps, the constables must keep wearing the heavy but polished metal helmets of winter.

In their airless slums, the poor perspired, too. Suddenly there were more of them at the end of June: The Imperial and Royal Telephone Administration dismissed three hundred workers, thus adding to the record number of jobless in recent years. After all, mobilization cost money, and the government must cut expenses somewhere. The discharged three hundred demonstrated on the Ringstrasse, joined not only by fellow unemployed but by some of the more affluent Viennese who had been waiting for months to have their first telephones installed and now would have to wait still longer.

The jobs were not restored; the premature heat would not let up. But a number of the disadvantaged benefited from the experience of their counterparts in America. The *Arbeiter Zeitung* reported that indigents of a still more sweltering metropolis, namely New York, found a bit of relief by spending the night outdoors. They'd bed down in Battery Park, hoping for cool breezes from New York Bay. To keep lights from flashing into their eyes, they'd turn their backs to the Statue of Liberty, already blazing brightly with electric bulbs for the Fourth of July. And so many a Viennese pauper made himself a bed of rags or blankets on a sidewalk. Instead of zephyrs from New York, he had whiffs from the Vienna Woods—and no Statue of Liberty by which to be either disturbed or deceived.

* * *

For men of means it was a very different summer. Like others of their class elsewhere, they dealt with the city heat by leaving it. But in contrast to their peers outside Austria, their travels often took them not to the newly chic but to the fashionable old: the Alps' Salzkammergut, traditionally the hunting and pleasure grounds of Habsburg.

Here, in the heart of this lake district south of Salzburg, lay Bad Ischl, the summer mecca of Vienna's theater world. Here Franz Lehár, composer of *The Merry Widow,* sovereign of the operetta, maintained a baronial chalet by the banks of the River Traun. Here, in a villa close by, his predecessor Johann Strauss had summered. At the Patisserie Zauner, Lehár munched Mohr im Hemd and exchanged gossip almost as delicious with tenors, sopranos, directors, conductors, actors of note, tragedians, and comic talents, all of whom also did their rusticating here.

The theater represented the most glamorous of the arts. One would think that its luminaries would stake out a vacation terrain of their own toward which their public would then flock. But this was Austria. Vienna's show folk, rather than create a new modish arena of their own, congregated around a spectacle of Habsburg ancien régime, produced bucolic-style, in Bad Ischl. In 1913 it was produced again.

A major figure in this scene was one of the stage world's own—Katharina Schratt, long a leading actress of the Court Theater. For twenty-seven years (before Franz Joseph had been widowed in 1898 and after) she had been the Emperor's lady. She still was. For twenty-seven summers the pair could be observed at Bad Ischl, his kepi bobbing alongside her flowered hat, his walking stick swinging close to her parasol, striding together between the snow-white lily beds and the bosky chestnut stands of the Spa Park.

By 1913 they looked like a pair bonded by a passion practiced through decades. What lay behind them instead was a quarter of a century of abstention. In 1888 Frau Schratt had offered to become her monarch's mistress. "Our relationship must be in the future what it has been in the past," the Emperor had replied (characteristically) by letter, referring to their chastity, "that is, if that relationship is to last, and it must last for it makes me so very happy."

These words had been written in his wife's lifetime; they remained in force after he was widowed. Celibacy would in the future, just as it had in the past, legitimize their ardor; restraint, well embellished, charmingly straitjacketed, would preserve the impulse forever.

And so Franz Joseph and Frau Schratt continued to be lovers in everything but raw fact. They never met between the sheets. Yet in Vienna or Ischl they practiced the entire range of stagecraft that surrounds the bed: all the ardent preambles of passion and the gallant postscripts, the avowals of desire, denials of indifference, impetuous confidences, embarrassed explanations, and the obligatory sulks and quarrels. These emotions they poured into countless letters. He addressed them to "My Dear Good Friend," she, to "Your Imperial and Royal Majesty, my Most August Lord."

They enacted their roles with a persuasiveness that appeared to obviate consummation. In Vienna, their play unfolded invisibly: behind the garden walls of Schönbrunn Palace or over the coffee table in her breakfast room across the street from Schönbrunn. But in Ischl the octogenarian swain and his fifty-year-old inamorata produced their romance in the open, beneath the summer sun. They simulated to perfection the trappings of a liaison.

It was a way of love, a way of life, that came natural to Franz Joseph, the weathered centerpiece of a patinaed court. Under his reign animation had petrified into decor. Decor—not dynamics—governed his affections as well as his politics. Both the Emperor's empire and the Emperor's affair were artifacts. Neither had much fleshly reality. Therefore both must draw their vigor, their tang, their long lives from etiquette and accoutrement. Both represented the triumph of form over substance. They were both masterpieces of survival through sheer style.

When Franz Joseph strode with Frau Schratt through Ischl's parks, detectives discreetly preceded and followed them. When he walked alone, he forbade all such protection. In Vienna there was his state coach with six snow-white steeds; his braided, epauletted retinue of equerries, adjutants, and chamberlains. In Ischl he furloughed them all. Protocol, too, took a holiday. Several times a week Franz Joseph strolled past the gate guards of the Kaiservilla, entirely by himself. This bearer of seventy-two august titles, this breathing legend that had occupied for sixty-odd years the West's most venerable and resonant throne, this master over life and death of many millions, this symbol holding together, against odds, an improbable empire ranging from yodelers on the Swiss border to muezzins chanting from minarets by the Turkish frontier—this near-divinity joined passers-by on the common sidewalk.

If the hour was very early, before seven, it found him off for his coffee with Frau Schratt in her Villa Felicitas. If it was later in the morning, he'd be wending his way toward the town church for Mass. He would stroll behind a babushka'd maid, laden with shopping, or next to a spa guest puffing a cigar. Often they didn't realize for seconds that The Presence was among them. In his blue uniform but without any of his countless decorations, His Imperial and Royal Majesty looked like any officer, long pensioned but still well barbered, trim, as he stepped with a certain circumspection off and on the curb. He glanced at the store windows as he passed and sometimes, like a typical vacationer, he squinted westward up the Ischl sky to see what the day's weather might bring.

Why? Why this charade of ordinariness? Perhaps for His Apostolic Majesty the ordinary had the allure of the exotic. His letters to Frau Schratt breathe a need for the commonplace. He inquires about the effectiveness of the garbage pick-up on her block in Vienna. And how comfortable were the new taxi cars in Vienna? As for himself, he will confess, in detail, that his corns hurt while he stood up to toast the King of Bulgaria. In other words, the Emperor wished to indulge a little in the plain prose of life—for the most part he was imprisoned in his own exaltedness.

And he may have had other reasons for impersonating a pedestrian in Ischl. In the Emperor's sundry capitals—Vienna, Budapest, Prague—the machinery of pomp manufactured the Habsburg charisma. In Ischl, Franz Joseph proved that he needed no courtiers, no supporting players, no footlights, no props. He could wreak magic alone, stepping over a dog turd on the Ischler Hauptstrasse. With a flash of wispy white sideburns on wrinkled cheeks, he could hush each street corner into a throne room. Traffic crunched to a halt at his sight. Drivers whipped off their hats. Women froze in mid-chat. The street turned into a tableau of bows and curtsies past which the Emperor ambled, responding now and then with a salute that seemed friendly but also a bit puzzled. It was as if he'd just been greeted by a nice fellow-officer whose name escaped him but which he might remember right after appreciating the Doboschtorte displayed there in the Patisserie Zauner's window.

For many years Ischl had seen Franz Joseph conjure imperial radiance next to a burgher storefront. But by the teens of the twentieth century his saunterings had taken on yet other aspects. In 1898 his Empress had been stabbed to death as she walked unescorted along the quai of Geneva. Since then even the presence of guards had been unable to prevent the spurting of royal blood. Earlier in 1913 an attempt had been made on the life of the Spanish King. The King of Greece had been murdered. Franz Joseph's solo rambles in Ischl were well-known enough to be downright provocative. Behind every doorway a revolver or a stiletto might be poised. What Franz Joseph was staging, after the gunning-down of Franz Schuhmeier, after the sudden Redl nightmare, was the theater of fatalism.

"If we must go under," he had remarked more than once to an aide-de-camp, "we better go under decently." Mortality was an art in Austria, in 1913. Passing through his mortal eighties, the monarch was its leading adept. He did not show how the end was to be avoided. He showed how it was to be risked and approached: with composure and balance and a certain stoic grace. He walked along the Hauptstrasse, through the homage of his subjects, among mingled scents drifting from the Spa Park: lilac, jasmine, rose, spiced faintly with the perfume of perdition.

8

ON JUNE 30, 1913, THE DISPUTE BETWEEN SERBIA AND BULGARIA OVER Macedonian territory reached its boiling point. Serbia, inveterate Habsburg foe, declared war on Bulgaria; Turkey, Greece, and Rumania joined the Serbian side. The Second Balkan War had started.

Throughout the first week of July, General Conrad belabored the telephone from Vienna to Ischl on behalf of yet another ultimatum to be fired at Belgrade. From the Belgian North Sea resort of Blankenberghe, the Crown Prince was on the wire, roaring for prudence and caution. And a cold rain kept coming down on the Alps around Ischl. The Emperor felt triply beleaguered.

"Dearest Friend," said his letter brought by courier on July

9 from his Ischl residence to Frau Schratt's Villa Felicitas a mile away.

> Dearest Friend:
>
> Just a few lines to welcome you back at the Felicitas. I want to thank you from the bottom of my heart that you came here despite the inclement skies in order to cheer me up . . . Let me ask if I may visit you as usual at 7 A.M. No reply will signify that you expect me. Therefore I will report to you tomorrow by telephone if I can come by foot or if the weather will force me into a carriage. In the former case, please leave the small door unlocked. In glad expectation of a much longed-for reunion.
>
> Loving you most deeply,
> Franz Joseph

He loved her most deeply, and never touched more than the woman's shoulder. Under clearing skies the air remained chill in Ischl; he walked without aides or surcoat to Frau Schratt's villa. Couriers brought him more bulletins from the Balkan War. The telephone ringing in his adjutant's office did not respect either the Alpine idyll in the window or an old gentleman's need for rest. Each day demanded another decision.

He vetoed the bend-or-break demand on Serbia that his Chief of Staff requested. He did permit his Foreign Minister to send Belgrade a monitory letter. He also allowed Conrad to tighten enforcement of conscription laws and to shore up security in the South Slav province of Bosnia by the Serbian border. Through cloud or sun Franz Joseph steered a policy that was mannerly, stately, steady, decorative. He directed it at a world of rude and enigmatic chaos.

On General Conrad's orders, the crackdown on draft evaders now also included those already past conscription age but who, once caught, would have to serve retroactively. Under that category came one "Hietler [*sic*], Adolf, last known address Männerheim, Meldemannstrasse, Vienna, present whereabouts still unknown in ongoing investigation," as the constable entrusted with the task had to report on August 22, 1913.

General Conrad also had three hundred suspected seditionists rounded up in Bosnia as well as Croatia. But instead of deterring, the action incited. At noon of August 18 a solemn Mass at the Zagreb cathedral celebrated the Emperor's birthday in the presence of the new Imperial Governor of Croatia, Baron Ivo Skerletz. As the Baron walked out of church, a Croatian house painter named Stjepan Dojčić lunged forward with a pistol. A moment later Baron Skerletz lay on the cathedral step, his elbow shattered by a bullet, bleeding through his heavily braided sleeve. A month later Dojčić was sentenced to sixteen years of hard labor. The policemen who dragged him from court to jail could not stop his shout: *"After me will come others!"*

They came and they kept coming. No sooner had Dojčić begun to serve his time than an informer's tip led to the arrest of a member of another terrorist group, also in Zagreb. One Lujo Aljinović, a student at a local teacher's college, was seized with a revolver in his pocket as he boarded a train to Vienna. Interrogated by the police, he less admitted than proclaimed his intention "to kill Crown Prince Franz Ferdinand and General Conrad for preparing to attack Serbia . . . Franz Ferdinand is the enemy of all South Slavs and I wished to eliminate this garbage which is hampering our national aspiration."

Unsettling news, disquieting fanatics, misunderstood Franz Ferdinand: "this garbage" was the South Slavs' most potent friend. However, Aljinović's venom showed that the Crown Prince and the General, those adversaries within the Emperor's innermost council, did have something in common, namely a would-be assassin. Therefore the Emperor forwarded Aljinović's threats to the Crown Prince—they might mitigate his animus against the General who was, after all, a fellow target of the same terror. As if in reply Franz Joseph received a copy of a letter sent by the Crown Prince to Count von Berchtold, the Imperial Foreign Minister. It dealt with General Conrad's desire to intervene against Serbia in the Balkan War:

> Excellency! Don't let yourself be influenced by Conrad—ever! Not an iota of support for any of his yappings at the Emperor! Naturally he wants every possible war, every kind of hooray! rashness that will conquer Serbia and God knows what else. The man's been driven even wilder by the Colonel Redl horror. Through war he wants to make up for the mess that's his responsibility at least in part. Therefore: Let's not play Balkan warrior ourselves. Let's not stoop to this hooliganism. Let's stay aloof and watch the scum bash in each others' skulls. It'd be unforgivable, insane, to start something that would pit us against Russia . . . Conrad is good and energetic in combat and in maneuvers, but when it comes to international politics in peacetime, the man is a harum-

> scarum maniac, unusable as an adviser because he sees his personal redemption only in a war which would be a disaster for the monarchy!

Hardly the sort of tone that created summer smiles in Ischl. The Crown Prince's letter set on edge what teeth were left to a very old and very civil Emperor. Franz Joseph was the realm's model of measured mannerliness. In this coarse new century, he felt, his empire endured as a last bastion of good form. Here leaders authenticated their position through their deportment. And this Crown Prince, this boor with his brawler's invective, refused to realize that Austrian statecraft had to be *acted* with propriety in order to be effectively executed.

"You know how he is," Franz Joseph would sigh when talking about Franz Ferdinand. "How" defined the angle of his complaint. To the Emperor's Viennese mind, the *how* of the man's actions superseded the *what.*

The *what* of the Crown Prince's letter happened to be a very astute view of Austria's international situation as well as of General Conrad's psychology—a view more insightful than that of any of the Emperor's other advisers. The *how* of the letter, though, was rough and raucous, and therefore cancelled its virtues. A messenger who did not perform the right bow before his Habsburg suzerain did not bring the right message.

"Don't let Conrad get out of hand!" bellowed the Crown Prince. "Tighten the damn leash!" The Emperor, offended, loosened the reins. Since he could finely modulate even a refusal, he loosened them only a nuance or two. His Majesty still vetoed direct military action against Serbia. On the other hand, he let Conrad counter Slav pressure with new stratagems aimed at Serbia's big brother, Russia. They were covert moves that tiptoed—which is often history's way of creeping from whisper to thunder.

* * *

Conrad's General Staff suspected St. Petersburg of encouraging sedition in the Austrian provinces next to Serbia. Therefore Conrad—with the Emperor's sanction, despite the Crown Prince's protests—had long encouraged anti-Tsarist revolutionaries exiled on Habsburg soil. This explained the "lethargy" of the Austrian police experienced so pleasantly by Trotsky. Toward Lenin the Austrian security apparatus was even more complaisant. In 1912 it had facilitated his move from France to Cracow in Austria, near the Russian border. Through this change of address, Habsburg intensified the undercover political warfare against Romanov.

Vienna instructed Cracow police: accommodate Lenin, infiltrate his conspirators not to hinder but to help him. In one of his earliest directives to the just-born St. Petersburg *Pravda,* Lenin had sponsored an article written by an Austrian agent. Now, in the summer of 1913, under All-Highest approval obtained from Ischl, clandestine operations like his were permitted to expand. The head of Conrad's Counter-Intelligence Bureau (once run by Colonel Redl), Colonel Oscar von Hranilović, was in charge of smoothing things still further for Lenin.

This convenient Bolshevik leader was allowed to visit Vienna in July 1913. He always enjoyed his sojourns there. (In a letter he once called the Austrian capital "a mighty, beautiful and vivacious city.") This time he came partly to consult doctors about his wife's goiter, partly to meet comrades in Vienna about the upcoming "summer conference" of the Bolshevik faction of the Russian Social Democratic Party scheduled (under the indulgent eyes of Habsburg authorities) in Austrian Galicia. Suddenly—from somewhere in the neighborhood of Vienna's Ministry of War—money floated into

Lenin's hands. Suddenly he could afford to place a large order with a Viennese printer: 10,000 copies of a proposed party resolution and no less than 50,000 copies of a proclamation to be smuggled into Russia; it commemorated the St. Petersburg Bloody Sunday when the Tsar's troops had massacred hundreds of workers and wounded thousands in 1905.

Leon Trotsky, the hero of 1905, chairman of the short-lived Soviet of that year, was in Vienna during this visit of Lenin's in July 1913. As we know, he had made the capital his headquarters, enjoying, like Lenin, the tolerance of the Austrian Counter-Intelligence Bureau. The two men, however, never met that summer for reasons excellent and ironic.

Their conflict was coming to a head just then; in fact, it carried echoes of the clash between Franz Joseph and his Heir Apparent. Lenin had established himself as virtual emperor of the Bolshevik wing of Russian socialism through his skilled, tireless manipulation of the Party's Central Committee. Trotsky had defined Lenin's imperial politicking as "egocentralism" whose manifesto read "I am confirmed by the Central Committee, therefore I am." As Franz Joseph's reign was ritualized daily through the intricacies of court etiquette, so Lenin finessed his leadership through the tenacities, the niceties, the ambushes, the rhetoric of factional infighting, an art he may have perfected from the camarilla politics of the Empire that was his host.

Trotsky, on the other hand, played a Franz Ferdinand role in the cast of Russian revolutionaries. He was the brainy, impolitic maverick of a newer generation. He had no patience with Lenin's steely-eyed craft of wearing down the Menshevik moderates within the Party. No, Trotsky, with the brilliance of his Western eloquence (honed at the Café Central), Trotsky through his role as pacifist among the Socialist sects, wanted to dazzle and conciliate Mensheviks and Bolsheviks into one camp—then sweep the unified Party into a revolution surging beyond Russia into the world . . .

Lenin dismissed this pipe dream of reconciliation. He also sneered at Trotsky's "absurd, semi-anarchist view that the maximum program, the conquest of power for a socialist revolution, can be achieved immediately . . ." Hence Trotsky's spit at Lenin ". . . that master-squabbler, brewing the deplorable brew of Party bickerings, that professional exploiter of backwardness in the Russian workers' movement . . . The entire edifice of Leninism at present rests on lies and falsification and bears inside itself the poisonous seeds of its own disintegration."

For August 1913 Lenin had scheduled his Summer Conference—another "bickering" Committee meeting—at his country residence in the Galician Tatra mountains. Trotsky stayed away from it, just as the Heir Apparent liked to stay away from the Emperor's villa in Bad Ischl or from the Imperial Palace in Vienna. In fact, Trotsky was off to Bulgaria to write about the new Balkan War.

Within four years, of course, the two revolutionary prodigies would (as Trotsky put it) "amnesty" each other of all their earlier disagreements. Trotsky would join Lenin as his co-architect of the Russian Revolution. But in the summer of 1913, another feud was cresting, also between a younger and an older leader. And this one hardened into a permanent battle that partisans are waging to this day.

On July 13, 1913, Freud left Vienna for the Bohemian spa of Marienbad. He was taking the cure for his rheumatism. He was also conditioning himself for the duel of his life. In a few weeks the Fourth International Psycho-Analytical Congress would start, and the man who would chair it, Carl Jung, whom Freud had installed as President and as his own Heir Apparent—this same Jung had turned against him. An insurrection threatened a precarious kingdom.

The International Psycho-Analytical Association had been organized as a monarchy similar to the realm in which its creator had been born. "Freud," wrote Ernest Jones, his most faithful Freudian, "Freud was too mistrustful of the average mind to adopt the democratic attitude customary in scientific societies . . . he wanted the leader to be in a permanent position, like a monarch . . ." who would exert ". . . a strong steadying influence with a balanced judgment, and a sense of responsibility . . ."

Franz Joseph couldn't have put it better. It was a view likely to have been inspired by Austria-Hungary's mosaic of contentiously hyphenated entities. Freud saw man's psyche similarly divided: id–ego–superego. The id, "the parliament of instincts," in Freud's words, resembled the lower legislature on the Ringstrasse, steaming with nationalist passions; the superego recalled the noblesse oblige of an older code to which the Austrian ethos still appealed with its feudal titles and the handkissing chivalry of its etiquette. The ego was the crown at the helm, steering the whole restive and cumbersome enterprise.

The International Psycho-Analytical Association consisted of members who must chart such tensions in their patients. Therefore they needed an organization much more powerfully centralized than (these are Jones's words) "old and relatively unemotional disciplines" like "geology and astronomy." To cope with the disorderly dramatics of the psychoanalysts' métier, a leader of hallowed power was required, a tiara'd ego whose office warranted not just election but coronation.

At a previous Psycho-Analytical Association Congress in

1910, Freud had overcome resistance from Viennese colleagues and anointed Carl Jung president. Under Freud's aegis the younger physician from Switzerland wielded the privileges of a Crown Prince. Talent as well as race had brought him to the top. Among Freud's many Jewish disciples, he had the advantage of being Christian. As Freud saw it, "Jews . . . are incompetent to win friends for the new teaching. Jews must be content with the modest role of preparing the ground." Jung was therefore most fit "to form ties in the world of general science . . . I am getting on in years . . . when the empire I have founded is orphaned, no one except Jung must inherit the whole thing."

But in 1913 the inheritor, the Franz Ferdinand of psychoanalysis, had not only committed but openly affirmed his high treason. He had discarded the theory of sexuality, a concept no less sacred to Freud than court protocol was to Franz Joseph. As protocol in the Habsburg palace, so sex in Freud's canon governed all aspects of the day; like the court code it was hierarchical: oral sexuality preceded anal in the development of man, and anal preceded genital. Jung recalls Freud's injunction on the first day of his, Jung's, presidency:

> "My dear Jung, promise me never to abandon the sexual theory . . . we must make a dogma of it, an unshakable bulwark."
>
> "A bulwark against what?" I asked.
>
> To which he replied, "Against the black tide of mud"—and here he hesitated for a moment, then added—"of occultism."

And now Jung, far from defending the bulwark, had begun to assault it. In a series of lectures given in London during the summer of 1913, he shifted emphasis from Freud's individual id to the idea of a collective unconscious. On certain aspects of dream theory he proclaimed "entire agreement" with Alfred Adler, Freud's foe. Most fatal of all was Jung's statement that psychoanalytic theory "should be freed from the purely sexual standpoint. In place of it I should like to introduce an energetic viewpoint into the psychology of neurosis."

By 1913 all this had become much more than an intellectual disagreement. The confrontation was now naked, bitter, man-to-man. A few months earlier, Jung, replying to one of Freud's admonitions, had suddenly lashed out in terms as personal as a slap:

> your technique of treating your disciples like patients is a *blunder*. In that way you produce either slavish sons or impudent puppies . . . I am objective enough to see through your little trick. You go around sniffing out all the symptomatic actions in your vicinity, thus reducing everyone to the level of sons and daughters who blushingly admit the existence of their faults. Meanwhile you remain on top as the father, sitting pretty. From sheer obsequiousness nobody dares pluck the beard of the prophet and to inquire for once what you should say to a patient with a tendency to analyze the analyst instead of himself. You would certainly ask him, "*Who's* got the neurosis?"

Such defiance was, purposely, unforgivable. Jung hurled it at Freud in an era when the distance between leader and led still remained sacral. In 1913 the Austrian Court Gazette still used routinely the phrase "by All-Highest Decision" because direct reference to the Emperor might compromise his transcendence. In 1913 Kaiser Wilhelm's anniversaries were still celebrated by subjects shouting *"Hurrah!"* while falling to their knees. In 1913 Russian film theaters showing a newsreel of the Tsar required the audience to stand at attention with heads bared; after the imperial image had departed the lights would go on, the anthem would be sung, and only then could the audience sit and the lights dim again to let ordinary shadows inhabit the screen.

Under this Zeitgeist the Jung rebellion came to pass. Indeed Jung's boxing of Freud's ear was lèse-majesté much worse than Trotsky's gibe at Lenin. After all, mutiny came natural to revolutionaries "vomiting their feelings like blood" as Rilke observed of arguments among Russian exiles. The International Psycho-Analytical Association, on the other hand, had seemlier ways. Though its members probed the underbelly of morality, they were *Herr Doktors* with academic dignities, well-shined shoes, watch-chain-festooned waistcoats, carefully knotted cravats. In 1913 they constituted a professional body, as subject as any other in the Imperial and Royal Crownlands of the House of Austria, to a hallowed sense of rank.

And Carl Jung's revolt shocked more than Alfred Adler's abandonment of the articles of faith two years earlier. In Adler's case the doctrinal often still veiled the personal. But in his letter Jung brazenly announced his intent "to pluck the beard of the prophet." He accused the founder of psychoanalysis of foisting his maladjustment on the psyche of his rivals. It went beyond heresy. It was a spit at the throne.

Freud's reply displayed well-mannered firmness à la Franz Joseph:

> We have a convention among us analysts that none of us need feel ashamed of his own bit of neurosis. But someone who behaves abnormally

> yet keeps shouting that he is normal gives ground for suspicion that he lacks insight into his illness. Accordingly, I propose that we abandon our personal relations entirely. I shall lose nothing by it, for my only emotional tie with you has long been a thin thread—the lingering effect of past disappointments . . .

These lines had been written early in 1913. But now it was July. In less than two months Freud would have to face Jung occupying the head chair of the Munich Psycho-Analytical Congress. The man he'd made President would now wield the gavel against him. This prospect loomed over Freud as he sipped the alkaline waters and walked the pinewood paths of Marienbad. The shadow under which he moved darkened as July approached, but it was a shadow that had engaged him all year. His latest manuscript, *Totem and Taboo,* dealt with the violent overthrow of a chief. As he would later admit, the theme contained an unconscious link to Jung, the usurper. And quite consciously Freud deployed *Totem and Taboo* as a weapon in this war. His essay explored the prehistoric lore of the "primal horde" from which the totem evolved. Freud was staking out systematically, possessively, areas of myth and primitive religion that were Jung's turf.

The king had counterattacked the rebel. But the king couldn't rest easy. A month of taking the waters from mid-July to mid-August did little to relieve his rheumatic right arm. "I can scarcely write," says his note from Marienbad to Ernest Jones; ". . . we had a bad time here. The weather was cold and wet." Nor was his mood sunny. His daughter Anna, who kept him company, would later report that this was the only time she remembered her father being depressed.

On August 11 the Freuds (daughter, wife, paterfamilias) traveled to San Martino di Castrozza, a lovely aerie of a resort 5,000 feet high in the Dolomites. Freud loved mountaineering but could spare little time for sparkling Alpine hikes. The Congress—and therefore combat with Jung—was now only a month away. His lieutenants in the International Psycho-Analytical Association were gathering around him at San Martino and took rooms next to his at the Hotel des Alpes. Sandor Ferenczi came from Budapest; Karl Abraham arrived from Berlin. Together they had long grim strategy sessions amplified by correspondence with Ernest Jones, Freud's field marshal in England.

The council ratified Freud's decision to continue his Franz Joseph stance: firmness, dignity, moderation. Neither Ferenczi nor Abraham was to assail Jung. Freud himself would read a paper—"The Predisposition to Obsessional Neurosis"—that was rather neutral in the context of the conflict. Only Jones would produce a paper criticizing, in measured tones, recent positions of the adversary.

Thus the battle plan; so the execution. When the Fourth International Psycho-Analytical Congress opened in Munich on September 7, Jung sat at a table apart from Freud with his phalanx of Swiss analysts. Two years earlier "the Crown Prince" had done his presiding with cordial humor. Now, at the 1913 Congress, his face was taut, his manner brusque, his gavel partisan. He cut off arguments, ruled inconvenient points out of order, recognized speakers whenever it suited his offensive against Freud. At the final session the filling of the next presidential term had to be settled. Despite everything, Freud suggested to his followers that they re-elect Jung, who therefore won the vote. But out of 82 members present, 22 withheld their ballots—an unprecedented and significant number. (To Jones, one of the abstainers, Jung spoke one short sentence that spoke racial volumes: "I thought you were a Christian.")

Freud's gesture was noblesse oblige of majestic proportions, a theatrical flourish masterfully Viennese. By comparison, his Zurich opponent looked mean and crude. When it was all over, Jung remained in possession of the title, but Freud walked away with much of his prestige and power intact. He could not arbitrarily strip Jung of the presidency. However, Freud proposed to his adherents that the Vienna, Berlin, and Budapest chapters petition Jung—without crass quarreling—to dissolve the International Association. On Jung's refusal they would quietly resign, thereby triggering resignations in England and America and signalling the probability of a new international group under Freud. All this needed to be done slowly, slowly enough for a face-saving interval during which Jung could evaluate the prospect and sue for peace.

The plan disquieted Freud's retinue. To them the moment called for outspokenness and action, not for gradual, indirect maneuvers. Jung was Serbia. Dr. Karl Abraham and Dr. Ernest Jones, Freud's two principal generals, took the line of General Conrad, the Austrian Chief of Staff: a harder, quicker, more damaging countermove must be made.

Of course the ultimate decision was Freud's. But in the days and weeks that followed, Freud, strangely enough, did nothing—nothing except hesitate.

The day after the Psycho-Analytical Congress ended, on September 10, 1913, Freud took the express from Munich to

Italy. In Rome he continued his hesitation in a way that was so ambivalent that he left two contradictory accounts of his sojourn. To Jones he wrote a letter mentioning the "delicious days" in the Eternal City. But later he would confess to the peculiar and pensive compulsion that marked his irresolute stay:

> Every day for three lonely weeks in September 1913 . . . I mounted the steps of the unlovely Corso Cavour where the deserted church [of San Pietro in Vincoli] stands . . . [Every day for three weeks] I stood in the church in front of the statue . . .

The statue was Michelangelo's monumental Moses, originally created for Pope Julius II's tomb in the Vatican. Moses mesmerized—and paralyzed—Freud during those unsure days after his collision with Jung. Of course, Rome itself had for years touched off an odd resonance inside him. Long before he had been able to afford traveling there, Freud's wishes and fantasies had centered on Rome to a degree he himself had called "neurotic" in lines to a colleague. The Rome fixation had also emerged in his self-analysis in *The Interpretation of Dreams*. Here he connected it to his boyhood worship of Hannibal, the Carthaginian (and hence Semitic) generalissimo who conquered much of the Roman Empire—except Rome itself.

In other words, it was Freud's conquistadorial self that wanted to complete a glory not attained by his hero. When he had finally reached Rome in 1901, he'd found his way quickly to Michelangelo's Moses, for that, too, was a familiar fascination ever since he had seen a copy of the statue in the Vienna Academy of Art. Like Hannibal, Moses was a great Semitic conqueror. He had overcome Egypt and had led his people to greatness without himself reaping its fruit: He had died outside the Promised Land just as Hannibal had not lived to capture the Capitoline Hill. But on that very hill, Freud had walked year after year since 1901, with much more than a tourist's abandon.

Was this his will for the conquistadorial absolute? Did he want to outdo his foremost models? Did he mean his conquests to exceed even theirs? His close friend Hans Sachs observed that "in the execution of his duty he was untiring and unbending, hard and sharp like steel, a 'good hater' close to the limits of vindictiveness."

"He reminded me of a conqueror," said Theodore Dreiser, who never met the man but knew him percipiently through his books, "a conqueror that has taken a city, entered its age-old prisons and there generously proceeded to release from their gloomy and rusted cells the prisoners of formulae, faiths, and illusions which have wracked and worn men for thousands and thousands of years . . ."

Such a chieftain might be flexible in strategy; he might array himself in sovereign, iron calm. But he must never compromise his purpose by one-thousandth of an inch. Freud usually aspired to all of these traits. But not during that Roman September of 1913. Not during those feckless weeks before his return to Vienna. It was Europe's last peaceful September before an irremediable explosion. It was the aftermath of his clenched confrontation with Jung. Back and forth Freud went along the via Cavour on his daily pilgrimages to Moses. Back and forth strode the doctor from Vienna with his graying beard and his conquistadorial bent. Peculiarly enough, he was trying to walk his way toward the idea of an unconquistadorial moderation; a moderation he saw embodied in Michelangelo's marble.

* * *

The statue in San Pietro represents a leader at a moment of imperious fury: Moses, just descended from Mount Sinai, finds Israel dancing around the Golden Calf (a totem!) and is about to dash the Tablets of the Law to pieces. Yet Freud, staring and staring at the curve and thrust of that enormous body, the fall of its robe, the curling of its fingers, reaches a startlingly different conclusion:

> I used to sit in front of the statue in the expectation that I should see how it would start up on its raised foot, hurl the Tablets to the ground, and let fly its wrath. Nothing of the kind happened. Instead the stone image became more and more transfixed, an almost oppressively solemn serenity radiated from it, and I was obliged to realize that something was shown here that could stay without change; that this Moses would keep sitting like this in his wrath forever . . .

But why should Michelangelo rein in this most unbiblical Moses? Because (writes Freud),

> Michelangelo modified the theme of the broken tablets; he does not let Moses break the Tablets in his wrath, but makes him be influenced by the danger that they might be broken and makes him pacify that wrath, or at any rate prevent it from becoming an act. In this way he had added something new and human to the figure of Moses, so that the giant frame with its tremendous

> physical power becomes only a concrete expression of the highest mental achievement that is possible in a man, that of struggling successfully against an inward passion for the sake of a cause to which he has devoted himself.

This Moses in Freud's essay "Moses of Michelangelo" is very different from the magisterial avenger in Exodus. And this is a very different Freud, acclaiming nothing less than repression.

But the surprise does not end here. Apart from inverting psychoanalysis, the essay ignores the Freudian approach altogether. Freud himself called it a "nonanalytic child" of his pen. He had no interest, when he wrote it, later in 1913, in probing deeper motives for Michelangelo's variation of the Moses theme. He doesn't dredge for disguised emotions. He deals, rather, with an overt political aim. Freud reasons that by presenting a restrained Moses, Michelangelo was warning the leader who had originally commissioned the statue, namely Pope Julius II, who

> attempted to realize great and mighty ends, especially designs on a large scale. The Pope was a man of action and he had a definite purpose, which was to unite Italy under Papal supremacy. He desired to bring about singlehanded what was not to happen for several centuries, and then only through the conjunction of many alien forces; and he worked with impatience in the short span of authority allowed him and used violent means.

The conquistadorial temper confessed to by Freud and observed in him by others—here Freud describes it in a negative context. The conqueror-Pope deserves Michelangelo's reproof.

And Moses, the martial pontiff of the Jews; Moses of the headlong valor; Moses, slayer of Egyptians and drowner of Pharaoh's army; Moses, the smasher of God's tablets; Moses who smote pagans the way General Conrad wanted to smite Serbs; Moses who ground the Golden Calf to bits and made the Israelites drink of it; Moses who had the Levites kill three thousand idolators—what happened to him?

Before Freud's eyes he vanished in the hot dust of Rome. In his stead rises a prophet who heroically resists his own vehemence.

It was in the spirit of the other Moses that Freud decided to end his summer hesitation over the war with Jung. He would forgo even the passive countermove of resigning from the Psycho-Analytical Association of which Jung remained the official head. As his paladin, Ernest Jones, wrote later, Freud would do anything he possibly could at this point to avoid an open schism at which the opponents of psychoanalysis could rejoice. Like his Moses he "pacified his wrath or at any rate prevented it from becoming an act . . . he struggled successfully against an inward passion for the sake of a cause to which he had devoted himself." For the sake of psychoanalysis he decided to wait things out quietly, at least for a while, at the end of the world's last calm summer.

9

On Sunday August 3, 1913, the Austrian resort of Bregenz marked its summer season with an unusual climax. It took place on the spacious promenade winding along the foothills that cup the eastern end of Lake Constance by the Swiss border. Many Viennese spent their summer holidays at this scenic, tonic spot, far from the urban dog days. With other tourists they strolled above the leafy shoreline to enjoy the view and the breeze of Central Europe's largest lake.

On August 3, however, the promenade drew a crowd extraordinarily large even for a weekend blessed by golden weather. On that Sunday the International Peace Conference held an open-air mass meeting there. Seven thousand pacifists converged on the lakefront, not only from the Austro-Hungarian Empire but from Germany, Switzerland, Italy, and France. Some 5,000 vacationers became their impromptu comrades. They heard the Viennese Socialist leader Karl Renner (Trotsky's debating partner at the Café Central and later first Chancellor of the first Austrian Republic in 1918 as well as first President of the second Austrian Republic in 1945). Renner talked about the timeliness of the occasion. Just a few days earlier the latest little Balkan war had ended. The Bulgarians, in full retreat, had signed an armistice with the Serbs, the Rumanians, and the Greeks. Hostilities had lasted less than a month. Yet Renner emphasized that modern weaponry could expedite a bloodbath very fast. For Bulgaria alone, a country of just over four million, the dead and wounded were estimated to exceed 150,000. In a war involving major powers like Austria, whole generations of young men would turn into corpses or into physical and mental cripples.

Therefore, said Renner, this latest peace just made in the Balkans was a peace that should make people think. It was an uneasy peace. At the Bucharest Conference where the victors' terms were to be signed into a treaty, the Serbs would emerge as the chief gainers. A strengthened Serbia might aggravate tensions at Austria's southeastern border. Belgrade and Vienna might goad each other into the most dangerous bravado. Because men had invented such efficient murder machines, peace had become more precious than ever. The life-saving necessity for peace was coming home to more and more people. That so many had gathered here for the cause of peace was a fact as bright as the lakeside sun.

Foghorns from steamers joined the applause. The throng dispersed into a spell of midsummer sweetness that lingered into fall.

* * *

When vacationers returned to Vienna they found in its streets a mellowing temper. The weather helped. During July and August frequent showers had punctuated sunshine. Rain had washed away most blossoms; but it had kept foliage juicy. As a result the proletariat of the outer districts, where their tenements adjoined the Vienna Woods, could stroll into green whose freshness ignored autumn. A few hellers would buy them a stick of horsemeat salami from stands by the vineyard inns; a few more coins would bring a bottle fermented from local grapes. Very soon they would lean against each other, sitting on the wine garden's hard wooden benches as happy as if on Sacher Hotel plush, singing of "the wine that will still sparkle when we no longer breathe, the girls that will laugh long after we are gone . . . ," enjoying an evanescent, convivial, inexpensive, very Viennese binge in a bower.

Possibly it was the clement air as well as the Party's stand on capital punishment that made the widow of Franz Schuhmeier, the murdered Socialist deputy, send a request for lenience to the Minister of Justice; the killer's brother remained a leader of the Conservative Party, but just the same she asked His Excellency to commute the death penalty imposed on the man who had assassinated her husband.

There were other amicable gestures, some quite unexpected. The first prominent fall event unfolding in the white-and-gold rococo of the Musikvereinssaal was not a concert but the Eleventh International Zionist Congress. Nine thousand attended, including a visitor from Prague, the labor-insurance official and would-be *littérateur* Franz Kafka, in town to give a speech at the concurrent Second International Conference on Accident Prevention.

His seven days in the Austrian capital pushed Kafka into insomnia, malaise, and the necessity for constant cold compresses. But another voice, then much more widely heard and known for its abrasive bigotry, took on a sudden *gemütlich* tone. The newspaper *Reichspost,* cutting edge of Austrian anti-Semitism, hailed the Jewish event in the Musikvereinssaal as proof of Vienna's cosmopolitan importance, its pre-eminence as a congress city.

In the fall of 1913 Vienna even seemed to make peace with the future without jeopardizing its stature as a virtuoso of the past. In this matter the Emperor himself provided an example. Until now he had shrugged aside the new century's contraptions. Franz Joseph's adjutants—never His Majesty—picked up the telephone. He never climbed into a motorcar unless forced by etiquette—say, in the company of an automobile addict like the Kaiser. But in Bad Ischl, on August 19, the day after his eighty-third birthday, he consented to view Mr. Thomas Edison's newest invention, the Kinetophone. This machine coordinated the wizardries of the film projector with those of the gramophone. At a special premiere in the Ischl Town Theater, the monarch and his lady took their seats in the first row. Frau Schratt heartily applauded the image of Enrico Caruso intoning *do re mi fa sol.* The Emperor's clapping was, well, polite. Still he sanctified new technology with his presence.

Forty-eight hours earlier he had made a move which, while also not necessarily enthusiastic, carried greater significance. He had dispatched a document with his seal to Bluehnbach Castle near Salzburg; this was one of Franz Ferdinand's hunting estates where the archduke was currently shooting stag. The sovereign's handwritten letter appointed his nephew Inspector General of all Imperial and Royal Armed Forces—the most powerful post given the Crown Prince so far. This elevation, a surprise considering the queasy relationship between the two, was effective immediately—and immediately made public. It, too, was seen as an ancient ruler's concession to tomorrow.

When the Court Train took Franz Joseph from Ischl back to Vienna on September 3, the city had been given, as it were, an All-Highest license to welcome modern things.

This it proceeded to do, with a baroque bow, of course. On some of the broader thoroughfares leading to the center of town, for example, the mayor established special lanes for motorcars in a hurry. Behind chauffeurs driving along these "fast strips" sat gentlemen registering, just as fast, the fall fashions of 1913. You could see them whiz by (at a velocity almost equaling the Crown Prince's Gräf & Stift) in suits of the latest English "country cut," tweeds of informal blue gray. And though it wasn't cool enough as yet, the ladies went even further, anticipating winter's first harbingers from the Paris fashion houses: Directoire collars high in back to plunge rather heedlessly in front, crêpe de chine dresses with ermine trimmings, huge "fantasy necklaces" of amber, coral, or lapis lazuli.

Most of such forward-minded feminine elegance could not be risked in automobiles. Their speed undid the perfection of the coiffure, not to speak of the plumage on the hat. No, ladies preferred the more leisured showcase of the fiacre. This horse-drawn cab, banned for a while, now received renewed municipal blessing. Indeed, to encourage fiacres against the proliferation of the fume-spewing taxi, they were permitted to dispense with set tariffs and to arrive at fares by mutual agreement. The fiacre, said the Mayor's office, would "return to the street scene a dear Viennese tradition."

Similar concerns touched a committee preparing, months in advance, the Industrialists' Ball—bound to be a highlight of the 1914 carnival season. The committee announced that there would be music from two orchestras as well as from six gramophone discs to be specially recorded in Buenos Aires by Los Caballeros; it was a band famous for that new rage, the tango (whose risqué modernity had just led Kaiser Wilhelm to forbid all German soldiers from even listening to it while in uniform). On the other hand—and all rumors to the contrary—Vienna's Industrialists' Ball would be opened by an eighteenth-century cotillion, according to custom. In the fall of 1913 the city seemed readier than ever to absorb onward thrusts of the future into its own timeless choreography.

The Habsburg government applied the technique to its increasingly huffy little Balkan opponent. Flushed with victory over Bulgaria, the Serbs had once more deepened their raids into Albanian territory. Belgrade argued that Vienna used Albania as a staging ground for agents who fostered sedition among Albanian ethnics within Serb borders. Vienna militants contended that these complaints were a blind for Serb expansionism growing more rampant daily.

In his Chief of Staff's office Baron Conrad paced, dictating letter after letter to the Emperor; each paragraph tried to impress on His Majesty the outrages Belgrade visited in Albania on Austria's stature. From Belvedere Palace the Crown Prince countered with a letter to Foreign Minister Count von Berchtold stating that "all such Serb horror stories leave me cold."

As always, the Emperor had to arbitrate. In the spirit of the fall of 1913, Franz Joseph's government decided to combine the latest of mailed fists with an old-fashioned diplomatic smile. The Minister of War, Baron von Krobatin, announced that four more dreadnoughts would be built at a cost of [illegible] million kronen each; the ships would boast every twentieth-century advance in armor and cannon; together they would constitute the most formidable task force in the Adriatic. At almost the same time Count von Berchtold held his fall reception for accredited ambassadors at the Ballhausplatz where he remarked, between toasts of champagne, that the sole purpose of Austrian strength was peace—especially peace with Serbia.

If Serbia didn't believe in pleasantries amidst goblets, it did take seriously the looming of the dreadnoughts. Early in October the Serbian Prime Minister Nikola Pašić visited Vienna. After an interview with Count von Berchtold, Pašić's office issued a communiqué: he and the Austrian Excellency could not agree on the issue of Austrian interference in the southern Balkans, but he did promise that Serbia would not invade Albania and he hoped that his pledge would fortify the possibilities of amity between Serbia and the Austro-Hungarian Empire.

Coming from the chief executive of a pugnacious upstart of a country, this was an almost chastened statement. Perhaps it also reflected a weakening of Serbia's international support that autumn. The saber that its protector could rattle was tarnished for the moment; the Tsar was beset by domestic trouble. Credit for that belonged, at least in part, to Lenin and therefore to Lenin's hidden hosts in Austrian Counter-Intelligence. At the Bolshevik summer conference in Austrian Galicia—held at virtually the same time as Freud's Psycho-Analytical Congress in Munich and as contentious and important—Lenin had forced through a controversial resolution: It directed the Bolshevik parliamentary deputies to the St. Petersburg legislature to form a caucus separate from the more moderate Mensheviks with whom they had till then formed a common Social Democratic front. In word and action they were now free to push their own much more drastic program.

Very soon the move made itself felt through much of industrialized Russia. The Bolshevik-controlled *Pravda* in St. Petersburg mercilessly scourged "Menshevik spinelessness" and Trotskyite "nonfactionalism." In the Duma, Bolshevik speakers called on workers to stop being slaves. Their fierceness unfettered, Lenin's men drew more attention from major trade unions. They also gained more influence. Scattered but steady strike activity spread in the factories, guided by Bolshevik headquarters in Austria. Here Lenin enjoyed freedom to operate and to politick in ways that made Habsburg smile. Occasionally Lenin smiled back. In his talks on the Nationalities Question he said more than once that Vienna handled the problem far better than St. Petersburg.

But in the second half of 1913 you didn't have to be a Bolshevik to consider Austria morally prettier than Russia. By autumn the damage from the Redl case was fading in Habsburg lands; at any rate it receded before the disgrace happening under Romanov. In October the Tsar's district attorney in Kiev prosecuted, with anti-Semitic zeal, a ritual-murder trial against a Jew named Mendel Beilis.

The spectacle reeked of medieval viciousness. Indignation ran through Europe, not least along the Danube. To support their brother so unjustly accused, Vienna's Jewish Community organized a huge meeting at the Musikvereinssaal. The famous (non-Jewish) physiologist Julius Wagner-Jauregg was among three Austrian scientists giving testimony in defense of Mendel Beilis's innocence. Internationally, on Beilis's behalf, a petition was addressed to the Tsar; notables signing it included Sir Arthur Conan Doyle, Engelbert Humperdinck, Anatole France, Käthe Kollwitz, Selma Lagerlöf, H. G. Wells, Frank Wedekind, as well as Viktor Adler, the Jewish leader of Austrian Socialism, and Hermann Bahr, the non-Jewish Austrian writer.

When the Russian court had to acquit Beilis in the first week of November, it was an Austrian variety-show producer who first offered him a personal-appearance contract worthy of his red-hot celebrity. Mr. Beilis begged off because of stress caused by the trial.

Meanwhile the first cold gusts helped yellow the leaves on oak and beech all over Vienna's parks. But whether or not it was the contrast to Tsarist barbarism, the Western Powers seemed to warm not only toward Austria but also toward its German ally. England's First Lord of the Admiralty, Winston Churchill, made a very well-tempered speech at Manchester; he noted an improvement in relations between his country and the Reich and proposed a mutual reduction in the building of new battleships. America contributed a friendly sound from even higher up. A German publisher brought out a translation of President Woodrow Wilson's *The State—Elements of Historical and Practical Politics.* It marked a highlight of the fall publishing season, not least because of the preface specially written by the author for this edition. In it the American President praised the profundity of German thought, which had furnished not only his book but many other American works with inspiration.

At almost the same time, Wilson's Secretary of State, William Jennings Bryan, chose an odd forum for displaying willingness to associate himself with things Austrian. The Vienna press reported his appearance in a variety show in Maryland also featuring a Tyrolean yodeler. Mr. Bryan's role in the entertainment consisted of a spectacularly orotund oration that championed peace among the world's principal countries, most of which he enumerated (omitting Mexico, against which the USA was preparing an ultimatum). This high-minded aria, euphonious with metaphor and legato vowels, he repeated for twelve performances. In an interview, his Excellency explained that only through fees for extra undertakings such as this could he foot the high representational expenses of his office. The Tyrolean received much less for his yodels. But then a Tyrolean yodeler was not an American gentleman, and an American gentleman—said Diamond Jim Brady in New York during an interview much quoted in the Vienna press that fall—an American gentleman required an income of $1,000 a day, plus expenses.

This, of course, was the sort of zany flash typical of America. But in the course of autumn of 1913, Vienna saw the international horizon brighten in a more important way. At Belvedere Palace the First Lord Chamberlain of the Crown Prince issued an auspicious statement. An arrangement informally discussed during the summer had been confirmed and could be publicly announced: His Imperial and Royal Highness, the Archduke and Heir Apparent Franz Ferdinand *and* his consort had been asked to join Their Majesties, the King and Queen of England, at Windsor Castle, for a shoot during the third week of November.

To be sure, this was to be a "private stay" for the Austrian couple—not a state visit, which would have implied an altogether august elevation for a morganatic wife. Still, the last time Franz Ferdinand's spouse had seen the English King, two years earlier, she had almost been smuggled into Buckingham

Palace as an incognito luncheon guest under the name of Countess of Artstetter. But now, at Windsor, the Archduke would have her officially at his side as the Duchess of Hohenberg. It was a protocol breakthrough; a coup scored by the Crown Prince over Prince Montenuovo, First Lord Chamberlain of the Emperor; an event registered instantly by Vienna gossip as a bulletin from the invisible front line running through the Court.

And there was that other arena, much less accessible to rumor, in which the Crown Prince did combat. Here the contest was waged through memos, usually top secret and livid; special couriers scurried from backstairs at the War Ministry to the "confidential door" of Franz Ferdinand's Military Chancellery at Belvedere Palace and back again. The temperatures sank in Vienna in the course of autumn. The thrust and parry heated up between Army Chief and Crown Prince, between Serbia's unappeasable foe and the volcanic apostle of restraint.

Earlier in the year the Archduke had mentioned that he might attend the Army's summer exercises planned for summer of 1914 at Sarajevo. Presently definite notice of his intention to participate was transmitted to the Chief of Staff by General Oscar Potiorek, Governor of Bosnia. The Crown Prince had chosen to convey "highest" information to the Chief of Staff through an officer of less senior rank. It was a pointed disregard of channels.

And the Chief of Staff, General Conrad, retaliated with some anti-Serb ammunition pointed directly at the Archduke's heart. Austrian intelligence in the United States had been watching Michael Pupin, the well-known professor of electromechanics at Columbia University and the head of Srpska Slega, an organization of Americans of Serbian descent. A student of Pupin's, one Dusan Trbuhović, had left America for

Serbia at the end of summer and during a farewell dinner for him at the Hotel La Salle in Chicago, the possibility of an attempt on Franz Ferdinand's life had been discussed in detail. This report Conrad sent on to the Archduke. It seems fair to assume that the purpose was not just to warn but to rattle His Highness, to shake him into a tougher stance toward the Serbs.

There is no evidence of a specific response on Franz Ferdinand's part. But that month he made devastatingly plain his position vis-à-vis Conrad.

For three days starting September 14, large-scale war games involving six divisions of the Austro-Hungarian Army were to unfold in Bohemia, on a terrain about fifty miles south of Prague. Conrad arrived on September 11 to prepare mock battles involving field telephone and telegraph as well as bomber aircraft. The exercises were to show how well the Empire could fight a twentieth-century war.

On the thirteenth, the Crown Prince's automobile roared up, followed by a huge detachment of horse. Instantly, brutally, he asserted his new rank of Inspector General, which gave him supreme command over all maneuvers. He cancelled a number of troop movements and changed the timing of all others—everything that Conrad had mapped out with such care. A three days' program was squeezed into little more than one, in order to make room for the Archduke's own plan.

Most of the second day went into a rehearsal over which the Crown Prince presided, frowning triumphantly astride his Lippizaner. On the sixteenth, he let his operation explode before the eyes of his wife and an assembly of Bohemian princes watching from a grandstand: Down the slope of Mount Tabor galloped tier upon tier of cavalry. It was a dust-wreathed extravaganza of hussar bravado. In real war it would have been mowed down—drawn swords, flowing capes, plumed shakos, and all—by laconic bursts from a few machine gun batteries.

The impresario of this passé magnificence was not one of your backward-minded Viennese. On the contrary, Franz Ferdinand preferred a powerful motorcar over the fastest thoroughbred. And in ordnance beyond the Army Chief's immediate sphere—the Austrian Navy, for example—the Archduke urged the most modern armaments. Franz Ferdinand had turned these maneuvers into a historial joke not because he liked antiquated valor but because he hated the Chief of Staff. To undo Conradian policy, the Crown Prince must undo Conrad himself in every way.

The horse droppings left by the hussar commotion had not yet been scooped when the Crown Prince barked at the Chief of Staff: *Why hadn't he attended field Mass?* Five minutes later, he barked at him again, this time in front of other generals: *Why had he permitted cars to park in the path of the cavalry attack?*

Conrad listened mutely. His handsome mustache twitched with his tic. He saluted and excused himself. He boarded alone his command train back to Vienna. He did not want to share his humiliation with his brother officers. But to his beloved Frau von Reininghaus he could pour out his heart about "...this battle-farce" the Archduke had put on, "...this ludicrous spectacle for amateurs and children" which "... the Archduke must have anticipated and intended because he must have known that I can accept all this no longer."

* * *

The day after his return from "the farce," on September 17, Conrad addressed to the Archduke a written request to accept his resignation, leaving it "to your Imperial and Royal Highness to most graciously decide what official form or reason should be assigned to my voluntary removal."

Franz Ferdinand had already picked out Conrad's successor—General Karl von Tersztyansky, head of the Budapest Army Corps. But at this juncture the Emperor himself intervened. At the moment the Balkan situation was still too unsettled, the military contingencies too unpredictable, for Austria to dispense with a seasoned commander like Conrad.

The Crown Prince was summoned to a discreet audience at the Hofburg. He returned to Konopiste where he exercised, furiously, his famed marksmanship on over a hundred heathcocks. Then he sat down to do something unusual, for him. Something quite Viennese: He smiled a fine smile over clenched teeth. "Dear General Conrad," he wrote on September 23, "Much as I understand your wish not to remain much longer in office, I do hope and trust that you shall be able to display in some other high position your inestimable abilities, your patriotic commitment and your generally admired qualities as a soldier for which we are much indebted to you. But for the moment I would like to ask you most earnestly, in the interest of a good cause and in my own name, not to change your command and to remain in your thorny office at least until spring, and thereby make a sacrifice to the Army and to all of us entrusted with its leadership."

The tone suggests anything but vintage Franz Ferdinand. These phrases are not only too humble, they are far humbler than the Emperor required. Strategy, not sincerity, produced the Archduke's compliments. If their intent was to tempt the General into overconfidence, they did their work well within a month.

Conrad, of course, withdrew his resignation. He had retained power with his dignity vindicated; his foe was beaten back, his opinion bolstered by the news of the day. Each week in October brought new reports of fighting along Albania's border with Serbia. Serbia claimed it was repelling an invasion. Albania, which consisted of tribal war lords shooting off Austrian rifles, accused Serbia of aggression. Conrad felt that the mounting chaos could only be resolved by a showdown with Belgrade. Since that might mean war with Russia, however, Austria needed to be backed by its own strong ally, Germany. Yet on just that point Berlin had been evasive, or worse.

On October 1, Wilhelm, writing to Franz Ferdinand, had been rather sympathetic to the Serbs; he had actually referred to "Albania's habit, incited by Turkey, of pouncing on Serbia . . ." This implied that the real inciter and protector of the Albanians, Austria, would ignite a needless conflagration from which Germany had a right to remain apart.

Conrad had been trying to enroll Berlin on Vienna's side. At an audience some months ago, he had—cautiously and respectfully—asked Franz Joseph to obtain some personal commitment from the Kaiser in case of a wider conflict. Franz Joseph's reply had been one short, brusque sentence. "It is the duty of kings to keep peace."

But that had been much earlier in the year, at a time less favorable to Conrad's cause, with Serb aggressiveness lying relatively low and the Crown Prince riding high as chief of the appeasers. Now, in October, it was the other way around. Now was the time to take by the horns that bull of bulls—Wilhelm II of Germany.

* * *

On October 18, 1913, the German monarch celebrated the one hundredth anniversary of the Battle of Leipzig, where Prussian, Austrian, and Swedish troops had vanquished Napoleon. Wilhelm, who loved to wallow in borrowed glory, wallowed away. He decreed a great tattoo in Leipzig; ordered the boom of guns saluting, the blare of trumpet, fife, and drum; convened a titled assembly of gold braids, of fringed epaulettes, of tunics sashed, starred, and bemedalled.

Dignitaries of the three victor countries laid wreaths at the foot of the gigantic monument built for the occasion. As leaders of the Austrian delegation, Franz Ferdinand and General Conrad then sat down at a table (set at the Gewandhaus for four hundred and fifty) to rise again and again to heel-clicking toasts proposed by the German Emperor.

After the banquet Wilhelm held a *cercle,* that is, an informal reception. And Conrad made his move. By way of paying his respects, he expressed his humble gratitude to His Majesty for underlining with this festivity the importance and the might of the alliance between German and Austrian arms in the past and thereby emphasizing its continued importance in present or future circumstances.

This was not idle courtesy. It was an overture to draw Wilhelm into any potential fracas not only with Serbia but its big brother in St. Petersburg. Revved up by the martial trappings of the fête, the Kaiser answered that, indeed, the German-Austrian alliance remained unshakable, unbreakable, undeterrable. And—undeterred himself by the presence of a Russian general to his left or by the frown of the Austrian Crown Prince to his right—Wilhelm added that this moment made him feel so close to his Austrian comrades-in-arms that he wished to be introduced to all of the officers in the Austrian delegation.

Conrad answered that he would be most honored to do just

that—and thereby pushed Franz Ferdinand beyond his boiling point.

"General!" the Crown Princely voice echoed across the hall. *"Are you the Austrian of highest rank here? Isn't it the privilege of the Austrian of highest rank to introduce other Austrians to His Majesty? And if that is so, why have you affronted me?"*

It was, of course, the Chief of Staff who had been affronted before an international audience that would regale chancelleries and palaces throughout Europe with this scene. Nonetheless the General must apologize to the Crown Prince. He must bow, no doubt deep enough to hide his tic. And he must pack all his bitterness into yet another letter to Frau von Reininghaus.

But he could not, as he had done four weeks earlier after the maneuver contretemps, propose again to quit as Chief of Staff. Tendering his resignation must not become a monthly tragicomedy. On his return to Vienna, Conrad resolved to do the opposite. He would gather all the powers of his office into a demand for a final reckoning with Belgrade. Just now Serb violation of Albanian sovereignty had been compounded by border crossings and pillage of troops from Montenegro, Belgrade's ally. Conrad sent a summary of "these provocations" to Franz Joseph together with a briefing on the support expressed by Kaiser Wilhelm in Leipzig: on the basis of such developments, the Chief of Staff requested the instant punitive invasion of Serbia.

To no avail. Conrad's was not the only account of the events at Leipzig. Franz Ferdinand reported to Franz Joseph that the General had interfered once more in vital diplomatic matters that went far beyond his military jurisdiction. His meddling, long irksome, had now become altogether insupportable at Leipzig. By broaching the question of international alignments, he had usurped the authority of Franz Joseph's Foreign

Minister, of the Crown Prince, indeed of Franz Joseph himself. Instead of Conrad's heedless firebreathing, the Archduke again urged prudence, enclosing a copy of his recent letter to the Foreign Minister: "Our country doesn't want war, as our countless difficulties with conscripts show . . . We can rid Albania of those Serbs by diplomatic means."

The Crown Prince won the day. Franz Joseph refrained from an invasion. He did activate some reserves. And he had his Foreign Ministry send Belgrade a note firmer than the Archduke wished but not immoderate in tone: Austria would have to "take proper measures" if foreign troops did not withdraw from Albania within eight days. A carefully coordinated demarche of similar nature was delivered by the Italian envoy in Belgrade on the same day, October 19. Italy's interest lay in foiling Serbian hegemony on the other side of the Adriatic; that interest was enlisted in the "diplomatic means" advocated by Franz Ferdinand.

On October 21, Serbia gave in. Its troops began to leave Albania. The Crown Prince could end his peace watch in Vienna. "My dear Berchtold," he wrote to the Foreign Minister on October 21, on his way to his country seat at Konopiste, glowing with relief, "I am so happy that war has been avoided . . . I've told you that if one approaches Kaiser Wilhelm with some deftness, avoiding Great Power Talk and other chicaneries . . . then he'll stand fully by us . . . and we won't need to resort to a single weapon or any Conradian Big Stick to make those [Serb] pigs hoof it back to their own borders . . ."

Indeed Kaiser Wilhelm stood so fully by Franz Ferdinand that he left Berlin two days later to visit the Archduke. Like all blusterers, Wilhelm was impressed by genuine intensity such as Franz Ferdinand's. The Archduke's ferocious peacemongering had ended, at least for a while, the Serbian crisis. Europe relaxed, and so did the two lords at Konopiste. The Archduke steered his guest's penchant for the grandiose into nonmilitary matters. His beaters saw to it that Kaiser Wilhelm shot eleven hundred pheasants during a two-day hunt. Then the Archduke led his companion through St. George's Hall in his castle, where he had collected no less than 3,750 representations of St. George slaying the dragon, from silk pennants to bronze statues to gothic carvings to jade cameos. During the tour the Austrian joked that Kaiser Wilhelm's naval-armaments race with Britain might not be necessary after all. Albion had already been bested right here: In St. George's Hall, this Austrian castle held more images of the patron saint of England than did Windsor.

The Kaiser laughed and went on to sniff specially bred late-blooming roses in the Archduke's park. For a while war would not yet be the principal sport of kings.

10

"ON TUESDAY, NOVEMBER 18, 1913," READS THE DIARY OF KING George V of England, "we got over a thousand pheasants and four hundred and fifty ducks."

It was a Tuesday at Windsor, marred by ugly winds and uncouth rain. Wednesday, much better behaved, brought a tally of "over seventeen hundred pheasants." Thursday, the King's party dispatched "about a thousand." Friday, "an awful day, blowing and pouring with rain, a regular deluge in the afternoon," nonetheless yielded a bag of "over eight hundred pheasants and nearly four hundred ducks."

Five very high-born huntsmen produced such mountains of cadavers: the King, three English dukes, and the guest of honor, Crown Prince Franz Ferdinand of Austria. Each day the

Archduke landed a disproportionately high number of birds. It was a feat much remarked on since the Austrian brought it off in the face of a difficulty. He was not used to English hunting habits. At the Windsor battue, beaters drove the birds into a much higher and faster flush than in Austria. As the Duke of Portland noted in his memoirs: "The Archduke proved himself first class and certainly the equal of most of my friends . . . Given enough practice in this country, he would have been the equal to any of our best shots."

Rough weather and fast pheasants weren't the only handicaps Franz Ferdinand overcame that week. One problem greeted him at the start, on Monday, November 17, when he and his Sophie arrived at the Windsor train station. There, ready to welcome them, they found King George in top hat and morning coat—alone. This fact, duly recorded in the Vienna Court Gazette, set off smiles of schadenfreude among the Archduke's foes, such as Prince Montenuovo, at the Habsburg court. To them the Queen's absence conveyed the absence of importance in Franz Ferdinand's morganatic wife.

If the asymmetrical reception reflected his Sophie's less-than-royal birth, the Archduke did not show the slightest annoyance. Usually, as we have seen, he disdained playing the Viennese Prince Charming. He was not in the habit of hiding his temper and took offense energetically. But when necessary, he could turn snarl into purr. Then his jagged mustache and the bright hard blue of his huge eyes conjured a most beguiling Austrian cavalier. Then he modulated bows, hand-kisses, gallantries, enthusiasms, compliments, to a nuance just right for the occasion.

Queen Mary—whose nonattendance at the station had been a protocol cause célèbre—was smitten. "The Archduke is most amiable," she wrote to her aunt. "He is delighted with everything and very appreciative of the beauties of this place, which of course appeals to me. He is making an excellent impression and is enjoying the informality of the visit. His wife, the Duchess, is very nice, agreeable, and quite easy to get on with, very tactful, which makes the position easier . . . In the Waterloo Gallery the Archduke was delighted at seeing portraits of his two grandfathers, Kaiser Franz and Archduke Karl, and we could scarcely drag him away. I was amused as I always feel the same way when I see any of the 'ancestors' pictures in a Palace abroad . . ."

Even a week after Franz Ferdinand's departure his appeal still glows in yet another letter of the Queen's: ". . . The Archduke was formerly very anti-English but that is quite changed now and *her* [morganatic Sophie's] influence has been and is good, they say, in every way. All the people staying with us who had known *him* before said how much he had changed for the better . . ."

True enough. Franz Ferdinand's earlier encounters with English culture had been collisions. The travel journals of his youth flay the arrogance of the English for "obliging everyone to follow their customs in every respect." But in 1913 it wasn't just his Sophie's "position" which made him honor those customs with such willingness and winningness. It was the darkening of the international horizon. It was the slowly hardening confrontation—over trouble in the Balkans and elsewhere—between the General Conrads in Britain, France, and Russia with *the* General Conrad in Austria and his colleague in Germany. To mitigate the confrontation, the Archduke mitigated his disposition, at least for a week at Windsor.

To that end he accommodated a habit he had once condemned in his journals as "being against the practice of all civilized countries"—namely the British way of toasting the sovereign of the host before toasting that of the guest of honor. With an especially suave smile Franz Ferdinand drank to the health of King George before he drank to Emperor Franz Joseph. On the chair opposite his at the dining room table of Windsor Castle sat Sir Edward Grey, England's Foreign Secretary, with whom he then chatted about subjects like Serbia and Albania without missing a beat of gemütlichkeit.

"Despite the private character of the visit," wrote the London *Times,* "it is quite clear that the Archduke's visit expresses good relations between the two ruling houses and that the good will shown by both sides includes the sympathies of the English nation."

The menu of the farewell dinner for the Austrian couple began with Consommé Britannia and ended with Charlotte Viennoise.

In Berlin, at almost the same time, the Tsar's Prime Minister visited his German counterpart, Theobald von Bethmann-Hollweg. At a banquet the Russian had positive words for his country's ties to Germany; after an indulgent sigh over "Austria's sometime somewhat willful deportment in the Balkans," he raised his glass "to an improved mood between St. Petersburg and Vienna."

Meanwhile London papers estimated that the Windsor shoot had netted over four thousand five hundred pheasants and more than a thousand ducks. An awesome, awful number. Yet as long as Princes slaughtered birds together, their soldiers would not slaughter each other.

11

IT WAS A FALL THAT SOOTHED VARIOUS DIFFICULT MOODS IN AUSTRIA. THE Crown Prince returned from England with a face that was almost unrecognizably sunny. Leon Trotsky enjoyed moving with his family from his modest summer quarters in the Sievering district to the unheated and therefore almost rent-free villa in Hütteldorf. Its seignorial spaciousness appealed to him; so did its cavalier disregard of the rigors of winter. The house breathed the sort of dash Trotsky liked to cultivate. If that dash was missing among his all too sedate fellow-socialists in Vienna, he found it in the gambits sparking the chessboards of the Café Central. He always liked to come back to the capital's intellectual jousts. And to his surprise he discovered himself in agreement with some aspects of Austrian diplomacy.

Part of the summer he had spent covering the latest Balkan war for his Vienna *Pravda*. The front had given him "a feeling of impotence before fate, a burning compassion for the human locust." But there were some locusts that touched him even more deeply than others. In the 1913 war, he clearly favored Bulgaria, the loser, who was Serbia's enemy and hence Austria's ally. Trotsky's reportage eloquently describes the pillage and torment visited on the Bulgarian countryside.

Vienna shared his sympathy for Bulgaria, though it manifested the feeling differently. Toward the end of November, the King of Bulgaria came to town and was received by Franz Joseph. The *Fremdenblatt* (which often served as the government mouthpiece) limited its characterization of the meeting to three words: "Brief and cordial." After all, Bulgaria, though defeated, was still Serbia's smoldering enemy. And Serbia, though recently disciplined by Austria's ultimatum, smoldered more hotly than ever against Habsburg. In view of Balkan inflammabilities, official Vienna affected restraint.

Unofficial Vienna, on the other hand, could pull out all the stops for Bulgaria. And if there was one person who incarnated the capital unofficially, it was Frau Schratt.

In her mansion hard by Schönbrunn Palace, the Austrian Emperor's lady gave His Bulgarian Majesty a soirée that stood out among all others of the season. It shone not only with the politically significant but also with the Court Opera's stars, including Maria Jeritza and Selma Kurz. From liver-dumpling soup to Sachertorte with raspberry whipped cream, La Schratt's damasked table knew nothing but delicacies. The hostess, obviously the Imperial surrogate, was at her bubbly and playful best; once more she proved why she had been Vienna's foremost comedienne. As for the Bulgarian monarch, the journal of the Court Theater's new director, Hugo Thimig, saw him "blooming, affable, elegant as always with a monocle, a lilac-colored waistcoast, a beautifully cut frock-coat, the

Golden Fleece worn on a black cord under a snowy white cravat, the Bulgarian military cross in his buttonhole . . . in buoyant spirits, with an excellent appetite." Just a few months ago he had lost nearly all of Macedonia to the Greeks and the Serbs. With this superb show of a dinner in Frau Schratt's salon he appeared to have regained it.

In 1913, autumn flattered the city. After some bewilderments earlier in the year, it was recovering its soul, that is, its theatricality. That became evident in the centennial of the triumph over Napoleon—or rather in the difference between Germany's celebration and Austria's.

In Leipzig the Kaiser had screamed glory at a throng of spiked helmets. But in Vienna something of a nostalgic ballet unfolded. On the Schwarzenbergplatz crested palatines on horseback produced a kaleidoscope of the Habsburg past. Around them assembled ninety-seven platoons, each differently arrayed, each from a different regiment of a different crownland, each glowing with the opulence of its particular tradition: Hungarian hussars in leopard skin and silvered bandoliers; Bosnian infantry with fez, dagger, and sash; the Tyrolean Imperial Rifles in their pearl-gray tunic trimmed with pine-green, their caps aflutter with white cockfeathers; the blue and yellow of marines from Trieste, the long sabers of Polish cuirassiers, and the scrolled spurs of Bohemian cavalry.

Above them all waved a forest of flags, pennants, ensigns, as well as ancient, brocaded gonfalons. Heraldic eagles rode the wind. They seemed to peer far beyond anno Domini 1913 into that medieval morning when Rudolf, the first Habsburg king, had arrived in Vienna as a young dynast with halberd and visor to defend the Faith.

But the wizard of the day was the man whose arrival was signalled by a trumpet blow. Like a rococo dream, the coach of state, all white and gold, drawn by six snowy Lippizaners, loomed up and came to a halt. Franz Joseph stepped out: The whole forest of flags sank at his sight, as if leveled by a gale. Eleven bands played the Imperial anthem. Thirty generals drew swords and lowered them to the ground before the Emperor. Cannons boomed their salute, and the bands swung into the "Radetzky March," a polka-like frolic of drum and horn by Johann Strauss Senior.

Franz Joseph proceeded to inspect the rainbow homage of his troops. His white sideburns gleamed, his limbs moved briskly. He had been on the throne for over six decades, a ruler timeless as his ruling house. An adjutant handed him a laurel wreath. He strode toward the statue of Prince Schwarzenberg, the Austrian generalissimo who had led the Allied armies to triumph over Bonaparte at Leipzig.

To lean the wreath against the pedestal, the Emperor bent his eighty-three years into the arc of a dragoon lieutenant kissing a countess's hand. He presented one of his best performances at a military ceremonial. It was as if he knew it would be his last.

And it was as if Vienna knew that the holiday coming up next would be the last All Souls' Day of the dear old Franz Joseph era. Finality brought out the artist in the Viennese. Fittingly the city displayed its mortuary genius that autumn. On All Souls' Day, November 2, Catholic Vienna commemorated its departed. In 1913 the date fell on a Sunday. The Church recommended that observances be postponed to Monday to avoid conflict with Sunday services. Most Viennese paid no heed. On Sunday, neither office nor factory could keep them from forming a city-wide cortege.

In the morning the streets began to empty into the cemeteries. By the hundreds of thousands, citizens were on the move, dressed in black, black from hat to shoes. The rich came in automobiles whose hoods were draped in black. Black-clad crowds streamed from the tramways. Public as well as private transport was at such premium that many groups hired vans—flagged in black—to take them to outlying graveyards.

They all carried sprays of asters—white bloom vivid against the darkness of the clothes and the gray of the sky. The flowers added yet more brightness to the graves. The night before, nearly each resting place had been given its own glow. Most mourners had placed simple lanterns or glass-covered candles by their plots. Next to noble mausoleums stood footmen in black garb, holding torches. Honor guards with black trimmings held aloft flares by the arcaded crypts of generals.

Into this sea of lights and griefs the throngs were pouring. All Souls' Day was as eloquent a pageant of the devout in late fall as May Day had been a parade of workers in the spring. An endless phalanx of black figures and bright blossoms moved to the beat of some soundless dirge. The bereaved laid down bouquets, hung wreaths, affixed festoons. They prayed for the delivery of their loved ones from purgatory. The choir of their murmurs enveloped the hiss of torches, the crunch of countless feet shuffling along gravel. Incense mingled with the asters' fragrance, with perfume from black-veiled women, and with whiffs of roasted chestnuts from vendors waiting by the cemetery gates. When the Viennese were finished with their dramaturgy, they would be ready for a snack.

The next day, newspapers evaluated graveside accomplishments. What tombs led the field in the most finely nuanced floral designs? At the giant Central Cemetery, Vienna's late and very popular mayor Karl Lueger scored the highest plaudits. Beethoven did very well. Johann Strauss Junior fell a bit short this year: His widow had overdone the garlands. Schubert made a comeback. Some recently deceased industrialists had to be placed at the bottom of the list; they were the victims of vulgar excess.

The city still mastered the esthetics of death. A good sign. A measure of how well, after Redl, Vienna had recovered its poise as 1913 waned to a close. It was poise elegantly maintained despite, and because of, doubts about the Empire's future. Vienna still considered itself the capital of a sensibility that was all the more finely tuned for its precariousness. The legend of this sunset sensibility attracted talents from all continents. They came to visit, to shine and to be judged, together with local talent, by the stringencies of Viennese sophistication.

Enrico Caruso arrived for his engagement at the Court Opera as Rodolfo in *La Bohème*. Ovations greeted his cadenzas. Yet at least one reviewer thought that the ensemble effect would have benefited if the star had taken more time to rehearse with the cast, and that the same problem flawed the marvels of his Don José in *Carmen*.

Maria Jeritza made an incandescent Minnie in Puccini's *The Girl of the Golden West*—except for a few instances of overacting.

A child of twelve electrified the Musikvereinssaal. Brilliantly he sped his violin through the difficulties of Paganini's "Caprices." Critics admired little Jascha Heifetz's virtuosity. They also wondered about his delectable blond locks: Was this a boy or a girl prodigy?

George Bernard Shaw did not come to Vienna, but his *Pygmalion* had its world premiere here, in German, at the Court Theater, almost six months before the first London production. Reviewers smiled judiciously at Mr. Shaw, the grizzled enfant terrible. They admitted that in this play he did less ranting and more entertaining than usual, even if, as the *Neue Freie Presse* sighed, the comedian in Mr. Shaw almost succumbed to the ideologue at the end.

Also at the Court Theater, one of the most unpredictable younger directors, Max Reinhardt, staged the passion play *Everyman* with touches sometimes breathtaking, sometimes self-consciously ingenious.

Franz Lehár's new operetta, *An Ideal Wife,* disappointed not because it was bad but simply because the composer had once more failed to match his *Merry Widow.*

The writer Thomas Mann visited to read early chapters of his new novel-in-progress *Felix Krull.* He aroused anticipation not only as the author of the best-selling *Buddenbrooks* but also as brother of Heinrich Mann, the pre-eminent name in German fiction. Readers crowded into the Urania lecture hall and found an interesting, taut, slim figure at the lectern. Some literary correspondents, though, felt that the author's voice could not do justice to his prose. It was too stolid, too flat a vehicle for the picaresque handsprings of his Krull; instead of smiling at his excellent villain, Herr Mann seemed always on the point of a sneeze.

Only one performer met every expectation. For two weeks that fall he was the star attraction at the Apollo Theater, the town's leading variety house. He was so famous that each evening the Apollo arranged the coming of his physical presence in stages, quite as if he were the messiah: At first the hall darkened and there flashed on a screen photographic slides of his earlier career—showing for the most part his bulging arms raised over the sprawled body of an opponent; then came motion picture clips of him pummeling a sandbag or running half a marathon, then newsreels of his most famous triumphs in the ring. Then suddenly the screen was whisked away, and there under a spotlight, standing naked to the waist, in the gleaming, formidable blackness of his flesh—the Heavyweight Champion of the World, Jack Johnson. He bowed, he punched two punching bags at the same time, he juggled bar bells as if they were swagger sticks, he boxed an opponent with one hand tied behind his back . . . only to be swallowed by darkness in which nothing could be seen but from which surged the recorded sound of a New York fight arena—a mob braying at a knockout count, an ecstasy that roared and faded . . . and transmuted somehow into music that, in turn, regenerated the spotlight. And here was the champion again, but now in white tie and tails, a gallant arm around his petite white wife in her ball gown. To Johann Strauss's "Tales from the Vienna Woods," athlete and lady waltzed their way into the very hearts of the audience. Night after night they brought the house down. Night after night, said the *Arbeiter Zeitung,* many of the poor came here to spend their bitterly earned kronen on the exploitation of tinseled brutality.

The Socialists brought to town a world champion of their own, this one from Germany. They invited Emanuel Lasker, the globe's best chess player, to appear at the chess club of the Arbeiterheim Café—the coffeehouse of the Workers' Center. Playing twenty-six games at once, he won twenty-two, drew four, and made a speech. The times were over, he said, when laborers had been poor, dumb, passive pawns. Now the worker was beginning to see himself as the central figure in the economy. He was no longer dumb, he had stopped being passive, and the time would come when he would no longer be poor. All he had to do was to use his mind fearlessly, and chess was a good way of sharpening his faculties.

England contributed a notable who also enlisted his talent in the cause of the underprivileged. The Volksbühne (The People's Stage) produced a German translation of John Galsworthy's *Justice.* In November the author himself traveled to Vienna to supervise rehearsals. The play told of the misfortunes of a junior clerk trapped in a class-biased criminal justice system. When the curtain came down on opening night, cries of "Author! Author!" resounded together with ardent applause. Mr. Galsworthy turned out to be too shy a gentleman to take a bow on stage. However, he was reported to be very pleased by the printed accolade in the *Arbeiter Zeitung* some days later.

Emile Zola was not alive to sojourn in Vienna that fall, but through his work he was John Galsworthy's comrade-in-the-arts. A film being shown in the working-class districts proved continuously popular. It was based on *Germinal,* Zola's harrowing, heart-breaking evocation of the coal miner's lot.

Not that Vienna's proletarians had to learn about wretchedness from a motion picture screen. Nor did they need the nasty Serbs to give them a sense of crisis. The prospect of winter was enough. How would they keep warm? Where find money for fuel? Bad times were getting worse. In Vienna manufacturing was on the decline. The ethnically fragmented Empire, with its many levels and styles of consumer demand, prevented the economies of standardized mass production practiced elsewhere in the West. Despite protective tariffs Austrian industry kept losing markets—inside and outside the borders—to competitors abroad. The machine shops, dominant employers in the capital's industrial precincts like Hernals and Ottakring, had to shut their doors against thousands seeking work: Nearly a third of the city's metal workers had lost their jobs over the past two years. Most cotton mills were open only four days in the week now. And construction had dropped so drastically that the Developers' Association appealed to the government for subsidies and for the lifting of import duties on certain building materials.

In the slums, dinner was a matter of makeshift and make-do. Horsemeat edged out even the cheapest cuts of pork. The "stale" counter in bakeries drew more customers than that selling fresh bread. Before the exhaust gratings of the great army laundries gathered nightly crowds, silent, ragged, fearful: The cold was holding off, but in case it came they wanted the warmth of laundry fumes. Others took refuge in the municipal warming rooms where they could rest, if not sleep, sitting upright on wooden benches; or they could try to crowd into the city's three Homeless Asylums—concrete warrens that offered straw cots and horse blankets. In 1913, vagrants had received such shelter half a million times in the fairy-tale metropolis of two million.

Before the year ended, just under fifteen hundred Viennese had tried to end their lives. Over six hundred succeeded, including a thirteen-year-old boy who hanged himself and a seven-year-old boy who jumped out of a window. Of course, a high suicide rate was a venerable Viennese tradition. Just as traditional were the ways of masking that kind of death. Even if it was self-inflicted in a Catholic city, it must not be denied sanctified ground: The bereaved family would procure a doctor's certificate stating that the deed was done *non compos mentis*. And though the death be threadbare, the funeral must be nicely dressed: The family would obtain burial loans from a bank, arrange for time payments with the florist, the casketmaker, the innkeeper. A last journey must brim with roses on a coffin of varnished wood with brass trimmings. And the wake must feature hearty wine and red meat in a well-heated inn.

For a long time, though, innkeepers did not need to light stoves for warmth. In 1913, fall refused to become winter. In fact, as if smitten by nostalgia, fall appeared to turn back to spring. Temperatures clung to the Fahrenheit fifties. At the start of December the thermometer even pushed past sixty.

There was no snow. Hence there was no call for snow removers. Thousands had hoped that their shoveling would earn them at least three kronen a day, a sum that would buy a stein of Pilsner for the shoveler and pig's knuckles with turnips for his family. To such people the mildness of the season simply meant more hunger.

On the other hand, they could go hungry in air better than in other cities. It was warm enough on many days in November, and even during the first weeks of December, to take an almost summery walk into the Vienna Woods. Here, in the foothills of the Alps, whose lovely slopes rose at the very point where the grim streets stopped, here the balm had tricked primroses, marguerites, dandelions, cyclamens into new bloom.

Since walking was free, whereas eating was not, a number of the jobless walked through the hills. Never mind that a little boy strolled along in shoes two sizes too big for him and laced with paper cord; or that his mother, bending down to search for some belated strawberry, wore a frock with a fire-sale stain. If you didn't look too closely, you saw a delightful

Viennese tableau: citizens taking their weekday ease in an arcadia beyond time.

Mid-December brought a brief bite of frost. But that added yet another scenic touch. Rime spangled the Vienna Woods. Nature became marquetry. The tiniest branch of bush or tree turned into a decorative detail, outlined in grained pearl. No matter how empty their stomachs, hikers moved through a landscape of jeweled pavillions.

When the hikers returned to the city, the woods came with them. Each street had its grove of Christmas trees for sale. And each such grove had a pauper standing by to help more moneyed citizens carry home a strapping pine. The chore would get him a few coins. Could he be blamed if he helped himself to a tip in the form of a branch broken off on the sly? In his one-room flat, the branch did nicely as a Christmas tree. His children took turns at pressing their little noses against the wood's break-off point: It let them smell the yule scent of tree resin. For heat his family had the kitchen hearth and the window's dusty sun, so unseasonably strong this year; for gifts, perhaps overcoats, bargained out of the local used-clothes store, wrapped in bright paper Mother had saved from the Christmas presents of 1912.

And if all that gave insufficient sustenance, Midnight Mass would give more. No parish church, humble or grand, lacked a crèche. The Christ Child in the stable glowed with consolation: poverty was the cradle of grace.

And then the city gathered itself up for the festive brink: New Year's Eve. December 31, though colder than most days preceding, was windless, crisply pleasant, luminous with stars. Following custom, a great crowd roistered toward the huge square in front of St. Stephen's Cathedral. The streets were parties on the go. Many merrymakers wore paper chains extravagantly colored, from which hung fantasy pendants. As they trooped toward St. Stephen's, men began to exchange hats with women—especially with those they did not yet know. The closer they came to the great church, the more ladies pranced along in top hats, the more men sashayed in frilly chapeaux. Onlookers from buildings along the way applauded, laughed, waved bright sheets from windows.

By eleven-thirty the square was full: It milled and whirled with dancing couples. At a quarter to twelve, they slowed. At five to the hour, they became quiet. All faced the Cathedral and looked up.

Up there, way up in the long looming of the gothic tower, hung Christendom's most formidable bell. Called "die Pummerin" (the Boomer), it had been forged in 1711 of the iron of one hundred and eighty Turkish cannon captured and melted down after the Grand Vizier Kara Mustafa had abandoned his siege of Vienna in 1683. For nearly two centuries afterwards the Boomer's deep, monumental voice had rung in solemn occasions; the entire cathedral, from spire to nave to gargoyle, had shaken to the swinging of its tonnage. Walls had begun to show cracks, and the city fathers, forced to protect the church from its bell, had stilled the Boomer in 1867. At every New Year's Eve since then a rumor would go through the streets: the Cardinal had persuaded the Mayor to let the Boomer speak this one night.

And now the first tremendous peal struck through the moment of midnight at the stars. Was it *die Pummerin* after all? The roar of the True Faith? The clarion of ancient victory? No one in the crowd had time to judge. Within seconds, a thousand other church bells across the city clanged into a chorus.

The sound overwhelmed the night sky and shivered constellations.

Gradually, after five minutes, the metal tongues stopped calling. Before the last echo died into the firmament, before the kissing and whooping started on the ground, there was a moment's silence.

A new presence had descended on the roofs.

The year 1914.

12

When thrust into a fresh expanse of future, the Viennese sought comfort in omens. They had a long-established New Year's pastime. Into an ice bucket filled with cold champagne they would throw molten bits of lead, and then, with a pair of tongs, hold up each bit for interpretation. From the shape into which the lump congealed they would extract clues to things to come. It was a game of fascinating ambiguities. Never had it been played more intensely than during the wee hours of that newest January first.

Very soon an event auspicious beyond doubt pleased the Imperial House. The young Archduke Franz Joseph became father of a healthy baby girl. She was baptized Her Imperial and Royal Highness, the most serene Adelheid Maria Josepha

Sixta Antonia Roberta Ottonia Zita Charlotte Luise Immaculata Pia Theresia Beatrix Franziska Isabella Henriette Maximiliana Genoveva Ignatia Markus d'Aviano von Habsburg. Twenty-one names garlanded a six-pound infant. Twenty-one more to strengthen dynastic continuity.

Fifty-two Viennese killed themselves that month. Most of them were poor and quite a few of them must have been prompted by the weather. On January 7, the full rigors of winter fell on the city at last. A blizzard, huge and angry, smothered the streets. A series of icy gales followed, blasting away for days.

The snow did provide jobs for shovelers. But many more were put out of work because the unrelenting, unending arctic gusts forced the closing of construction sites. Nearly every day police blotters recorded the finding of frozen bodies of indigents: in an unused bowling alley; in a crude tent by the banks of the Danube; even in an abandoned mausoleum in the Central Cemetery.

All this did not dampen toasts to the baby Archduchess in loyalist taverns all over town. Nor did it diminish the flow of congratulations from the world's ruling families to the Hofburg. Even the King of Serbia sent a telegram. Three days later, though, a statement of a rather different nature issued from Belgrade. The Serbian Crown Prince Alexander and the Serbian Prime Minister Pašić would go to St. Petersburg "to discuss the international situation."

In Vienna, the Chief of Staff General Conrad deemed the visit a further hardening of the Serb-Russian coalition against Austria. In his eyes the development fit a larger pattern. Conrad's French counterpart, General Joseph Joffre, was already in St. Petersburg to expedite a loan of 550 million French francs. Why? For the explicit purpose of modernizing Russia's western railroad system, so vital in speeding troops to any war between a Russian-French-English entente and the German-Austrian alliance.

In his memos to the Emperor, General Conrad detailed his warnings together with two requests: (1) to strengthen garrisons along Austria's border with Russia, and (2) to obtain authority for the Ministry of War to draft more conscripts for a longer period of time, in order to match the recent French law lengthening service from two to three years.

This was how the head of the war party reacted to the first stirrings of the new year. But in his audiences with the Emperor, the Crown Prince refuted Conrad's points with his own, in his own pungent style: (1) Talk of impending war between the Great Powers was criminal nonsense; it so happened that the Duke and Duchess of Portland would be Franz Ferdinand's guests at Konopiste in March; at that time Duke and Crown Prince would plan details of a visit to Austria by King George of England in September to shoot roebuck with Franz Ferdinand—after a respectful courtesy call on Franz Joseph, of course. So much for Western hostility against Austria! (2) It was precisely the swelling of Austrian garrisons at the Russian border that gave idiot hotheads in Paris and St. Petersburg a pretext to heat up the military mood in their countries. That sort of cannon-waving was not policy—it was stupidity.

Franz Joseph listened to the arguments of both men. Then he acted—like Franz Joseph. His government did introduce a bill in parliament that would extend the present conscription law; he did not increase the permanent garrisons by the Russian border.

To the Viennese such news was routine hissing and scuffling in the corridors of power. Politics were not uppermost in the town's mind during that first arctic month of 1914. The very poor kept busy fighting their way through the daily crisis of survival—to stay warm, to stay fed. Others, more fortunate, prepared for the excitement of the carnival.

Of course a number of young men did have to pay attention to military matters. Anticipating the more comprehensive conscription bill (it would harvest 32,000 more recruits annually), General Conrad tightened draft implementation. The long hand of his apparatus reached an Austrian who had already thought himself safely escaped.

Shortly after New Year's, the War Ministry's Conscription Bureau succeeded at last in tracking down the whereabouts of Adolf Hietler [*sic*]. On the afternoon of January 18, a German detective entered Schleissheimerstrasse 34 in Munich and found on the third floor, in a room sublet by a tailor, the man he wanted. He arrested Hitler for violating the military service regulations of an allied state. The next day the fugitive was brought to the Austrian Consulate where he was ordered to report to the Army Induction Center of his native province, Upper Austria, in Linz.

Whereupon Hitler sat down to write one of his most voluble and mendacious letters. The real reason for evading the Austrian draft had been his revulsion against serving as "a pure German" in the multiracial Habsburg forces. Yet the petition he now addressed to the Linz Magistracy, Section II, ascribes his failure to register to the monetary and spiritual straits of a loyal, impoverished, high-minded youth with lofty artistic aspirations:

> the main reason making it impossible for me to honor your summons is that it has not been possible for me to muster the sum necessary for such a journey at such short notice.
>
> In the summons my profession is specified as "artist." Although I have a right to that designa-

tion, it is nevertheless only conditionally appropriate. While it is true that I am earning my keep as a painter, I do so only since I am entirely without assets (my father was a government official) and therefore require an income to finance my education. I can devote only a fraction of time to financial gain since I am still completing my education as an architectural painter. Therefore my earnings are extremely modest, just sufficient for subsistence purposes. I submit as proof of the above my tax returns and request that you will be good enough to return the same to me. My income is estimated at 1200 marks at the very best, an estimate that is too high rather than too low, and does not mean that I earn 100 marks a month. Oh no. My monthly income is subject to great variation but is very poor at the moment because the art trade sort of suffers winter doldrums at this time in Munich . . .

Concerning my failure to register for the army in the fall of 1909, I hope you will have the kindness to realize that this was for me an immeasurably bitter time. I was an unexperienced young man without financial support, and too proud to accept subsidies or to ask for them. Without any help, dependent only on my efforts, the few kronen I earned barely sufficed for a room to sleep in. For two years I had no companion other than worry or penury, no comrade except continually gnawing hunger. I have never known the beautiful word "youth." Even today, after five years, I retain souvenirs of that time in the form of chilblain sores on my fingers, hands, and feet. And yet

> I cannot recall the period without a certain satisfaction, since I am now past the worst. Despite my wretchedness and despite the dubious surroundings in which I had to suffer it, I did keep my name free of stain. I have maintained a spotless record in the eye of my conscience and in the eye of the law—except for that one omitted military registration, the necessity for which I was not even aware of.
>
> I beg most humbly that my petition be received in this spirit and sign
>
> most respectfully yours
> Adolf Hitler
> artist

Here is a picture of deprivation raised by a man who—unbeknownst to anyone around him—pocketed the comfortable income from two legacies. In style, his self-portrait to the authorities resembles the stilted landscapes Hitler was selling at the time in Munich (earning a bit of extra money he didn't need since he lived below his means). In emotionality this supplication recalls his rantings in Vienna's Männerheim. But now he was using a well-calculated Austrian mixture of protocol and pathos, make-believe and baroque deference. It worked.

The Linz magistracy granted his request to appear at the Salzburg Induction Center since that venue was closer to Bavaria and "the journey therefore more affordable to the petitioner." And at Salzburg, following a physical examination on February 5, 1914, the Hitler file was closed with the conclusion: "Unfit for military or auxiliary service; too weak; incapable of bearing arms."

13

SAFELY BACK IN MUNICH, HITLER CONTINUED DOODLING HIS WAY TOWARD destiny. At the same time two young Bosnians joined him in an eerie partnership. The three never met. Hitler stayed in Bavaria. The other two lived in the Bosnian capital of Sarajevo; yet during those early months of 1914 they took the first decisive steps toward triggering the first global war without which the man in Munich could never have started the second.

The zealotry of the two in Bosnia ran opposite to that of the one in Bavaria. His obsessive nationalism was German; theirs, Slav. Still, all three had trouble with the Vienna authorities, and all three were art-minded malcontents. Only the Bosnians' esthetics—in contrast to Hitler's—were anything but Victorian.

At twenty-three, the older of the Bosnian pair, Danilo Ilić seems to have been a rather complicated radical, alloying as he did his nationalism with Marxist and anarchist leanings. He supported himself as proofreader for the Serbian-language paper *Srpska Riječ* in Sarajevo. Tall, attenuated, neurasthenic, he always wore a black tie "as a constant reminder of death." His stomach ulcer kept him as conveniently out of General Conrad's army as "weakness" kept out Hitler. Ilić cultivated unorthodox modern literature. Early in 1914 he spent much of his spare time translating into Serbo-Croatian Maxim Gorki's *The Burning Heart,* Oscar Wilde's essays on art and criticism, Leonid Andreyev's *The Dark Horizon,* Mikhail Bakunin's *The Paris Commune and the Idea of the State.* At the same time others among the Young Bosnians, the secret society of which he was part, translated Kierkegaard, Edgar Allan Poe, and Walt Whitman's "Song of Myself."

Ilić had been introduced to the works of Nietzsche by a fellow Young Bosnian barely eighteen years old named Gavrilo Princip. Princip, a slight youth with a high, furrowed forehead and eyes of a startling pale blue, was taciturn, restless, absorbed in books and given to actions baffling to his family. He had little patience for the banalities of the Commercial High School into which his parents had placed him. Like Ilić, he savored the darker writers. For his nickname he chose "Gavroche" after Victor Hugo's boy-hero in *Les Misérables*. Besides Nietzsche, he idolized the most pessimistic of Serb poets, Sima Pandurović.

But Ilić and Princip did not gloom the day away in literary introspection. Like the other Young Bosnians they wanted to implement the rebel's view of society, as conjured in their favorite literature, with rebellious action. They aimed to free the Serbs of Bosnia from the dead hand of the Church, from stale tradition and primitive custom, from everything that stifled the unfolding of the individual and the emancipation of women. Above all, they wanted to tear away the shackles put on their people by the Austrian Empire. They burned to unite all Slavs now under the Habsburg's yoke and join them with their brethren in Serbia and Montenegro into one free and glorious South Slav state.

"The whole of our society is snoring ungracefully," a Young Bosnian wrote of the period. "Only the poets and revolutionaries are awake." Ilić and Princip were not only ardently awake but incandescently ascetic. Like most of the Young Bosnians, they did not drink or smoke or engage in sex (just like abstemious young Hitler). One member of the group, who had gotten to know Trotsky while a student in Vienna, wrote the Russian in 1914: "You must believe me when I tell you that all of us follow the rule of abstinence."

Ilić and Princip observed it passionately. The blood of their young manhood must surge only for the freedom of their fellow South Slavs.

At the news of the Second Balkan War in 1913, Ilić had *walked* from Sarajevo to Belgrade (to save money and to escape detection) and joined the Serb army as a volunteer. Hence his nickname "Hadzija" (after the Muslim pilgrim, the Hadji). The Balkan War had also drawn Princip to Belgrade where he had tried to enlist in the *komite*, the irregular Serb units operating in guerrilla style. But Princip had been rejected, being too young and small. Now, in the first months of 1914, he was back in Sarajevo, back in the tedious school from which he'd already been expelled once for joining an anti-Austrian demonstration. He hated blackboard and homework. He lived for his meetings with Ilić and the Young Bosnians. Inside him grew the need to do something worthy of his favorite verse, Nietzsche's lines:

I know whence I arrive
Unsatisfied like the flame.
I glow and writhe.
Everything I embrace becomes light,
Everything that I leave becomes coal.
Flame am I, surely.

What or whom could this inexorable flame burn? With Ilić and his comrades he had discussed killing the Austrian Governor of Bosnia-Hercegovina, General Potiorek. Yet Potiorek, though the most visible oppressor in the land, was just a tool. It was the heart of Habsburg that must be struck. Toward the end of January, Princip received a letter from a Young Bosnian in France, saying that Franz Ferdinand would be visiting Paris under circumstances favorable to an assassination. By some accounts, Princip replied in his and Ilić's name that he wanted to use the chance to eliminate the tyrant but that he would first acquire weapons and training in Belgrade.

Of course Franz Ferdinand was not the anti-Serb ogre that seared Princip's mind. And of course the two never met in France. Yet their paths began to converge in February 1914.

Around the first of that month, Princip did leave Sarajevo, ostensibly to continue his high school education in Belgrade. His brother paid the fare for a detour on the way. Princip stopped over at his native village of Grahovo, in Western Bosnia. Here he was marooned for some weeks by the same giant blizzards that smothered Vienna. And most of that time, his mother was to recall, he spent brooding, staring at the snow.

* * *

Gavrilo Princip knew nothing of the actual politics or personality of Crown Prince Franz Ferdinand. And Franz Ferdinand did not even know of Gavrilo Princip's existence. However, the Crown Prince had heard of another youth, equally modern in his malaise, down to a susceptibility to Nietzsche. He was one of the few Austrian artists who, like the Young Bosnians, saw a radical connection between art and society.

His name was Oskar Kokoschka, and at twenty-two he had come to the Archduke's attention through his play, produced at a modernist art-students' theater in Vienna in 1909. Also on the bill was a dramatization of *The Birthday of the Infanta,* a bitter fairy tale by a literary hero of the Young Bosnians, Oscar Wilde. Kokoschka's *Murder, Hope of Women,* consisted of a chaos of screams, stabbings, and poetic fragments about love practiced as a bloody trial of combat. It happened that the audience included some Imperial Army soldiers from Bosnia's Sarajevo who didn't share Young Bosnia's enthusiasm for the avant-garde. They helped start the lusty riots that followed. The Crown Prince read the newspaper reports the next day and reacted characteristically. "Every bone in that young man's body," he said about Kokoschka, "should be broken."

It pleased Kokoschka that his work had touched the higher spheres. How wonderful to *épater le prince*! He stuck to his ways, though painting rather than playwriting became the instrument of his notoriety. Encouraged by his mistress Alma Mahler (composer Gustav Mahler's widow), he had developed, in the early teens of the century, an expressionist imagery at once febrile and morbid, putrescent and electric. Considering Kokoschka's temper and considering Alma's responsiveness to any passing male of talent and virility, their affair was at first oddly stable. Often it produced what was for Kokoschka atypical bliss. But during the first months of 1914 this, like many other things in Austria, began to change.

The couple met in a villa in the Semmering, an idyllic Alpine hamlet near Vienna. One day Kokoschka opened the door to find their trysting chalet literally slimy with an orgy of toads. The warty creatures had escaped from a tank to sliver and hop, slaver and mate, all over the living room rug.

Recently Kokoschka had begun to suspect Alma of finessing an affair not only with the architect Walter Gropius but with Rudolf Kammerer, a prominent biologist experimenting with frogs. And here seemed to be viscous proof of the second liaison: bulge-eyed, twitching couplings before a window filled with snowy splendor.

The sight altered Kokoschka's angle of invention. For more than a year he had been at work on *The Tempest*, one of his central masterpieces. Wild swirls of color suggest a man and a woman resting in what could be either a bed afloat in clouds or a boat adrift in a stream. Some powerful force curls the two against each other—a force that apparently changed nature and color after Kokoschka's encounter with the toads early in 1914: he started to re-tint many of the picture's vibrant Bengal reds to a colder and more ominous blue-green. Ardor dissolved toward phosphorescence. Tenderness turns into trap. "The boat in which we two are being tossed about . . ." Kokoschka would later write to a friend, "is a house big enough for a whole world of pain which we have gone through together. And I am going to the war, secretly. After . . . [this painting] I should really go under." "The Tempest," wrote a critic much later still, "has been interpreted in our day as a potent metaphor of 'collapse, dissolution, *finis Austriae*, the end of time.' "

"Finis Austriae" is the wisdom of hindsight. In January 1914, the Hitlers, the Princips, the Kokoschkas were either disreputable or, worse, unknown. Vienna concerned itself not with the end of time but with the beginning of carnival. Countess Jenny von Haugwitz hosted the first highlight of the merry season. She gave a "streamlined" ball in the newly redecorated Directoire salon of the Hotel Imperial. The evening prescribed "an automotive theme" for costumes and saw many a shapely Rolls-Royce, Daimler, and Mercedes-Benz cruise across the parquet.

The Bank Employees' Club tried to top its Bankruptcy Ball of the previous year with a Banknote Forgers' Fest, and nearly succeeded. Even lower class celebrations set high standards. For example, the Public Bath Attendants' Ball at the Stahlehner Hall announced that persons in clown suits would not be admitted for that was much too common, unoriginal, and old-fashioned a disguise. And so a mob of goggled aviators and formidably hatted suffragettes converged on the door.

The Laundresses' Ball did introduce—though only briefly—some dissonance. The ball itself was fun: lively with authentic pinch-them! young laundresses in the striped stockings and ribbonned blouses of their trade. But most of the young Society bucks who had come to take the girls home "to have their trousers ironed" had to face the next day with their garments as creased as ever. The laundresses refused even the lordliest offers for private breakfast. Early in the morning they went straight from their ball to the Ringstrasse to join their unemployed sisters in a protest march.

For Vienna that was a somewhat too modern way of capping a carnival night. One week later the Ball at Court in the Imperial Palace* provided a lesson on how to pay one's respects to the future more delicately. The old Emperor himself played teacher. He inaugurated the dancing by turning the

* The last such ball ever held.

first few beats of the first waltz with the young, pretty Zita, wife of his grandnephew, the Archduke Karl, who was second in succession. This necessarily discomfited the Crown Prince since his morganatic spouse Sophie did not rate an Emperor's waltz on so formal a night. But after returning from the dance, the monarch resolved the embarrassment. He turned to Franz Ferdinand, standing very stiffly at his side. Would Sophie have the kindness, Franz Joseph asked, to join him at his table together with Karl, Zita, and, of course, Franz Ferdinand himself?

It was a finely balanced distribution of affabilities. Though he left intact every nuance of precedence and protocol, the old gentleman breathed a new feeling of mutual cordiality into three generations of the ruling family.

On a night shortly thereafter the Habsburgs held their own private family ball. As the carnival's most exclusive affair, it came to pass in the Imperial Palace Apartments of one of the younger Archdukes, Peter Ferdinand, and his Archduchess Marie Christine. Not even an orchestra intruded. Discreetly, a string quartet played Haydn behind a screen. Servants noted that despite its august character the gathering was unusually warm this year, with many Highest hugs and kisses.

The next day, Shrove Tuesday, brought the ultimate in public social glitter. The Duke and the Duchess of Cumberland, bearers (despite its Anglo-Saxon name) of a crest long eminent in Austrian blazonry, gave their annual *matinée dansante*, from 4 to 10 P.M. The scene was the Palais Cumberland, once summer château of Empress Maria Theresa. Guests danced in the great ballroom whose roundness conformed to their waltzing and whose frescoes amplified the merriment divinely, catching gods and goddesses at play. The buffet was served in the renowned "treasure suite" with its silvered furniture. Jewelry ministered to gastronomy. Footmen offered caviar on silver plate, pheasant on gold. Each guest departed with a box of chocolate truffles wrapped in silver and stamped with the Cumberland escutcheon.

Most left in happy haste. For on the same night the Princess Croy-Sternberg presided over an excitingly new-fashioned benefit ball for the Red Cross in the new Konzerthaus. There a thicket of potted orange trees and tromp l'oeil screens, ablossom with orchids and bougainvillea, created the tango tropics in an Austrian winter.

Then midnight turned into the morning of February 25—Ash Wednesday. Lent started. Carnival was over. But in contrast to the previous year, the carnival spirit lingered. In 1914 Vienna seemed to be clinging to fun. The weather gave a hand. After the longest frost in years, March blew in with mild, moist, yeasty breezes. All over the Vienna Woods yellow-pink crocuses leaped out of the ground, tiny harlequins unabashed by melting mounds of snow. In the Danube lagoons, larks trilled and swooped above trees not yet in bud.

Spring was ambushing the austerity of winter with little guerrilla galas here and there. And the capital's diplomats marked the end of the ball season with yet another event. It was an official, political, real-life costume party that lasted much longer than one evening. It was called Albania.

14

VIENNA'S ALBANIAN FLING HAD HAD A PRELUDE OF SOME FOUR HUNDRED years. For that long the Albanians had lived and seethed under Turkish rule. Partly Christian, mostly Moslem, each of them intractable, they were mountain tribes roaming the interior of the Balkan peninsula on the Southern end of the Adriatic. When the Turkish sultanate began to collapse at the turn of the century, Albania became booty. Italy wanted a part of it as its foothold in the Balkans. Greece craved a piece. Belgrade coveted its coast line for access to the sea. And just because Belgrade wanted a section, Vienna wanted all of it: all of it in the form of a Habsburg client state, to show that Balkan hegemony would not be shared with Serbs but belonged to but one realm—Austria.

Still, a bit of sharing had to be tolerated. In 1913 a London conference of Europe's leading countries (the Central Powers as well as the Western Allies) had awarded the Albanian Kosovo region to Serbia. Some snippets went to Greece. The rest of the territory, with the major part of its inhabitants and its anarchy, was to be an independent nation.

The nationhood of that nation did not exist. But Vienna guaranteed the integrity of the phantom. After all, Austria was the illusionist among the great powers. The London Conference made Italy co-guarantor, a partnership Vienna largely, and politely, ignored. It did not want interference and certainly did not need help.

Shortly before New Year of 1914, Austria had persuaded the Conference to appoint William, Prince of Wied, ruler of Albania. The Albanian term for that office was *mbret*. The Prince of Wied did not know how to pronounce *mbret*. He was, however, very good at enunciating *Hohenzollern-Sigmaringen*, the royal house of Rumania to which he was related. A tall, fair-skinned Teuton lordling, he had never laid eyes on any of the swarthy goatherds and maize-growers who were now to be his people. He did not speak a syllable of their language. He had never set foot on their land. He had no idea of Albanian customs, traditions, politics, vendettas, difficulties. Most people of "civilized" Europe shared his ignorance. Until it became an international controversy, Albania had been a *terra incognita*—a remote labyrinthine confusion of ragged chiefdoms. To "guarantee" such a country under such a *mbret* meant to conjure it out of a plumed hat.

And just that was a chore congenial to the fabulists by the Danube. During the first three months of 1914, official Vienna conjured away with the skill born of experience. After all, the Habsburg domain had managed to disencumber itself of most connections to drab reality. By 1914 the Austrian Empire was a chimera ancient, iridescent, and almost plausible through its perennial re-invention. Since the Empire's survival depended on it, such self-fabrication was a very serious business. Fabricating "Albania" was not—not quite. But the Albanian challenge tapped a talent the governing Viennese loved to exercise, and so they applied their gift to this game.

As the decorations for the last costume ball of carnival 1914 were dismantled, the city buckled down in earnest to the construction of the Albanian fantasy. Its hero, the Prince of Wied, planned to enter his fairyland in March. For his escort Vienna recruited an Albanian Volunteer Brigade for which a wonderfully imaginative uniform was devised; it combined hussar and dragoon motifs with the Balkan tang of a fez-like helmet. These colorful apparitions made a fetching background to another design, namely the monochrome elegance of the Prince's state dress: tunic, trousers, tassels, and braids shading from gray to black, setting off the blaze of medals on his breast, a few of which were also freshly concocted.

Vienna then proceeded to style special Albanian postage to welcome the new potentate. A stamp series displayed the Albanian double eagle (looking like a nephew of the Habsburg bird) superimposed on two dates: 1467 and 1914. The first designated the victory of Skanderbeg, Albania's legendary champion, who had vanquished the Turks back then; the second spoke of the national redeemer now, getting ready in his tassels of gray and black.

At the end of February 1914, the *mbret* still could not pronounce his title. On the other hand, he had a very successful last fitting. Therefore he was ready for statesmanship.

He began a triumphal progress south. The Austrian state

yacht *Taurus*, guarded by three cruisers, floated him down the Adriatic. On March 7 he stepped onto a red-carpeted dock in the harbor of Durres; behind him, a retinue of sashes and cummerbunds that resembled a toy version of the Habsburg court.

At three that afternoon the *mbret* displayed himself on the balcony of the biggest local house that was still within the protective range of Austrian naval guns. A well-rehearsed crowd of Albanian folk—the men in starched white kilts, the women in very laundered babushkas—waved flags with the nephew-double-eagle and intoned Albanian hoorays. Flowers were tossed, white doves released, blessings uttered by mullahs and Greek Orthodox priests—all on cue. The chorus of *Aida* could not have done better.

After the enthusiasm subsided punctually, the *mbret* held his first State Council. It addressed three problems. (1) What were the best shoots in the most secure areas? (2) What game was there to shoot? (3) What European princes should be invited to the hunt?

Official Vienna smiled. Serbia was not amused. "I saw," said a skeptic among the witnesses, "the beginning of a tragic operetta."

A week after the Prince of Wied came to Albania, the Bosnian schoolboy Gavrilo Princip came to Belgrade. Wied's advent as *mbret* produced headlines all over Europe. Princip's arrival was noted only in the police registration form he filled out on March 13, 1914, in a cheap lodging house at 23 Carigradska Street. Very soon the Prince of Wied became forgotten news. Today, three quarters of a century later, Princip is celebrated as Yugoslavia's principal martyr; a bridge in the capital bears his name; a museum documents his life; his footprints preserve his memory in concrete.

But in March 1914, he professed to be just another student at the First Belgrade High School. He was preparing himself for his sixth-class examinations: that was the reason for his stay as stated on the police form. For that purpose his family paid his expenses. The weekly remittance they sent him was not a huge sum; still, it put a certain burden on what his father earned as village postman in Austrian Bosnia.

The postman had no idea that Gavrilo spent much of his money and his time at the Golden Sturgeon Café on Green Wreath Square, one of Belgrade's major marketplaces. The Golden Sturgeon served hot tea on rusty tables to a special breed of students; they sipped, huddled, whispered, and hardly ever bent over a copybook. Most were from Austrian Bosnia—beardless firebrands who had volunteered for Serbia during the Balkan wars. Now it would be dangerous to return. A sympathetic Serb government had extended scholarships to many of them—but school-bench sitting was dull for young men who had seen action. Study bored them. Politics consumed them.

They all hated the Austrian regime which they saw throttling their native land. They all pronounced "Habsburg" with a hiss. But Gavrilo Princip's hiss came from a depth remarkable in a body so thin and small. He did not talk much. But his pale blue eyes could flash a light that stopped the talk of others. There was a hypnotic edge to his low voice, his quiet, constant movements, even to his silence. The friends he made at the Golden Sturgeon became a following.

One of them was Nedeljko Cabrinović, formerly a student, currently an employee of the Belgrade State Printing Office. In the last week of March, Cabrinović received a letter from Bosnia with no message inside the envelope—only a newspaper clipping. He met Princip for lunch to show it to him. It had been cut out of a Sarajevo daily and contained the news that the Archduke Franz Ferdinand would be visiting that city in the course of the June maneuvers.

Gavrilo Princip read the story. He said nothing, for a while. Then he asked Cabrinović to meet him at the Golden Sturgeon again, in the evening. Cabrinović did. Again they shared a rusty table. Princip ordered mint tea, which he sipped wordlessly, shifting slowly in his chair. After a few minutes he motioned Cabrinović to walk with him into the adjacent park. He led his friend to a remote bench in the dark. They sat down. Princip spoke at last. Softly he asked his friend whether he would help him kill the Crown Prince of Austria. Silence. Cabrinović nodded. Silence. In Princip's blue eyes gleamed the light of a distant lantern. "I will find the weapons," Princip said. Silence. They shook hands. Together they walked back to the Golden Sturgeon Café.

This happened on March 27, 1914. Earlier on the same day, some three hundred miles west of that Belgrade park, the Crown Prince of Austria had a difficult encounter.

The setting seemed pleasant enough: a fine spring morning on the wave-slapped jetty of Miramare, a romantic seaside castle just outside Trieste. Franz Ferdinand was watching the giant snow-white German yacht *Hohenzollern* steam toward him across the bay. It flew the Kaiser's personal ensign with the motto *"Gott mit uns!"* A flotilla of German cruisers foamed the waters in its wake. As the *Hohenzollern* came closer, Wilhelm II became discernible, grasping the rail valorously at the prow. "My God," the Archduke burst out at his adjutant. "He's got that damned carving knife on! I forgot mine!"

The "carving knife" was a naval dagger with an anchor-shaped hilt that Wilhelm had invented as an accessory to his All-Highest naval uniform; he had gifted Franz Ferdinand with a copy. "Fetch it for me!" Franz Ferdinand said to his adjutant. "He'll expect me to wear it! Get that blasted thing—right now!"

The Archduke often let his ill temper fly but hardly ever at the expense of Wilhelm II. If he did now, it was because too many vexations beset him in March of 1914. Some were old and familiar: those little, jeweled, poisoned arrows shot at him by the Vienna court. The very ground on which he stood that moment, the Castle Miramare, had been used against him. As a personal possession of Franz Joseph, Miramare lay under the jurisdiction of Prince Montenuovo, First Lord Chamberlain of the Emperor and foremost enemy of the Crown Prince. Montenuovo could not forbid Franz Ferdinand to use the castle for a spring sojourn or for a setting in which to entertain the German monarch. The Crown Prince's wife, on the other hand, was not the Crown Princess, nor were the couple's children archdukes. According to Montenuovo's malevolently stringent interpretation of Habsburg house rules, Franz Ferdinand's morganatic loved ones did not have the right of residence in one of the dynasty's own manors. After all, their Highnesses were not Imperial but only Serene.

Naturally the First Lord Chamberlain's spite always came sugared in courtier phrasing. His letter to the Crown Prince had expressed "regret to be unable to make Miramare arrangements for their Serene Highnesses without an express All-Highest command which the undersigned [Montenuovo] devoutly hopes your Imperial and Royal Highness [Franz Ferdinand] will obtain."

In other words Franz Ferdinand must do once more what he had been forced to do on previous occasions: go to the humbling length of appealing personally to his All-Highest Uncle Franz Joseph. Only then could his Sophie, his daughter, and his two sons sleep under the same roof with him in Miramare.

Still, Miramare was a fitting mise-en-scène in which to welcome the most grandiose of all Prussians during this stopover on his Adriatic cruise. The *Hohenzollern* had docked. A 21-gun salute boomed from the Austrian dreadnought *Viribus Unitis*. Wilhelm strutted down his gangplank, a naval peacock in white and gold. Braids, froggings, epaulettes, medals, and "carving knife" invoked every variety of overgorgeousness.

And yet: The same witnesses reporting Franz Ferdinand's earlier frown also speak of the cordiality that marked this dockside meeting just as it did most other encounters of the two men. Franz Ferdinand often referred to Wilhelm as *"Europas grösster Mordskerl"* (Europe's No. 1 devil of a fellow). Never mind lapses of taste or questions of judgment—the sheer spectacle of the German's bravado impressed the Archduke, a bravado unchecked by any authority above the Kaiser's head or by an astute brain inside it. Franz Ferdinand's mind was saddled with both. He was wary of Wilhelm's sovereign excesses. He also envied and admired them.

At any rate it was politic to greet fulsomely this fulsome personage. Franz Ferdinand, being chronically embroiled with the Vienna court, needed support from the Berlin Emperor who was Vienna's preeminent ally. And that morning, in the brilliant sunshine on the jetty (with Franz Ferdinand's "carving knife" fetched just in time), there was something else to be gained from the German: The stature of the Archduke's wife benefited from Wilhelm's vanity. The Kaiser fancied himself as graceful a hand-kisser as any Austrian. He loved to prove it on Austrian territory. As he lowered his All-Highest mustache over Sophie's less-than-archducal fingers, she partook of Imperial cachet: Another skirmish had been won against the Montenuovo camarilla.

But at Miramare loomed other issues of greater relevance to the world at large. The Crown Prince broached them at lunch in the castle's marble dining hall. He was, he confided to Wilhelm, unhappy about all that *mbret* ado in Albania. His own choice for the Albanian throne, the Duke Wilhelm von Urach, a much more capable candidate, had been turned down by Vienna. This weak, silly *mbret* worried the Crown Prince because of Serbian repercussions. If the Austrian-backed ruler tottered, the Serbs would try to grab more Albanian territory, even to the point of a confrontation with Austria. And, Ferdinand added, it wasn't just the Albanian situation, it was also the Hungarian attitude that made the Serbs pugnacious. The Hungarians provoked not just Belgrade Serbs but Serbs inside the Austro-Hungarian province of Bosnia; there a Magyar civil administration imposed Hungarian as a teaching language on many schools with a majority of Serbo-Croat students; in other ways, too, the Hungarian hand lay heavy on the land. And to be frank, the Archduke said, taking a deep breath, it was right here that the Kaiser could be of vital help. After all, Wilhelm wielded great influence with Count Stephan Tisza, the Hungarian Prime Minister. Any move to make the Hungarians see a tiny bit of reason would be of tremendous value. Would His Majesty be kind enough to take it under consideration?

By then guest and host had reached post-prandial liqueurs. The Kaiser savored his brandy. Well, yes, to be sure, he said, those Hungarians could be rascals. And Tisza, whom he had received in audience while coming through Vienna the other day, indeed Tisza was a rascal, too, but an absolutely first class rascal, clever and fast as you had to be in your dealings with all those Balkan bandits, Bulgaria, Serbia, and what not; yes, Tisza was really a true statesman worthy of Franz Ferdinand's trust—in fact, come to think of it, at the German fall maneuvers to which Franz Ferdinand must come as his, the Kaiser's guest, maybe Tisza should be invited, too; the King of Italy had just accepted—what a jolly foursome! It would iron out all sorts of differences. Also show how Germany, Austria-Hungary and Italy stood together—England and France better not plan any stupidities against the Central powers. A fall maneuvers foursome—capital idea! Meanwhile, how about enjoying cigars out on the terrace?

On the terrace the two princes lit Cubans and reclined in wicker chairs. They blew smoke rings across the blue-gold Adriatic. The Kaiser had chosen to bypass Franz Ferdinand's request for help against the Hungarians. Franz Ferdinand was not in a position to press his case. His august caller disliked arguments that clouded good scenery or spoiled the pleasures of tobacco. It would not do to risk a crucial friendship.

Cigars finished, the Crown Prince accompanied the Kaiser on an inspection tour of an Austrian battleship. Time for the *Hohenzollern* to steam on to Corfu. Wilhelm kissed Sophie's hand good-bye. Austrian cannon boomed their salute while Wilhelm was piped aboard his yacht. Then Franz Ferdinand could rid himself of his German Grand Admiral's uniform. He could toss away the "carving knife." He could not shed his frustration.

In Vienna's Hofburg a few days later Franz Ferdinand briefed his monarch on what he called, unsmiling, "an interesting meeting, more fruitful on some difficulties than on others, such as the awful Hungarian problem." Franz Joseph's answer was a cough. He had a cold. He did not ask for amplifications. He did not consider Hungary a more awful problem now than it had been for, say, the last forty years. His nephew was always throwing at him "problems," "difficulties," "awfulnesses." It was one thing for Franz Ferdinand to keep preaching peace with Serbia. That was serviceable. It offset the war cries of General Conrad. But must he preach peace so turbulently? Problematizing Hungary? Exaggerating Serb complications? Discomfiting Franz Joseph's old age? His nephew always rushed at him with one direness or another, no matter how kind Franz Joseph tried to be. Right now he had been kind again: Despite Montenuovo's advice, he had invited the Crown Prince's morganatic family to stay at the Imperial Palace.

They did not stay there long. At first they planned to remain until the opening of the racing season on Easter Sunday. But within forty-eight hours the Crown Prince had had enough of Vienna; enough of the impassivity of its Emperor; enough of the myopia of its government; enough of the snideness of its court. He summoned his Lord Chamberlain who in turn mobilized his footmen and chauffeurs. Then the Crown Princely caravan of automobiles roared off to Konopiste. They left behind nothing but a dark fierce cloud of dust.

15

VIENNA'S FIRST TURF GALA OF 1914 PROCEEDED WITHOUT THE HEIR APparent glooming in the Imperial Box at Freudenau. That in itself added to the verve of the occasion. What's more, the weather smiled. April 12 turned out to be an idyllic Easter Sunday. Not one cloud flawed a sky that was only a nuance paler than the dominant fashion color that spring: Capri blue. The Princess Montenuovo, wife of His Majesty's First Lord Chamberlain, displayed the hue delightfully in her ensemble: a blue gown trimmed with white moiré and tango-yellow ribbons, topped by a collar of snowy lace. Many thought it brave of her to subject her generous figure to the narrow cut mandated by Paris.

Of course the younger, slimmer crowd could better accommodate French couture. But quite a few of them were missing from the aristocrats' boxes or the haut bourgeois grandstands. They'd been seduced by another attraction of newer vogue. At Aspern Airfield an "Aeronautical Parade" had drawn so many of the jeunesse dorée that their Rolls-Royces, Austro-Daimlers, Gräf & Stifts, and Mercedes-Benzes overflowed the parking space. They all watched the heavens that had become a stage. A fighter plane of the Imperial and Royal Air Force looped the loop, a double-decker towed a flock of gliders, a giant eight-passenger "bus-plane" disgorged parachutists whose green-and-scarlet umbrellas floated down the sunshine.

The same Easter Sunday in Vienna also featured a third spectacle. It was a dual demonstration on the Ringstrasse against two kinds of unemployment. Some six thousand workers who had recently lost their jobs were marching with placards demanding work. Another crowd protested the dissolution of Parliament. Bickering between German and Czech deputies had slowed down legislative business. This had given Count Karl von Stürgkh, Prime Minister of the Austrian half the Austro-Hungarian Empire, the excuse to invoke the notorious Paragraph Fourteen of the realm's constitution. It allowed him to declare the parliamentarians unable to exercise their function and to suspend the Vienna (as distinct from the Budapest) parliament. Until new elections would be called—in the indefinite future—the Stürgkh administration would be answerable only to the Emperor.

Paragraph Fourteen had been invoked before. It had caused ructions before that had been shrugged off before, but never with the concision of the remark reportedly made on Easter

Sunday at the Freudenau track. It was attributed to the Prime Minister himself and might be just flippant enough to be his. Count von Stürgkh had to watch the early races alone in his box; when the friend he had invited finally appeared, he blamed the lateness on a traffic back-up caused by demonstrators on the Ring. "I suppose," the Prime Minister was much quoted as saying, "I gave them spring fever."

Once Minister of Education, Count von Stürgkh had started his career as an academic, a frequent resort for impoverished nobility. He was rather pedantic by nature and perhaps for that reason often forced the sort of humor that would make him competitive with the cynical wit of his colleague, Count von Berchtold.

On that Easter Sunday at the track, Berchtold was spooning coffee ice cream a few boxes away in the Jockey Club enclosure. As we know, Count von Stürgkh was Prime Minister only of Austria while Count von Berchtold's office of Foreign Minister encompassed all of Austria-Hungary, with interests far beyond the yawps of complainers on the Ringstrasse. Perhaps it was a sign of how uncouth the times had become that professional concerns should intrude on his Sunday leisure.

Friends kept dropping by between races, always on some agreeable pretext. Ladies offered the Berchtolds chocolate truffles from silk-lined boxes; gentlemen kissed the Countess's hand and complimented her on the Capri blue feathers of her hat. And all along they touched on certain questions. The rumors, for example, about the Tsar's daughter being betrothed to the son of the Rumanian king. Would that align Rumania into Russia's pan-Slavic stance against Austria? And the stories about impending Russo-British naval exercises off German ports—was that to develop the encirclement of the Central Powers? And could one include in that category the 250 million francs France recently loaned Serbia for armaments? And how serious was the Serb-fomented mutiny that had broken out against the *mbret*, Austria's friend on the Albanian throne? And was it true about a clash between Austrian and Italian advisers on the *mbret*'s Inner Council? And speaking of Italy, in a confrontation between the Triple Entente (Russia, France, Britain) and the Triple Alliance (Austria, Germany, Italy), how reliable would Italy be?

"And who," Count von Berchtold answered, "will win the Prezednit handicap this afternoon?"

His friends laughed. His ice-cream-spooning sang-froid reassured them. The Foreign Minister leaned back in his box seat, in black top hat and gray topcoat, one slim knee crossed over another. A grandee with stables of his own, he knew how to document his racing judgment. Sacher (named after the torte) figured as winner of the handicap. The Foreign Minister, who always weighed the latest intelligence, had learned of a slight problem with the favorite's right foreleg. He bet on Radoteur.

Radoteur came in first. The Foreign Minister ate a chocolate truffle.

The next day, Monday, April 13, Count von Berchtold boarded his salon car in Panama hat and spats. He was off to a sub-tropical clime: Abbazia, the palm-dotted Habsburg resort on the Adriatic, not too far from Miramare where the Crown Prince had, unsuccessfuly, smoked a cigar with the Kaiser.

In Abbazia the Foreign Minister would be holding a more felicitous meeting—a conference with his Italian counterpart. A few little points needed to be discussed. One of them concerned Albania: Italy wished to participate in the industrial progress of that brand-new country but found Vienna a shade insensitive to its economic interests there. For its part, Vienna felt occasionally baffled by exaggerations in the Italian press about the "oppression" of Italians in South Tyrol.

Count von Berchtold did not entirely succeed in smiling away all differences between himself and his colleague, the Marchese Antonio de San Giuliano. But the Count, an impeccable host, did treat the Marchese to a dirigible lunch that offered poached salmon, cold champagne, and the view of a long stretch of Illyrian coastline from the gondola of a Zeppelin cruising fifteen hundred feet high. The Count also gave a great garden party in the Marchese's honor, at a seaside villa hung with Chinese lanterns and filled with the music of strolling violins. To top it all off, he motored with the Marchese to the Imperial and Royal stud farm at Lippiza where the famed white Lippizaner horses performed the subtle arts of dressage for his Italian Excellency. After five days of gastronomy, scenery, and *politesse*, the Austrian Foreign Ministry could announce with satisfaction that Italy remained as firm a member of the Triple Alliance as ever. Then Count von Berchtold returned to Vienna on April 19, in time for another Sunday demonstration on the Ring.

But what country in Europe did not suffer such bouts of "spring fever"? Austria's potential adversaries were hardly immune. In Serbia, the opposition withdrew all its deputies from the Belgrade parliament, alleging unconstitutional practices by the government in budget matters. In Russia, four thousand workers walked out of the Treugolnik rubber factory in St. Petersburg. They were joined by thousands more at the Siemens electric plant. Comrades in industrial installations in

Moscow and Riga followed suit until the strikers numbered nearly one hundred thousand. In France, the elections set for May produced daily clashes between supporters of President Raymond Poincaré, who wanted to keep the three-year conscription period, and the followers of the Socialist leader Jean Jaurès who insisted on reducing it. Even England was losing the last of its Victorian seemliness in 1914. In April dozens of special *Save Ulster!* trains rolled almost daily into London. They brought demonstrators who flooded through the streets with shouts of "*Ulster will fight and Ulster will be right!*" The Protestants' orange banners cursed the Catholic Irish for wanting to reduce Ireland to the Pope's footstool. In Dublin green cadres of the Feinians marched for self-government. By the Thames, Parliament shook with debates over the Home Rule Bill. The issue convulsed the British Isles.

By comparison, the disturbances in Vienna seemed almost minor. Most played out on the Ringstrasse where the architecture absorbed much of what tumult there was into the histrionics of the façades.

Spring absorbed the rest. Even the most bilious townsman couldn't help knowing that the Vienna Woods undulated only a few streetcar stops away. And here the lilacs exhaled their sweetness, the baby leaf waved its miracle green, and the zither called from the vintner's garden. Together they seduced politics into pleasure.

Soon the only enduring controversies appeared to be deliciously traditional: Was this year's wine as good as last season's? Had the Court Opera been right in turning down Richard Strauss's *Ariadne auf Naxos*? Could a soprano like Maria Jeritza, who made her mark as Elsa in *Lohengrin,* sing Adele in *Die Fledermaus*?

How pleasant, the answers. Yes, the new year's wine promised to match its predecessor. Yes, La Jeritza did prove to be a marvelous Adele. And something in Viennese logic justified the rejection of *Ariadne.* This logic concluded that the city's talent was not modernist like Richard Strauss; that the phrase *"Wien bleibt Wien"* (Vienna remains Vienna) summed up the city's virtuosity; that timelessness, not timeliness, expressed its soul.

Princess Pauline Metternich seemed to prove the point. This grand dame was the ancient but ever-buoyant daughter-in-law of the Chancellor who had been Napoleon's nemesis. At the end of April she gave an *Alt-Wiener Jause,* that is, an Old Viennese High Tea where select company in Biedermeier dress enjoyed delicacies and three-quarter time offered in the style of a century ago.

That was how the haut monde perpetuated *Alt Wien.* For the people at large another *Alt Wein* rose up in the Kaisergarten. The Emperor's garden was the Imperial Palace pleasance, and for the occasion His Majesty admitted the public to its lawns. Here they found highlights of a time that was no more, sculpted of papier-mâché, meticulously reproduced in scaled-down size after old paintings or illustrations in yellowed books: razed landmarks like the original Court Theater, romanesque churches perished in wars, early baroque mansions consumed by fires. Reborn here, all their turrets, pediments, gargoyles presented themselves once again to the gaze of a twentieth-century public.

Wien bleibt Wien. More than ever Vienna remained itself at the end of April 1914. And just then it learned something that was not quite imaginable.

The First Lord Chamberlain issued an announcement. His Majesty's cold, having turned into bronchitis, had now developed into pneumonia. Leading specialists were in attendance. His Imperial and Royal Highness, the Crown Prince, had been summoned from Konopiste to the capital.

Franz Joseph had reigned for sixty-six years. Firmly, if secretly, the notion had established itself, somewhere deep back in the mind of the town, that he would reign for another six hundred. Now Vienna must deal with the absurd possibility that he might not.

16

NEVER HAD THE HUGE GATES OF THE IMPERIAL PALACE GROUNDS IN SCHÖN-brunn opened to so many humble vehicles—to quite ordinary taxis. From their doors emerged the physicians who were trying to keep the monarch alive. Grand automobiles of dignitaries also rolled into the broad graveled driveway. Sentinels presented arms as their passengers emerged: Count von Berchtold, Minister of Foreign Affairs; Count von Krobatin, Minister of War; Count von Stürgkh, the Premier. But unlike the doctors they were not admitted to the All-Highest bedside. His Majesty was too ill. They could only leave their reports, their respects, their wishes, and their prayers.

Often the serious-faced Excellencies would then direct their chauffeurs to drive from Schönbrunn, in Vienna's southwest, to Castle Belvedere in the southeast. Here the Heir Apparent resided and waited—but not for them. Other visitors' cars remained parked far longer at the Belvedere. They belonged to members of the Crown Prince's shadow cabinet about to move into the sun.

Who were these, and what did their comings, goings, stayings, portend? In the late April days of 1914 such questions dominated a third meeting ground, namely the restaurant Meissl & Schadn. Its façade on the Kärntnerstrasse pictured all five continents, reflecting the concerns of its clientele: key officials of sub-cabinet rank of the Ministry of Foreign Affairs and the Ministry of War. They would be the caretaker team between monarchs. In a special back room of Meissl & Schadn—the *Extra Stüberl*—they enjoyed the establishment's vaunted Tafelspitz while caucusing on the problems of transition in the Palace.

It was bound to be dramatic. They'd already heard that almost the entire court planned to stand down the moment last rites were administered at the All-Highest bed. The First Lord Chamberlain, Prince Montenuovo, had in hand letters of resignation written in advance by himself as well as by equerries, adjutants, lords-in-waiting. These instruments would be signed and dated minutes before the old Emperor's death. That would prevent the new ruler from cashiering the retinue *en masse* with a consequent loss of their pensions.

But the prospect of Franz Ferdinand striding toward the throne also raised an issue far graver than retirement benefits of cup-bearers. The back room at Meissl & Schadn worried over nothing less than civil war.

At Castle Belevedere a post-accession plan had been drawn up. To anyone in the upper circles of government its content held few secrets. It would implement the Crown Prince's absolute determination to remove the Hungarian Prime Minister

Tisza and to change Hungary's suffrage laws by which Tisza maintained power. At present the electoral system was heavily skewed in favor of the landed gentry—Tisza's political base. The new Emperor would grant equal votes to all Magyars. Agricultural workers, landless and therefore voteless until now, would be able to ballot their bosses out of office. Three million Croats, semi-enslaved within Hungarian borders, would gain a strong voice against their suppressors. Beyond that, Franz Ferdinand intended to radically revise the constitution of the entire Habsburg realm. Under him "Austria-Hungary" would be superseded by a "United States of Austria." With the Empire federalized, many present bedevilments would vanish.

Other nationalities would not starve while Hungarian barons feasted. Vienna's central control would apply to military and some financial matters. Outside of these, the Crown would respect and enforce the autonomy (cultural or otherwise) of Bohemia, Croatia, Slovenia, Galicia, Transylvania, Illyria, Dalmatia, and—neither last nor first—Hungary. To all such domains the Emperor of Austria would serve as equitable King. He would give his Slavic subjects the parity which had long been their due.

Of course none of the Meissl & Schadn habitués had ever heard of an article an obscure Bolshevik had compiled in Vienna the year before. Had they read Stalin's "Marxism and the National Question," they would have been astonished by its structural resemblance to Franz Ferdinand's scheme. At any rate, most of the sub-Excellencies at Meissl & Schadn admitted that the post-accession plan made sense; perhaps urgent, one-minute-before-midnight sense. And just because it made sense it would make trouble.

Hungary's bearded, formidable Prime Minister Tisza no

doubt anticipated Franz Ferdinand's intentions. He was not the man to put up with them. The Meissl & Schadn consensus believed that Tisza might not hesitate to mobilize the Hungarian militia against the new Emperor. He had practically said so. "If Franz Ferdinand wants to use the army against me," Tisza had been quoted even before the present crisis in the old Emperor's health, "I will have the last word." And this is what the Crown Prince had said loudly, to the head of his Military Chancellery shortly after the Emperor had fallen ill: "Twenty-four hours after I am in, Tisza will be out."

The Meissl & Schadn crowd had even gotten word on who was to put Tisza out. The car of Joseph von Kristoffy, a former Hungarian Minister of the Interior, could be found more often in Vienna than in Budapest these days—usually at a side entrance of the Castle Belvedere. He was Franz Ferdinand's choice for Premier of Hungary. By that same entrance, just as often stood the automobile of General Karl von Terstyanski, the Crown Prince's favorite to succeed General Conrad as Chief of Staff. He was already commander of the Budapest garrison. His assignment: to make Tisza reliquish his office, if necessary by force.

Tisza, however, had an iron grip. It seemed inevitable that after Franz Joseph's death the implacable new sovereign would collide with the immovable Hungarian. Would the monarchy become a battlefield? Through what constitutional juggling or political stratagem could one contrive a compromise? Or did the problem no longer permit a peaceful option? The sub-Excellencies at Meissl & Schadn sighed. To bring their parleys to a Viennese conclusion they liked to order Linzer torte, another *spécialité de la maison*. But when they walked out of the restaurant into the May evening, it was not the taste of the torte that lingered. It was the sigh.

* * *

The All-Highest illness weighed on the city. Pacers in the corridors of power failed to enjoy a fine spring. So did Vienna's lesser folk. They couldn't afford to probe the Empire's future over bone china and Bohemian crystal. Instead, they gathered on plain benches of the vineyard inns in the Vienna Woods. The moon dappled the beech leaves, the wine gladdened the tongue, but the idyll was laced with apprehension. People stared into their goblets. They shook their heads over the latest medical bulletins from the Palace. Those doctors had become so terse. It wasn't right that the kindly, ageless legend of Franz Joseph should terminate in "severe pulmonary complications." The phrase seemed too blunt and newfangled—something like the frown on Franz Ferdinand's portraits.

The plain people on the plain benches knew hardly anything pleasant about their future ruler. His long absences from the capital implied little fondness for Vienna. His official stare revealed nothing. And so the people tried to fill that sullen void. They talked about an article series featured in the tabloid *Illustrirtes Wiener Extrablatt* just then. Its subject, though dating back almost twenty years, was timely. It concerned another Habsburg sickbed; Franz Ferdinand himself had lain in that one, in 1895, when tuberculosis had been eroding his lungs.

Then, too, the bulletins had grown terse. But the Archduke's fierce will had prevailed not only over the disease but over its exploitation by his enemies at Court. Quickly and quite publicly the camarilla had written him off as successor. Ceremonials and privileges of an heir apparent had been transferred to Franz Ferdinand's younger and much flightier brother, the Archduke Otto. Until then Otto had been famous chiefly for the champagne-happy night during which he had strolled through the Sacher Hotel lobby naked except for the badge of the Order of the Golden Fleece hanging from his neck. That had not kept the Emperor's First Lord Chamberlain from asking Otto to inaugurate theaters, open bridges, visit new hospitals. From 1894 to 1895 the Court Gazette had treated Otto as the de facto Crown Prince. And even after Franz Ferdinand had regained enough fitness for a longer journey, he had not been included in the great state visit of 1896. Archduke Otto had accompanied Emperor Franz Joseph to St. Petersburg for a meeting with the Tsar.

Of course the *Illustrirtes Wiener Extrablatt* could only hint at the high-altitude malice of those years. But now, in late April of 1914, the stories around it ran as vintage gossip through Vienna's inns: Perhaps the bitterness of his young, sick years had put the scowl on Franz Ferdinand's face? Perhaps the aggravations of his morganatic marriage had deepened it? In the inns, people wondered, conjectured, drank. For a while they felt a bit better. How good to merge Franz Ferdinand tales into Habsburg legendry, to fit him into a traditional scheme! Encouraged, the vineyard drinkers sang a song written just a few months earlier. It came from the pen of a municipal bureaucrat yet it had grown to be the rage all over Europe; it had even spread to England and America. The whole world was hymning something fragile and sweet:

Wien, Wien, nur Du allein
Sollst stets die Stadt meiner Träume sein

Dort wo die alten Häuserln stehn,
Dort wo die lieblichen Mädchen gehn . . .

(Vienna, Vienna, none but you,
Can be the city of my dreams come true

Here, where the dear old houses loom,
Where I for lovely young girls swoon . . .)

Actually "Wien, Wien" was just the latest and by far the most famous example of the genre *Wiener Lieder*. Over a hundred *Wiener Lieder* had been composed in the last eighty years. All were songs of lyric wistfulness. They sighed of a love not for a woman or a man but for Vienna; for that rainbow of a town fraying away exquisitely between vineyard and Danube; for streets in which the girls were beautiful *because* the houses were old; for a world whose doom was its enchantment.

In April 1914 the people on the wooden benches sang "Wien, Wien," to serenade their sick, dear Emperor. Actually he had become dear only after he had become ancient. But he had been ancient for so long, he seemed to have been dear forever. For generations those silver sideburns had generated fond stories, wonderful rumors, reverent speculations. Austrian patriotism centered on this ikon of infinite anecdotes and wrinkles. Still, the day must come when six horses draped in black would bear him away; when the most unsentimental of Archdukes would roar up in his motorcar to take possession of the Imperial Palace. What then?

Neither the firmament's glimmer above nor the reflections in the Danube below answered the question brooding over the vineyard hills. And so the people in the leafy inns resorted to their only ready remedy: to drink; to gossip antique Habsburg gossip again; and, again and again, to sing *"Wien, Wien . . ."*

Another tune attained enormous popularity in Vienna's springtime of 1914—the first international hit of a young American composer, Irving Berlin. It was frequently featured by modish restaurant orchestras like the one in the Ringstrasse's Grand Hotel. But during late April and early May the music there played to an unusual number of empty tables. Franz Joseph's pneumonia was taking its toll in these plush precincts, too. The succession, with its perils and uncertainties, loomed ahead. A sudden decline had shaken the stock market. Many of the more loose-pursed tycoons were retrenching and that included patrons of the Grand Hotel restaurant. Nevertheless, some habitués kept coming to enjoy Stuffed Whitefish à la Radziwill (a renowned virtuosity of the chef's) and to keep *au courant* with Mister Irving Berlin. Among prominent diners figured Hermann von Reininghaus, the young brewery grand seigneur, and his dusky wife Gina as well as the third element of the triangle, General Conrad, the Chief of Staff.

The presence of the beloved—even when encumbered by her husband—always cheered the General. What's more, the good weather promised him, a passionate mountaineer, some fine Alpine tours. But as Gina noted in her memoirs, his smile looked rigid in those days. With reason. The General shared all of Vienna's fear for the old Emperor. In addition, he must face the probability that the new monarch would dismiss him in disgrace, would send him packing summarily, together with the Hungarian Prime Minister Tisza even as the coffin of Franz Joseph was carried into the crypt of the Capuchin Church.

Of course an exit in May would only accelerate somewhat the General's timetable. In the spring of 1914 he had resolved to wait for the Sarajevo maneuvers at the end of June, and then to resign. It was enough. He had been harassed too often by Franz Ferdinand, rebuffed too often each time he requested the punishment of Serbia—which was fomenting a rebellion in Albania right now. Too often had he been frustrated for the sake of "this foul peace which drags on and on," as he had put it in one of his secret letters to Gina von Reininghaus. The same letter vibrated with impatience for a "war from which I could return crowned with success that would allow me to break through all the barriers between us, Gina, and claim you as my own dearest wife . . . [a war that] would bring the satisfactions in my career and private life which fate has so far denied me."

He would be denied them forever when Franz Ferdinand mounted the throne. Still, at the Grand Hotel restaurant he could bear with fate a little better because here it was cushioned with Gina's closeness. When the orchestra struck up that rousing new air from America, the General rose to his feet, bowed, requested Herr von Reininghaus's permission to ask Frau von Reininghaus for the honor of this dance.

It was granted. General and lady walked to the parquet floor. They began to sway in each others arms. The vocalist sang, in Viennese English, the song most popular throughout the Western world that spring of 1914:

Come on and hear, come on and hear
  Alexander's ragtime band,
Come on along, come on along,
  It's the best band in the land,
They can play a bugle call
  Like you never heard before,
Make it so natural
  That you want to go to war . . .

17

REPERCUSSIONS OF FRANZ JOSEPH'S PNEUMONIA SPREAD SOUTHWARD TO the Serbian capital. Before the news reached him there, Gavrilo Princip had been focusing steadily, unblinking, on a climax that drew nearer each day: the June war games of the Austrian Army near Sarajevo, captained by the man who must be killed, the Archduke Franz Ferdinand.

To help him in the deed, Princip had recruited Nedeljko Cabrinović in Belgrade. In Sarajevo itself Princip's old confederate Danilo Ilić was waiting. But by April Princip decided that the assassination of the Habsburg Crown Prince was an enterprise requiring yet another partner. He picked Trifko Grabež, a fellow lodger in his rooming house at 23 Carigradska Street in Belgrade.

Grabež, too, had been a former high school student in Austrian Bosnia who had crossed the border into Serbia and now lounged about Belgrade coffeehouses between odd jobs. But Grabež's exile differed from Princip's. It lacked politics. In a dispute over grades, Grabež had punched his teacher in the nose before running away. Vagabonding, adventuring, womanizing, appealed to Grabež much more than ideology. Yet Princip liked the lad's pluck and brawn. And so thin little Princip began to talk to Grabež, whose muscular frame towered over him. He kept talking softly, steadily, in the seclusion of his room. Unblinking, he talked with a voice barely audible yet of an overwhelming intensity. When he finished, the big fellow had become the little one's obedient disciple. In two days, juvenile delinquent had changed to zealot. Grabež was ready to do anything at his leader's command.

Princip had now collected the manpower for his kill. He still needed arms and the training to use them. The Young Bosnia organization, whose members met on coffeehouse terraces, would be of limited use. Young Bosnia's program included action to flesh out its anti-Habsburg slogans. But too much of its energy went into the production of patriotic verse.

Princip turned to a far tougher group. Its name never saw print. But it was led by a man whose photograph sometimes appeared in Belgrade newspapers that spring: an enormous Serbian Army officer, as heavy as he was tall, monolithically bald, with a brute black mustache jutting from a Mongolian face. The caption under his picture identified him as Colonel Dragutin Dimitrijević, Director of the Intelligence Bureau of the Serbian General Staff. But at Belgrade's political cafés one knew much more than that about him. There, whispers referred to him as Apis—the sacred bull of ancient Egypt.

Like his namesake he was a myth to his adherents. No ordinary earthly concerns tethered him: no wife, no lover, no family, no children, neither hobby nor recreation. He was not the liver of a life but the demon of an idea. At night he slept a few hours at his brother-in-law's. The rest of his time he spent in the Belgrade Ministry of War, in an office whirring with telephone wires, telegraph keys, decoding devices, couriers arriving and departing. Restaurants and theaters did not exist for him. He was beyond normal frivolities. All his waking hours served one unmerciful passion: to carve Greater Serbia out of the rotting body of the Habsburg Empire.

Eleven years earlier, in 1903, Apis had been among a band of officers who had dynamited the doors of Belgrade's Royal Palace, hunted for the Austrian toady, King Alexander, cornered him in a closet with his Queen, perforated the couple with revolver bullets, hacked their bodies up with sabers, and thrown them out the window.

The assassination had placed on the Serb throne the present, much more anti-Viennese Karageorgević dynasty. A few years later Apis had become leader of Ujedinjeje ili Smrt (Union or Death)—a society known in the coffeehouses by a murmured nickname: The Black Hand. Though its membership included some cabinet ministers and General Staff officers, it had no official sanction or recognition. Its nationalism was far more radical than that of the Serbian government itself. Initiates said that Prime Minister Pašić had appointed Apis Intelligence Chief in order to keep track of the man, to co-opt and control him. Nevertheless, Apis's Black Hand had killed King George I of Greece the previous year, in 1913, for repressing Slav minorities. No doubt the Black Hand had other plans along this line, very clandestine ones. In the coffeehouses the classified section of the Belgrade daily *Trgovinski Glasnik* received close scrutiny. Here the Society placed innocuously phrased items in the Situations Wanted column; properly deciphered, they were Black Hand messages to its various cells.

Part rumor, part fact, such things sifted through the mists

shrouding the group. In April 1914, Gavrilo Princip knew one thing for sure. He must reach Apis or at least one of his men. They would help him achieve his purpose.

Just before the month ended, he made contact. Through an intermediary he met an authentic agent of the Black Hand, the Serbian Army Major, Voislav Tankosić. The encounter began awkwardly on the terrace of the Acorn Garland. As soon as the two shook hands, they recognized each other. Twenty months earlier, during the First Balkan War, Princip had come to Belgrade to volunteer for the Major's guerrilla force operating against the Turks. Tankosić had turned down the sixteen-year-old schoolboy for being too young, too short, and too frail. Now Princip was eighteen; despite the adult mustache he had grown, he was as short as ever and looked even thinner. But his light blue eyes did not blink as he explained, softly and calmly, that he would need guns and bombs to blast away the Crown Prince of the Austro-Hungarian Empire in Sarajevo.

This time Major Tankosić did not reject the stripling out of hand. He told him to stand by. "Someone" would have to be consulted.

"Someone"—obviously Apis—took his time. A week passed. Princip relayed his impatience to the Major. Tankosić sent back a message: "the boy" should read the newspapers; Franz Joseph had fallen mortally sick, and Franz Ferdinand, as the new monarch, would have better things to do than bother with summer maneuvers in Sarajevo. The whole thing was off.

"The boy," Princip, sent back a note: He did not give a fig

about the Emperor's illness. He would kill Franz Ferdinand whether he wore the crown or not, whether he came to Sarajevo or not. Nothing was off. Now, what about the weapons?

Shortly thereafter a runner came with a second message to Princip's room: "You and your friends, go to Topcider Park now." Princip rounded up Grabež and Cabrinović, shepherded them to Topcider, one of Belgrade's more deserted parks. The three were easy to spot—a thin little youth, flanked by two older, taller companions. As the trio approached the park's main entrance, a man waiting there raised his hand slightly.

He led them to a remote spot in the greenery. He gave them a wooden box containing three revolvers and a cardboard box filled with ammunition. He pointed to the stump of an oak tree shaped rather like a human body. He showed them how to load; how to aim; how to fire.

He showed them day after day. The sun shone, the pistols blazed, the Park echoed, the oak stump splintered. When the two weeks' course was over, Princip emerged as the best student. From a standing position "the boy" scored six hits out of ten shots at a distance of more than 200 yards. At a distance of 60 yards he scored eight absolutely perfect hits. And he was almost as sharp a marksman while running. Grabež and Cabrinović did not match his skill but had become fair shots.

After their last class the three went to the Golden Sturgeon café for a discreet celebration. Since Princip enforced abstinence, they ordered mineral water. His blue eyes did not blink and he did not smile when he asked his friends to raise their glasses to the health of the old Emperor of Austria. His Majesty's recovery would bring Franz Ferdinand into convenient range. At least on one coffeehouse terrace in Belgrade, it was an exciting spring.

18

IN SARAJEVO, DANILO ILIĆ NURSED THE SAME MURDEROUS HOPE FOR Franz Joseph's recuperation. Ilić, Gavrilo Princip's earliest co-conspirator, was awaiting his fellow-assassins' arrival in the Bosnian capital.

Meanwhile he began to write for *Zvono*, a new Socialist paper with avant-garde leanings. Though only a very junior comrade, he lost no time in attacking the Socialist Party leadership in Bosnia. "It is strange," he wrote, "that the words of our Party bosses should accord with those of the Austrian Foreign Minister who favors independence for Albania while denying the same right to the South Slavs . . . The consequence of such foolish Socialist leadership is a diminishing Socialist consciousness."

Now, the bosses of Bosnia's small Socialist Party received their cues from headquarters of the much larger movement in Vienna. Which is to say, they were guided by Viktor Adler, doyen of working-class opposition throughout the Habsburg Empire. In assailing "the bosses," Ilić really assailed Adler—not quite fairly.

Adler's *Arbeiter Zeitung* often did mock the farce of Albanian independence. It often did deplore the suppression of South Slav autonomy. But in 1914, Austrian Socialism also felt the need to combat the spread of unemployment, the pauperization of the employed in their slums, the acceleration of armament production everywhere. In this press of problems, Adler's support of Slav rights was incidental rather than insistent. Ilić felt it was inexcusably casual.

There were other differences between Ilić and Adler; between the Sarajevo Socialist itching to get an Archduke into his gun sights, and the Vienna Party chief championing, but not forcing Liberty, Fraternity, Equality. Ilić was the son of a cobbler; Adler, the scion of a stockbroker. Ilić was twenty-four; at sixty-two Adler was the Emperor's junior by more than twenty years and yet, in Ilić's eyes, also a worn dynast ruling his domain too long. Ilić, always in white shirt and black tie, was an unrelentingly neat rebel. Adler, on the other hand, with his gray mane uncombed, his thick glasses loose on his nose, his perpetually strained voice (whose cracked eloquence struck Trotsky)—Adler must have seemed to Ilić like the *Herr Professor* of a passé revolution.

Yet Ilić and Adler had surprisingly much in common. Nationalism with a Nietzschean twist had launched them both into politics. Ilić had joined Young Bosnia, the student group of teetotalers. Their South Slav "Will to Power," fueled by Nietzsche, troubled Austrian authorities in 1914. Nearly forty years earlier Austrian authorities had been troubled by Adler's friends for similar reasons. In Vienna, police agents had monitored a student organization that mixed vegetarianism, populism, and a pan-German weltanschauung into a radical brew. At its meetings young Gustav Mahler had pounded out "Deutschland, Deutschland über Alles" on the piano, young Viktor Adler had declaimed insurrectionary verse, but its lodestar—like Young Bosnia's decades later—had been Friedrich Nietzsche, then still alive and unwell, seething brilliantly among his sleeping potions and headache pills. Indeed on Nietzsche's birthday, October 18, 1877, Viktor Adler had signed a letter to the master, acclaiming him as "our luminous and transporting guide."

What had inspired Adler's group in the 1870s appealed to Princip and Ilić in 1914—Nietzsche's pronunciamento that for the fulfilled life man needed to be doubly divine: divine like Dionysus, god of the orgiastic joy harvested from the heroic deed (a deity often represented by an Apis-like bull!); divine also like Apollo, god of the serenity harvested from contemplative reason.

Now, in the spring of 1914, Ilić's friend Princip acted out the Dionysian principle of his favorite Nietzsche poem:

> Everything that I leave becomes coal.
> Flame am I, surely . . .

Dionysian bullets were singing through a man-shaped tree stump in a Belgrade Park. In Munich, Adolf Hitler—another young temperance fanatic—was burning to lead a Dionysian master race. (Hitler's last birthday gift to Mussolini in 1943: *The Collected Works of Nietzsche.*) In Vienna during the Great War, Viktor Adler's son Friedrich—named after Friedrich Nietzsche—would commit a Dionysian crime; he would shoot and kill the Austrian Prime Minister von Stürgkh at the restaurant Meissl & Schadn. Adler Senior, however, as befits an elderly asthmatic revolutionary of middle-class origins, had fallen back on Nietzsche's more sedate Apollonian aspects. By 1914, he no longer saw the superman as the hero of some magically wild folk poem but as a rational social being, no longer as the superb Teuton but as the emancipated proletarian. To help the worker liberate his brethren, the Party must give him an education.

The new proletarian didn't need to storm the Bastille. But he had to master a syllabus. Only by unshackling his mind could the worker free himself of injustice. "The revolution of consciousness," Adler had written, "must progress along with the revolution in economics."

By 1914, Viktor Adler had been spearheading that revolution for twenty-five years. Since he had led it in Vienna, he'd had to lead it *against* Vienna. He had to fight the *genius loci* that let the poor waltz through their poverty. He had to take on the élan with which the city painted carnival across squalor; fight the handkissing done in rags; fight the wine songs sung by starvelings; fight the heraldic fairy tales framing lives of grime.

"One thing is needful," Nietzsche had said, "namely, giving style to one's character." Victor Adler made the worker acquire character by cultivating a new style. Instead of whining sentimental ditties about Alt-Wien, Socialist choirs rehearsed songs about union organizers. Instead of all that tavern reminiscing about Empress Elizabeth, the people rediscovered the revolution of 1848 through slide shows at the Party's Adult Education Centers. Instead of dissipating their leisure with alcohol or gambling or prostitutes, they joined the Party's Gymnasts' or Alpinists' or Bikers' clubs. The Party organized and sanitized the workers' lives, and thus vitalized their resistance against exploitation.

Through all that, Austro-Marxism had produced "the world's most educated proletarians." Furthermore it elected a plurality envied by its competitors. At the Austrian Parliament dissolved in 1914, the Socialists commanded 84 out of 504 members. This stood out as an impressive number in a legislature that was a crazy quilt of many little ideological patches.

Yet the nature of the Party's strength also produced its insulation. It was a quasi-Nietzschean elite operating in a most un-Nietzschean ambiance. To become strong, it had purged its members of their Austrian indulgences. Adler had fashioned a political masterpiece against the Viennese grain; therefore its strength stood isolated. Other parties might have connected with it in terms of common strategy, if not program. But in character the Socialists were too alien for coalitions or even negotiations. Austro-Marxism lacked the leverage of brother movements in other countries.

In 1914 even more than in previous years, Viktor Adler knew that his Party must not be a weak link of the international workers' alliance. Shadows had begun to jut across Europe's borders. Governments of major powers speechified louder than ever about national interests, patriotic valor, and automated battleships. France heard German sabers rattling. Germany protested its encirclement by England, France, and Russia. Russia denounced Austria's pushiness in the Balkans. And Austria countered sharply; statements from Count von Berchtold's Foreign Ministry on the Ballhausplatz, editorials in the Ballhausplatz-inspired press, all used an especially martial tone to prove that Habsburg was not crippled by the illness of the Emperor.

Yet at the same time the masses had grown more sensitive to the menace of war. In Germany, Rosa Luxemburg had just been tried for inciting troops to mutiny: If Germans were asked to murder Frenchmen—she had said in public—Germans would refuse. A court had sent her to jail for a year, but the sentence did not dim the pacifism of German Socialists or the popularity of their party. In the Berlin parliament their plurality topped their comrades' in Vienna. No less than 35 percent of all Reichstag deputies wore the red ribbon in their lapels. In France, the people would go to the polls on May 10; all signs pointed to a Socialist triumph bound to reduce the three-year conscription. In Russia the Tsar must face strikes spreading to armament factories.

Socialist advances elsewhere would soon stare Austro-Marxism in the face. It was in Vienna that the leaders of Europe's proletariats were to convene for the fiftieth anniversary of the founding of the Socialist International. Their meeting was scheduled to begin on August 23 at the Grosser Musikvereinssaal, with Viktor Adler as host.

The prospect charged Adler's agenda in the spring of 1914. It was time to overcome the insulation of his Party; to show comrades abroad and at home that Austrian Socialism could contribute crucially to the International's chorus: "More Bread, Fewer Guns, No War!"

For such a purpose, May Day of 1914 would be an exhilarating reveille. Most of Viktor Adler's politics appealed to the intellect. But May Day spoke to the body's sensuousness. Therefore it was only appropriate that Viktor Adler had invented the May Day March in the apartment later occupied by Sigmund Freud at Berggasse 19: May Day stoked the Socialist libido. The great march ritualized and rhapsodized ideals presented by the Party much more soberly during the rest of the year. In brief, May Day's Apollonian orderliness had always carried Dionysian voltage. No wonder that the sight of the march had overwhelmed Hitler at twenty-three, or that its memory in Hitler's brain would later set brown-shirted ecstatics goose-stepping behind the swastika. No wonder May Day had electrified Gustav Mahler, Viktor Adler's cohort in their Nietzschean salad days. As Socialist leader, Viktor Adler defined May Day as a "waking call." As mature composer, Mahler intended to title his Third Symphony *The Gay Science* (in tribute to Nietzsche's book of the same name) and began its first movement with a "*Weckruf*" (waking call) to rouse the dormant Nietzschean life force. No wonder that Richard Strauss was to remark that whenever he conducted Mahler's Third he would always imagine, during the First Movement, "uncountable battalions of workers marching to the May Day celebration in Vienna's Prater." No wonder that Mahler at the end of his career, by then the aging apolitical Director of the Vienna Opera, had suddenly recaptured the ardor of his youth on a May First. Leaving an opera rehearsal, he had run into the workers' procession by accident, joined it on impulse, stuck with it to the very end, and came home at night "vibrant with brotherliness."

That had been in 1905. Now it was 1914. Mahler was dead. Viktor Adler was old, suffering from cardiac edema. Yet he remained as determined a workers' leader as ever. This year of all years, the May Day march needed juice, resolve, will. Yet just this year the march faced unusual jeopardy. At any moment the Emperor might die. His successor Franz Ferdinand might cancel all celebrations. True, so far Franz Joseph had survived a fever that would have killed most other octogenarians. Yet his very lingering posed a problem for May First. In many an Austrian Socialist there lurked a covert monarchist. Would there be a reluctance to join the Red festival while the father of the country fought for breath?

* * *

At most of the twenty-five May Days so far, the sky had been clear and comradely in Vienna. This year weather forecasters were wary. Still, May 1, 1914, dawned with a plenitude of sun. What's more, the Emperor's pneumonia did not dampen class consciousness. Workers poured out of the slums. By the hundreds they gathered as craft groups at many different assembly points: tailors, bakers, mechanics, glove-makers. By the thousands the groups merged on the Ringstrasse, adding multitudes as they went. By the tens of thousands they crossed the Danube Canal bridges. As a host of hundreds of thousands they converged on the Prater. There in the park they were the First Movement of Mahler's Third become flesh, ready for the crescendo.

At that point it was just past noon. Above a moving sea of heads the heavens had turned from blue to gray. But clouds had become irrelevant. There was such brightness surging through the streets: band after band intoning the "Internationale" or playing workers' songs; banners calling for an eight-hour day; banners demanding apartments with plumbing; banners condemning alcohol as the capitalists' confederate; banners exhorting the government to recall Parliament, to spend less money on guns, to ease conscription, to keep peace.

Arms locked, the marchers chanted their grievances and sang out their hopes. And this May Viktor Adler had added a new touch—"Red Cavalry," made up of battalions of bicyclists. Their legs pistoning in unison, their bike wheels festooned with red carnations, they held trumpets to their mouths and made the town echo with fanfares that galvanized onlookers into cheers. Topping it all were delegations from abroad as heralds of the International's Congress to come: carpenters from Germany in their guild dress of top hats, black scarves, and gray bell-bottom trousers; French steel workers in blue aprons and metal caps; booted Italian miners waving lit lanterns.

The entire, enormous crowd came to a halt on the largest Prater meadow, just as the first drops fell. Thunder overrode the greetings of the intial speaker. Within a minute rain flooded down. Hail peppered the deluge. The throng fled into the Prater's inns, restaurants, and coffeehouses. Here labor's holiday continued in jam-packed solidarity but also in an unscheduled key. Had the weather held, the workers would have listened in orderly rows as orators outside exhorted them to valor and temperance and discipline for the ongoing struggle. Now, munching sausage, sitting on each other's laps or even on banners condemning liquor, they toasted their comradeship with bottles of Gumpoldskirchner. Of course at the Inn to the Brown Stag where Viktor Adler himself had taken refuge, one drank only coffee or orange soda. Still, Adler must have known that this May Day had come to an end more Viennese than planned.

19

SPRING WAS TAKING A PRECARIOUS TURN FOR ALL THREE OF VIENNA'S GRAND old men. The downpour spoiled Victor Adler's fête; it exacerbated his asthma for the next few days. Helpless stethoscopes surrounded Franz Joseph's bed. And the patriarch of psychosomatic medicine found his health in straits just as his Emperor's pneumonia reached a crisis. The coincidence may not have been coincidental.

During the winter of 1914 Freud had been suffering intermittently from colitis. In mid-April his symptoms persisted to a worrisome degree. He began to suspect a tumor of the colon.

Things were greening and sprouting in the Vienna Woods, but this spring the doctor lost his taste for mushroom hunts. He felt too tired for noontime walks around the Ring. What energy he had, he gave to his work and to the fisticuffs disguised as monographs within the International Psycho-Analytical Association.

Especially to the last. The association's politics, like those of the Balkans, had been steadily tensing. Until the end of 1913 Freud had hoped if not for peace, at least for a truce with his Swiss adversary, Carl Jung. In the course of the year Freud's allies had rallied around him in lectures and papers; they'd directed a scholarly scorn at the "dogmas from Zurich" (particularly at Jung's de-sexualization of the libido into general psychic energy). Freud himself, however, had refrained from all personal sallies. As if to fortify his restraint he kept refining his "Moses of Michelangelo," that essay in praise of conciliation. Yet at the same time he took a certain partisan pleasure in the response to his recent *Totem and Taboo.* The psychoanalytic intellegentsia took note that *Totem* scintillated on the symbology of primitive man, the very field Jung claimed as his own.

In early 1914 Freud had begun to take a more decided role in the campaign. He used a paper begun during his Roman summer of 1913. Then, between trips to the Moses statue in the Church of San Pietro in Vincoli, he had blocked out "On Narcissism: an Introduction." Later, in Vienna, polishing the essay during the spring of 1914, he fashioned it into something of a stiletto: He included a very pointed though still civil revision of Jung's ideas on the subject.

Meanwhile the enemy was not sitting still. Jung was preparing to pluck once more at the prophet's beard through upcoming lectures in Scotland. Rumors to that effect filtered fast to Vienna. As if to confirm them, Jung publicly protested against Freud-inspired "aspersions on my *bona fides*" and resigned as editor of the *Psycho-Analytic Yearbook.*

For Freud this was a signal to stop all appeasement. He had

long repressed the militancy of his resentment. The speed with which it surfaced now can be gauged from two sentences from two different letters. "I have no desire for separation," he had written about Jung on June 1, 1913, ". . . perhaps my *Totem* paper will bring on the breach against my will." On January 12, 1914, he wrote, working on another paper, ". . . I expect that this statement of mine will put an end to all compromises and bring about the desired rupture."

General Conrad could not have expressed better *his* impatience with formal ties to a foe. After all, Belgrade still maintained diplomatic relations with Vienna, just as Jung was still President of Freud's International Psycho-Analytical Association. In contrast to the General, however, Freud wore the crown of his realm and could fire off ultimatums at will. "This statement" that would cause "the desired rupture" was a manuscript he had started just before New Year's when he also labored on "Narcissism" and "Moses of Michelangelo." For Freud it was a season of astonishingly diverse industriousness that continued as the months grew warmer and his colitis worse. Yet regardless of other worries or chores, Freud kept working on this "statement" designed to kill all "compromises" with the Jungians. He wanted to publish it in the next issue of the *Psycho-Analytic Yearbook* from which Jung had just resigned.

The "statement" was a "polemic" as Freud himself more closely defined it. Its title: "On the History of Psycho-Analysis." Despite the neutral tag, it articulated (in the words of the editor of Freud's Standard Edition) "the fundamental postulates and hypotheses of psycho-analysis to show that the theories of . . . Jung were totally incompatible with them."

* * *

Advance word of the Freud offensive reached Jung in the early months of 1914. Soon afterward the Freud-controlled *Internationale Zeitschrift für Psycho-Analyse* loosed a barrage of hostile comment at Jung-influenced monographs. The strategy took. On April 20 Jung completed the breach. He resigned from the Presidency of the International Psycho-Analytical Association.

"I am tired of leniency and kindness." Freud made that confession in a letter of May 17, three months after finishing the Moses essay in which he had embraced leniency and kindness. How well tuned he was to the world's mood in 1914. How quickly his Apollo had changed to Dionysus. And how mortal he remained, just like the world's other Dionysians. In mid-May his intestinal symptoms, ever worsening, forced him to comply with his physician's demand. He submitted to a detailed examination by a specialist on cancer of the colon.

20

On May 12, 1914, two men in civilian clothes, yet attended by orderlies, had tea in the sitting room of a hotel suite in Carlsbad. One of them had obviously come to the spa for a purpose other than a cure. At sixty-two General Conrad was trim and fit, still a terrier primed to pounce. The tic of his left eye punctuated his energy, the crispness and speed of his motions. His handsome face, topped by the mane of gold and gray, glowed with a tan earned on horseback during spring maneuvers.

His German counterpart slumped in an armchair as though he were much more than only four years older. General Helmuth von Moltke, Chief of Staff of the Kaiser's armed forces, needed the healing waters badly. Ungainly, flabby, bald, he was not at all well in stomach or kidney. Nor fortunate with certain wrinkles in his disposition. To offset these he read Nietzsche as the Muse of Power and he often talked about Thomas Carlyle's books showing that history was made by heroes. Still, he couldn't help proclivities odd for the principal warrior of the Junkers. He was a cello-playing Christian Scientist with a penchant for esoteric cults. At night, when nobody was watching, he translated Maurice Maeterlinck's *Pelléas et Mélisande* from the French. He suggested a frayed, bruised poet, possibly androgynous, definitely overweight.

The Kaiser called Moltke "der traurige Julius" (sad Julius). High-echelon wags in Berlin claimed that he was not sad, just hurting with bruises from his falls from the saddle. As a source of many a grin, the horsemanship of the Chief of Staff contributed to the lighter side of official life in Berlin. One of his celebrated tumbles had been in front of the equestrian statue of his uncle, *the* Helmuth von Moltke, the great Field Marshal von Moltke, victor over Napoleon III in the war of 1870.

The comparison afflicted the lesser von Moltke all his life. So did the conflict between his duty, which must be remorseless, and his intelligence, which was considerable. "The next war," he had told the Kaiser a few years earlier, "will be a national war. It will not be settled by one decisive battle but will be a long wearisome struggle with an enemy who will not be overcome until his whole national force is broken . . . a war which will utterly exhaust our own people even if we are victorious." Yet here he sat, in May 1914, discussing the next war. It was von Moltke's job to map out the catastrophe of victory.

Of course General Conrad suffered from none of his colleague's pangs or qualms. He had journeyed to Carlsbad ostensibly to underline in person what he had written Berlin in several memoranda; namely that Serbia's provocations in Albania and elsewhere could no longer go unanswered. Belgrade, he told the German Chief of Staff, was presuming too much on the patience of Conrad's Imperial masters (an allusion to Crown Prince Ferdinand's pacifism and the caution of Franz Joseph, now so sick). A day of reckoning was at hand. It would put the German-Austrian alliance to a test. Conrad said he wanted to make sure that he and his Berlin confrère agreed on all the mechanics of the partnership.

Conrad, in other words, was fishing for reassurance. If Russia and France rushed to Serbia's aid, could Austria count on instant, unconditional German support? Conrad did not ask the question outright. But it hung in the air. Obviously it was the reason for his visit.

In his response von Moltke had to take into account *his* Imperial master's philosophy. The Kaiser preferred easy braggadocio to nasty hard work like conducting a major war. And so von Moltke said that he hoped the world's peace would not be hostage to some petty Balkan adventurism. But he also said—swallowing a liver pill with a bitter grimace—that Kaiser Wilhelm was not the kind of leader who ever let his guard down. Germany could not ignore recent developments like those huge French loans to Russia and Serbia that were so plainly meant to finance armaments; or Russia's feverish overhaul of her transportation system to speed troop movements to the German border. The Triple Entente—von Moltke shrugged a weary shoulder as he referred to the camp consisting of Russia, France, and Great Britain—always carried on about German aggressiveness. These countries didn't realize that Kaiser Wilhelm would never raise his mailed fist except in defense of his or his ally's legitimate interests. All the hysteria in the Russian press, for example, about the naval implications of the recent widening of the Kiel Canal. True, German battleships could now steam directly from the North Sea to the Baltic. But that was a safeguard necessary in view of moves made by the Triple Entente—like the joint British-Russian fleet maneuvers planned in the Baltic Sea.

Conrad nodded with a vengeance: just what he was always emphasizing in Vienna—the Central Powers were only catching up—in fact, not catching up fast enough, wouldn't His Excellency agree?

Von Moltke's counternod lacked his colleague's vim. Still, it was a nod. Yes, von Moltke said. Russia in particular was moving swiftly toward readiness. The later the showdown, the worse. "Before I took my leave," Conrad would write in his memoirs, "I again asked General von Moltke how long, in his view, the double war against Russia and France would last before Germany could turn with a strong force on Russia alone. Moltke: 'We hope to be finished with France six weeks after the commencement of operations, or at least finished to a degree that we can transfer our main strength to the East.' "

Colonel Edward House, Woodrow Wilson's adviser, did not eavesdrop on this scene. But he happened to be touring Europe at that time on a mission for the American President. He was to collect information for a plan by which Wilson might calm down the continent. And the American did catch the mood producing conversations such as the one in Carlsbad. "The situation is extraordinary," he reported on May 29, 1914, from Berlin to the White House. "It is militarism run stark mad. Unless someone acting for you can bring about a different understanding, there is some day to be an awful cataclysm. No one in Europe can do it. There is too much hatred. Too many jealousies."

It turned out that the White House must tend to belligerence much closer to home. American nationals had been abused in

Lenin in 1914. *Culver Pictures, Inc.*

Stalin ca. 1914. *Culver Pictures, Inc.*

Hitler amid the crowd acclaiming the German declaration of war on Russia. Date: August 1, 1914. Place: Odeonplatz, Munich. *Culver Pictures, Inc.*

Dapper Leon Trotsky's passport photograph, 1914.

Viktor Adler, leader of Austria's Socialist Party. *Bildarchiv d. Öst. Nationalbibliothek*

A married couple in love: Archduke Franz Ferdinand and his morganatic wife, Sophie. *Bildarchiv d. Öst. Nationalbibliothek*

Chess players and kibitzers at the Café Central. *Werner J. Schweiger*

Ball at the Imperial Palace in Vienna. *Bildarchiv d. Öst. Nationalbibliothek*

Caricature of Karl Kraus, Vienna's preeminent satirist, peddling his periodical, *Die Fackel*. *Die Muskete*

General Conrad von Hötzendorf, Chief of Staff of Austria's Armed Forces. *Bildarchiv d. Öst. Nationalbibliothek*

Emperor Franz Joseph strolling with his lady love, the actress Katharina Schratt, in Bad Ischl. *Bildarchiv d. Öst. Nationalbibliothek*

Sigmund Freud with his daughter Anna on summer holiday in the Dolomites shortly before his confrontation with Jung at the International Psycho-Analytic Congress in Munich in September 1913. *Mary Evans-Sigmund Freud Copyrights, Colchester*

Emperor Franz Joseph in his hunting costume in Bad Ischl. *Öst. Staatsarchiv-Kriegsarchiv*

The assassin Gavrilo Princip *(right)* with his co-conspirator Trifko Grabež *(left)* and a friend on a bench in Belgrade's Kalmedgan Park, May 1914. *Bildarchiv d. Öst. Nationalbibliothek*

Count Leopold von Berchtold, Foreign Minister of the Austro-Hungarian Empire.
Bildarchiv d. Öst. Nationalbibliothek

June 12, 1914, sixteen days before the assassination: The Kaiser visits Franz Ferdinand at Konopiste. *From left to right:* The Archduke in the uniform of the 10th Prussian Uhlan Regiment; his wife, the Duchess Hohenberg; the Kaiser in hunting costume, having his hand kissed by one of the Archduke's sons.
Archiv Günther Ossmann, Wien

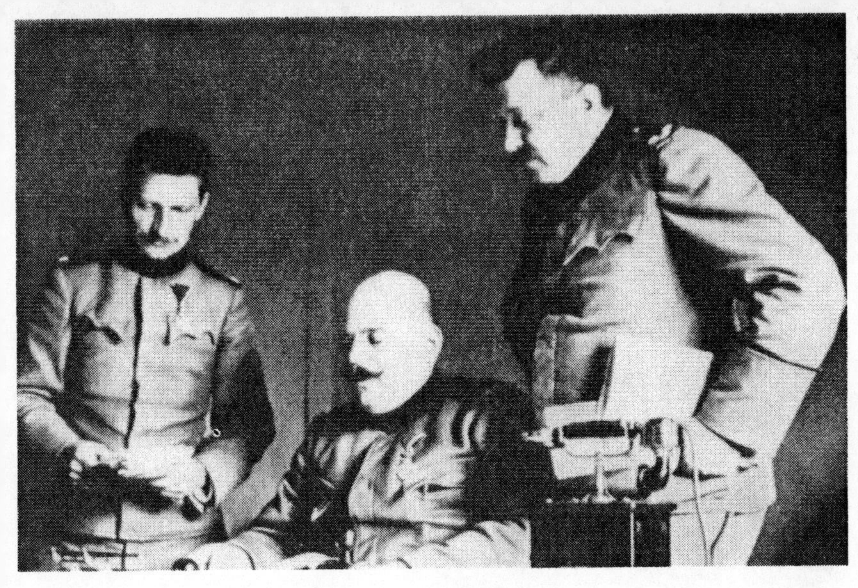

The Chief of Serbia's Intelligence Bureau, Colonel Dragutin C. Dimitrijević, flanked by aides. Also known by the code name "Apis," he was the head of the Serbian terrorist organization The Black Hand, which funded the assassins. *Bildarchiv d. Öst. National-bibliothek*

Konopiste. The esplanade leading to the rose garden at Archduke Franz Ferdinand's castle. *Bildarchiv d. Öst. National-bibliothek*

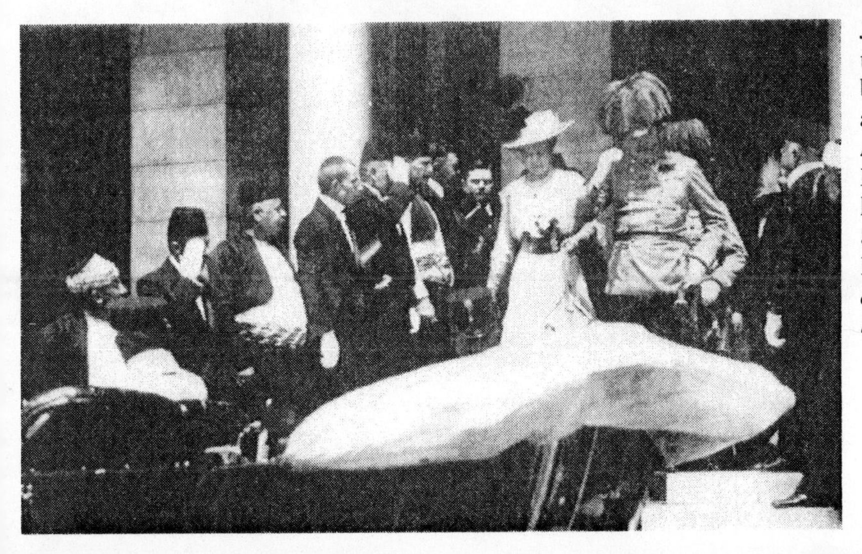

June 28, 1914, ten minutes before the assassination: Archduke Franz Ferdinand and his wife leave Sarajevo City Hall. *Bildarchiv d. Öst. National-bibliothek*

The death car: Franz Ferdinand and his wife in the back seat with Count Harrach standing on the running board. *Bildarchiv d. Öst. Nationalbibliothek*

The assassin Princip just after his arrest. *Culver Pictures, Inc.*

Mexico. In April, Marines had seized Vera Cruz. By May the United States stood on the brink of war with its Southern neighbor. Woodrow Wilson faced too much New World trouble to straighten out the Old.

But the arithmetic of the militarism alarming Colonel House was indeed awesome. Despite Socialist resistance, the Berlin parliament had raised the peacetime strength of the German military establishment from 660,000 to nearly 800,000. The three-year conscription period added enormous striking power to the French army. Within four years Russia's preparedness program had increased her forces by 500,000 men to 1,300,000, and her forces were growing still. In a similar span Austria had expanded her army from 400,000 to half a million. "We spend half as much on armaments as Germany," wrote the Socialist *Arbeiter Zeitung* soon after the Generals' High Tea at Carlsbad, "yet Austria's gross product is only one-sixth of Germany's. In other words, we spend proportionately three times as much on war as Kaiser Wilhelm. Must we play Big Power at the cost of poverty and hunger?"

As these words were published on May 29, a cold spell shivered through the Vienna Woods. Twenty-four hours later the sun returned. Again lilacs flashed, cuckoos called, kites soared above apple blossoms in the hills wreathing the city. At almost the same time the First Lord Chamberlain made a smiling announcement at Schönbrunn Palace. The congestion in His Majesty's lungs had cleared. Most signs of pneumonia were gone and so was the fever. The august patient was making a strong recovery. In fact, His Majesty's physicians had reason to hope that he would be able to return to a normal schedule in about two weeks.

* * *

The legend of Franz Joseph could continue, perhaps, forever, in the flesh. And from the trivial to the crucial, everything seemed to change for the better along the Danube. Nevetle, a yearling from the stable of Foreign Minister Count von Berchtold, came in first at the Freudenau races in Vienna. This brightened the wit of upper officials supping at Meissl & Schadn. They were familiar with certain perfumed coaches often waiting at a side entrance of the Minister's offices at the Ballhausplatz. To them the fact that his filly had won the Con Amore handicap signified that—with the Emperor improved—the Count's continued tenure would also continue his luck in the conduct of affairs, be they foreign or female.

Indeed, private sport aside, the Foreign Minister could point with satisfaction to news important to the world at large. At a meeting with legislative leaders he quoted a statement just made by the French Prime Minister: It expressed deep admiration for the wisdom with which Franz Joseph—so recently restored—guided the destiny of the realm. Count von Berchtold also mentioned that the King of England had confirmed his intention to hunt with Crown Prince Franz Ferdinand in Austria come fall. For Serbia the Count had words of hope and moderation. (Of Albanian complexities he said nothing, possibly because they were simply too complex: On the one hand, the insurrection against the *mbret* had caused half his government to resign and himself to seek refuge on the Italian warship *Misurata;* on the other hand, the *mbret* had created yet another decoration, the Order of the White Star of Skanderbeg, whose glitter on the breasts of some disorderly majors re-ordered things to the point where the *mbret* could slink back to his capital again.) On the whole the Austrian Foreign Minister was happy to conclude that Cassandra wails about the imminence of war were as unfounded as earlier evil rumors about the imminence of the monarch's death.

Berchtold was not the only one to exude optimism. Early in June his Berlin colleague Chancellor von Bethmann-Hollweg sent the German ambassador in London a note whose cheer contrasts with the grimness of the generals at Carlsbad just a couple of weeks before. The German Chancellor said that he could not blame Russia for wanting a stronger voice in the Balkans and that "I do not believe that Russia is planning an early war against us. Whether it will come to a general European conflagration will depend entirely on the attitude of Germany and England. If we two stand united as guarantors of European peace . . . then war can be averted."

A few days later, on June 24 (three days before Archduke Franz Ferdinand's arrival in Sarajevo), the German ambassador reported a most amiable chat with Sir Edward Grey, the English Foreign Secretary: "The Secretary said that it was his endeavour to go hand in hand with us [Germans] into the future and to remain in close contact over all the questions that might arise . . . As regards Russia, he had not the slightest reason to doubt the peaceful intentions of the Russian government. Nothing could take place that would give this relationship [between Russia and England] an aggressive point against Germany. He believed moreover that lately a less apprehensive frame of mind on the question had been gaining ground with us in Germany . . . " The Foreign Ministers kept soothing, the chimneys of gun factories kept smoking.

At the other end of the political spectrum, Vladimir Lenin did not anticipate war. When the Socialist International had called an Emergency Conference in Basel in 1912 on the threat of a worldwide conflict, he had not bothered to attend. Soon afterward he'd written to Gorki: "A war between Austria and

Russia would be a very useful thing for the revolution in all of Eastern Europe, but it is not likely that Franz Joseph and [Tsar] Nikolosha will give us that pleasure."

Now, in May 1914, Lenin had no eye for international clouds. It was not war between nations that was on his mind but the battle between factions within Socialism. He spent his huge energies on carving out an ever stronger Bolshevik position vis-à-vis the milksop Mensheviks and all other rivals contending for leadership of the revolutionary movement. From Poronin in the Galician mountains, on the Habsburg side of the Austrian-Russian frontier, Lenin's letters and couriers kept streaming into the Tsar's territory. They carried instructions on how to increase still further the circulation gains of the St. Petersburg *Pravda* that had put the Menshevik paper *Luch* out of business; how to spread Bolshevik control of the Metal Workers' Brotherhood so that Bolsheviks would dominate related trade unions as well; how to encourage a trio of Moscow millionaires—who hoped to liberalize the Tsar by encouraging pressure from the savage left—in the financing of Bolshevik activities. Lenin's chief purpose that spring: to present an array of Bolshevik voices as powerful as possible at the Unity Conference of all Russian Socialist Party segments set for July 1914 in Brussels, and then to march fully mobilized into the Congress of the Socialist International to open in Vienna on August 26.

Meanwhile Dr. Sigmund Freud girded for intramural grapeshot at *his* Congress—that of the International Psycho-Analytical Association scheduled for September 1914 at Dresden. Now, three months earlier, it was apple-blossom time in Vienna and at Berggasse headquarters "war" meant "Jung."

After all, relentless pressure from Freud's forces had just

pushed the Swiss psychiatrist out of the presidency of the International Psycho-Analytical Association. Some sort of counterblow from Zurich must be expected. Yet June started the way May ended—quite clemently.

For one thing, evaluation had been completed of the tests Freud had undergone—with excellent news. There was no sign whatsoever of any intestinal tumor. Soon afterward Freud's symptoms subsided. His fear of cancer vanished together with his Emperor's pneumonia. As for the Freud-Jung front, the first salvo from the enemy was subtle rather than searing. Jung fired it by way of his address to the British Medical Association in Aberdeen: "The Unconscious in Psycho-Pathology." The speech abolished psychoanalysis, at least in Jung's vocabulary: He didn't so much as mention the word. But except through omission he didn't attack Freud's movement either; at one point he even credited his former mentor with calling attention to the importance of dreams.

Of course that sort of gesture furthered the aims of ill will by a show of good manners. At the same time it produced a sort of lull. Freud could—almost—return to normal business. He devoted himself to the famous Wolf Man case. Here Freud traced a phobia of wolves to the patient's glimpse, at a very young age, of his parents copulating *a tergo*. In truth, one aspect of the paper was yet another chapter of the anti-Jung argument. Jung held that such primal scenes were usually a neurotic fantasy. Freud maintained they were real. But in the Wolf Man paper he softened the collision between dogmas by admitting that the difference might not be "a matter of very great importance."

The war with Jung was on, but at this point it did not require any very ugly waging. Freud looked forward to his summer cure at Carlsbad in a mood much brighter than that of the two chiefs of staff who had taken the waters there some weeks earlier.

21

VIENNA PERKED UP DURING THE LAST WEEKS OF SPRING. AT ONE OF Princess Metternich's famed "mixed dinners," industrialists heard from courtiers proof of Franz Joseph's complete recovery: Once more His Majesty was taking walks in the Schönbrunn Palace gardens with his one and only Frau Schratt. This unofficial but adorable bulletin lifted the stock market to the level from which it had dropped at the onset of the All-Highest illness.

The weather was genial. It had the good taste to rain only at night. The sun seemed to have melted away most angry demonstrations along the Ringstrasse. Those controversies still left in town showed a luscious Viennese sheen. At the Café Central, Havanas were puffed, mochas were sipped, chocolate éclairs were being forked as the disputants faced the issues: Was Gustav Mahler's adaptation of Hugo Wolf's *Der Corregidor* really as calamitous as some reviews complained? Or did its problem reside not in the music but in the flawed presentation? And was the culprit of that flaw an opera management known for its anti-Mahler bias after the great maestro had passed? And for how long would that same straitlaced management keep Richard Strauss's voluptuous *Salome* out of its repertoire? And, still speaking of the Court Opera, did diva Selma Kurz deserve *ten* curtain calls for her Lucia di Lammermoor? Shifting to ballet, what about Pavlova's Directoire dress—wasn't that a bit out of key when she danced the gavotte, no matter how dazzling her entrechats? And had Frank Wedekind enhanced his own play *Samson* by not only directing it but also taking on the role of Og, King of the Philistines? Or was it time for that rather weathered eroticist to let go of the greasepaint?

Outside Austria thornier themes drew grimmer contestants. In Great Britain, it was Irish against English as well as English women against English men. Suffragettes threatened to kidnap members of the royal family who would then be ransomed for the right to vote. The King could no longer take his morning ride through Hyde Park. Shouting ladies kept waylaying his horse. In France, the Socialist victory at the May elections showed popular resentment of the three-year conscription term while at the same time hardening President Poincaré's insistence on it; the conflict produced daily mêlées between people and police. Russian strikes stopped factory wheels from Moscow to Tiflis. The Duma at St. Petersburg had become so rowdy that even the nicely cravated Alexander

Kerensky of the usually well-behaved Labor Party had to be escorted from the chamber for causing a disruption.

But it was Serbia—Russia's protégé, Austria's bane—that shook with the most severe domestic turmoil. In Serbia the opposition between the two most powerful political camps sharpened toward a showdown. Prime Minister Pašić led one side; his Radical Party stood for measured nationalism. As nationalist, Pašić proclaimed Serbia's right to defend her interests (and pocketed, some said, commissions from the French firm Schneider-Creuzot, which was producing arms for Serbia's defense). But as a man of measure, Pašić feared that excessive action against Austria would risk a crisis before Serbia was ready. He suspected that zealots, mostly officers, would use war to usurp the government.

Pašić's chief opponent was the chief zealot: Colonel Apis, officially head of Army Intelligence, secretly leader of the Black Hand. Apis would accept nothing less than the most drastic fulfillment of the Serb cause, above all the breaking of Habsburg chains that bound Slav brethren in Austrian Bosnia.

In the spring of 1914, Belgrade simmered with the incompatibility between Pašić and Apis. The Prime Minister dismissed Apis's main supporter in the cabinet, Minister of War Miloš Božanović. Apis's side retaliated through the periodical *Pijemont.* "A gang of men without conscience," it said about Pašić's party in May 1914, ". . . this government cannot be tolerated for a moment or rebellion will break out in our country." Apis had no public connection to the paper publishing the attack. Yet Belgrade recognized him as the target of the counterattack when the Minister of the Interior banned *Pijemont.* Gendarmes summoned from the countryside patrolled Belgrade's streets: Serbia's other armed force had been alerted against an army coup.

Vienna took note of Serb frictions but not of their deeper implications. Just at the end of May, the Chief of Austrian Intelligence—the one man in Vienna most likely to know Belgrade behind the scenes—retired abruptly. Apis's Habsburg counterpart, Colonel "Ostrymiecz" von Urbanski, was pensioned off. (The War Ministry did not deny rumors that he had been caught selling to a film producer memorabilia of his late associate Colonel Redl, the famous and now posthumously cinemagenic traitor.) The loss of its director disoriented Austria's information gathering service. Yet even at its best it would not have sniffed out an event in Belgrade of which not even the Serbian Prime Minister had an inkling.

Underground, in the cellar of a shabby house, three young men went through a ceremony whose consequences would explode over millions of square miles of the world above.

On the night of May 27, 1914, Gavrilo Princip and his two disciples walked down seven steps on Krakjice Natalije Street into a small room in the basement. They were met by a figure robed and hooded in black.

"Who among you three speaks for the others?"

"I do," said Princip, the youngest and smallest.

"Do you know one important reason why you are going to execute this mission?"

"Because the Archduke Franz Ferdinand is the oppressor of our people."

"Do you know when you are going to execute this mission?"

"When the oppressor comes to Sarajevo."

"When will that be?"

"On June 28. That is another important reason—that day. He dares to come there on St. Vitus Day."

"And what is a third important reason?"

Princip hesitated. He knew that on St. Vitus Day, June 28 of the year 1389, a Serb hero had penetrated the lines of the conquering Turkish army to stab its generalissimo Sultan Murad to death, thereby establishing the date for the Serbian national holiday. He knew that the appearance of a Habsburg prince on South Slav soil on just that day was a sneer at Serb pride and a second important reason for vengeance. But Princip could not think of still another important reason.

"There are many reasons," he said.

"We do not expect you to know that other special reason," the black hood said. "Very few people know it. Colonel Apis knows it. The Archduke has a special weapon. He will use it if we let him come to power. He will use the lie of moderation to steal our people's sympathy. Then he will oppress us doubly. You did not know that?"

"No," Princip said.

"Even in our country the Prime Minister uses the lie of moderation to keep himself in power. Did you know that?"

"I have heard of it."

"Are you ready to fight such liars with all means?"

"Yes."

"Are the three of you ready?"

"Yes."

Pause.

"You may go into the next room."

The next room was lit by a single candle on a table draped in black, against walls also draped in black. The candle flickered at three men sitting behind the table in black robes and black hoods. Before them, arranged in a circle around the flame, lay an unsheathed dagger, a skull, a crucifix, a revolver, a bottle with a death's head label. This was the altar of *Smrt ili Zivot,* the Bosnian arm of Colonel Apis's Black Hand.

The black hood in the middle motioned the three youths to step forward. Line by line he began to recite the oath, which they repeated after him, line by line:

"I swear by the holiness of the cross . . ."
"I swear by the preciousness of liberty . . ."
"I swear by the sun that warms me . . ."
"And the earth that nourishes me . . ."
"I swear by God in heaven . . ."
"By my ancestors' blood . . ."
"By my honor and my life . . ."
"As true as I am a Serb and a man . . ."
"That from this day on until the moment of my death . . ."
"I shall remain faithful to every law of this organization . . ."
"I shall be ever ready to sacrifice for it . . ."
"To suffer for it . . ."
"To die for it . . ."
"And I swear to take all its secrets with me to the grave . . ."

The hooded men rose to their feet. Each man reached into the pocket of his black robe. Each pulled out a little cardboard box. Each box contained a capsule of cyanide. The three hooded men handed the three little boxes to the three youths. Each of the hooded three embraced each of the youths. Not another word was spoken. The candle was blown out. The three hooded men remained in the dark. The three youths groped toward the door.

The next morning, on Thursday, May 28, 1914, Princip and his two companions boarded a steamer anchored at a Belgrade dock. They carried small suitcases and wore loose overcoats. Under his coat, each of the three had two bombs tied around his waist. Each also carried a revolver in one trouser pocket, ammunition in a second pocket, and in a third, instantly handy, the capsule of cyanide.

It was a misty, sleepy day. Slowly the ship began to plow upstream on the river Sava, westward toward Sarajevo.

22

Eight days later, on June 5, His Excellency Jovan Jovanović, the Serbian envoy to Vienna, bowed himself into the gold-on-white rococo of the office of the Habsburg Minister of Finance Leon von Bilinski. For intricate Viennese reasons Bilinski doubled as Minister in charge of the Austrian province of Bosnia-Hercegovina; in that capacity he ushered his visitor to a chair. Bosnia abutted on Serbia, and the visitor had come on a queasy errand.

After an exchange of courtesies all the more elaborate for the tension between the two countries, Jovanović ceremonially cleared his throat. It was his duty, he said, to express a certain concern of the Royal Serb Government, namely the forthcoming participation of His Imperial Highness the Archduke Franz Ferdinand at Austrian Army exercises to be held in the Sarajevo area. Since these exercises were to take place in territory adjacent to Serbia and since they coincided with Serbia's National Day, they might provoke some regrettable actions.

"Regrettable actions?" the Austrian asked.

Yes, very regrettable, the Serbian envoy said. Under the circumstances an Austrian Army soldier of the Serb race might be misled into loading his rifle with real bullets to aim it at His Imperial Highness. Therefore the Serbian government earnestly hoped that the Austrian government would want to shift both the time and the place of the maneuvers.

It was Count von Bilinski's turn to do some throat-clearing. He replied that, first of all, the police reported peace and quiet in Bosnia, including the Bosnian capital Sarajevo. Furthermore the army exercises would take place nowhere near the Serbian border. Lastly, he had no doubt whatsoever that His Imperial Highness, the Archduke Crown Prince, enjoyed the full loyalty of the entire Austrian Armed Forces. Or did his Excellency have specific information to the contrary?

The Serbian envoy said, no, he could offer nothing specific. The concern of the Serbian Government simply reflected the general mood of the Serbian people.

Count von Bilinski gave a civil nod. His Excellency's remarks, he said, would receive the consideration they deserved. Meanwhile he was grateful to His Excellency for taking the trouble to visit him on such a lovely day. The Serbian envoy, on his part, thanked the Minister for extending him so gracious a reception. And the mendacities of etiquette continued until the gold-on-white doors closed on the encounter.

* * *

Of course the envoy's visit *had* been prompted by some quite specific information. It had been relayed to Serbia's premier Pašić by his Minister of the Interior: A contact at the frontier had reported that on the night from June 1 to June 2 three young men, heavily armed, had been spirited across the river Drina which separated Serbia from Austrian Bosnia.

The purpose and identity of the youths were not known. Known to the Prime Minister, however, were the ways of the Black Hand. Known, too, was the Archduke's forthcoming presence in Sarajevo as well as the Black Hand's motives for turning him into a corpse. Decked out in Serb patriotism, they aimed at sedition against the Serb government. A murder of that enormity would cause an imbroglio convenient for the Black Hand—a chance to seize power.

Prime Minister Pašić could not idly turn his back while such a scheme moved forward, could not let killers, dispatched by Apis across the Drina River, continue toward the Archduke. He must warn Austria. But the warning must be masked. After all, Apis was still Chief of Serbian Army Intelligence. Pašić had not been able to dislodge that bald monster. By giving Austria specifics about a possible assassination, he might be giving away clues leading to the complicity of a high Serbian official and so incriminate the whole country. Hence a compromise: Pašić instructed his envoy to alert Austria but to omit any genuine details.

In Vienna Bilinski did as he was done to. He was just as cunning about not telling the truth—just as careful. He told neither the Archduke nor the police nor the army nor Austrian Intelligence about that visit to his office. He, too, had politic reasons.

Bilinski disliked General Potiorek, the Austrian Military Governor of Bosnia, a Serb-eating hotspur of the General Conrad stripe. If Bilinski passed on these vague, probably meaningless whispers of the Serb envoy, they would eventually benefit Potiorek. Despite their unreality, Potiorek would use them to vindicate his bias, strengthen his position. This, in turn, would heighten his insolence toward Bilinski who was his nominal superior as Minister in charge of Bosnia. And Potiorek was already insolent enough.

Potiorek had appropriated a privilege belonging to Bilinski. He, not Bilinski, had made the arrangements for the Archduke's sojourn in Bosnia; worse yet, he had then sent the Archduke's program to all ministries except Bilinski's. On top of that, Bilinski had not even received an invitation to the state dinner! Why should Bilinski play Potiorek's intelligence-assistant and feed Potiorek every scrap of information that might or might not be authentic, that might or might not help Potiorek to do his job?

Bilinski retaliated with his silence. And General Potiorek did his job by his—uninformed—lights. Of the 22,000 troops deployed near Sarajevo for maneuvers, he detailed only an honor guard for the Archduke's route in the city itself. This was to show that under Potiorek's govenorship Belgrade's propaganda had been unable to shake the allegiance of the population to the Crown: His Imperial Highness required no extra protection in Sarajevo.

But in areas other than security Potiorek launched preparations aplenty. Throughout June telegraph keys kept clicking between Potiorek's office and the archducal chancellery at Belvedere Palace in Vienna. What wines would His Imperial Highness prefer at various dinners? Would Highness like to approve the seating at all the tables? Did Highness wish to specify menus? As for the horse His Imperial Highness would grace, what would be the best saddle and which the most comfortable stirrup length? And what was Highness's exact weight, so as to select the proper mount?

There was a moment, peculiarly enough, when all these questions seemed to be asked in vain.

That moment had come the day before the Serbian envoy's visit to Bilinski. On June 4, Franz Joseph received his Heir Apparent in audience. It was the first meeting between uncle and nephew since the older man had recovered from his illness. In contrast to some previous encounters, this one seemed to proceed quite cordially. But after expressing his pleasure at seeing the Emperor so well, the Archduke made a rather unexpected reference to his own health. He had not felt very fit lately, he said. The weather down in Bosnia was bound to be hot in mid-summer. He had been asking himself whether he was in a condition to undertake the journey.

Franz Joseph looked at Franz Ferdinand. The Archduke appeared to be as robust as ever. A bit curtly the Emperor asked if the purpose of this conversation was to inform him that Franz Ferdinand did not wish to go to the Sarajevo exercises.

Oh, he did wish to go, Franz Ferdinand said. But he would be grateful if he could bring Sophie along; his wife was always a boost to his constitution.

The Emperor confessed himself puzzled. After all, he said, Sophie usually came along on maneuvers—Franz Ferdinand needed no special permission for that purpose. Yes, the Archduke said, but what he meant was that with His Majesty's gracious approval he, Franz Ferdinand, would like to have Sophie with him during the subsequent state visit to Sarajevo itself. Her presence would certainly lighten the burden.

Franz Joseph was ancient but not slow. He understood what Franz Ferdinand *really* meant: to make Sophie the Crown

Princess at least while the two were in Sarajevo. At her husband's side she would share all the homage shown to the Crown Prince.

A tiresome issue, a tiresome audience. "Very well," Franz Joseph said. "If you go, let her go with you everywhere. Now do as you like."

That ended Franz Ferdinand's reluctance about Sarajevo, which had been no reluctance at all but rather a basis for negotiations now successfully concluded. Never mind the old man's gruffness—it was his consent that mattered. As the Archduke took his leave he kissed the Emperor's hand heartily as never before.

Never before—certainly not on Habsburg soil—had Sophie received the ceremonial respect she would soon be shown at Sarajevo. And never before had the Archduke been quite so confident of himself and of his future. The tubercle bacillus was the only assassin he truly feared. Some years earlier he'd asked his personal physician for a hand-written note: "*I, Dr. Viktor Eisenmenger, hereby certify that His Imperial and Royal Highness the Archduke Franz Ferdinand has been entirely cured of tuberculosis and that he will never suffer a relapse again.*" When anxious, he would reach for the pocket where he always carried "my life certificate."

His staff saw him reach for it much less often in the spring of 1914. His hypochondria was receding. As for bullets or bombs, he had always been a fatalist. "Precautions?" he'd once said to his secretary. "Bodyguards? I put up with them, but that's all rubbish. We are at all times in God's hands. Worry paralyzes life."

Of course, he was not nearly as philosophical about challenges thrust at him by sworn enemies—the likes of General Conrad or the Emperor's First Lord Chamberlain Prince Montenuovo. Yet in June the Archduke scented victory even in that arena. He discerned it in the Emperor's consent on Sophie. He saw it—ever since the Emperor's illness—in the quality of bows and curtsies greeting him. They seemed less rigid, more spontaneous. He didn't crave acclaim as the Kaiser did, nor encourage it even indirectly like Franz Joseph. Playacting the Lord Affable was not his forte. He disliked indulging the people unnecessarily because he hated indulging himself (even his hunting mania was a pursuit as relentless on his comfort as it was on the lives of ducks and deer). But now he sensed, if not popularity, a readier acceptance of his imperial destiny.

23

For the Archduke it was a euphoric month. On Sunday, June 7, three days after his audience at the Palace, he attended the Vienna Derby. Last year he'd stayed away. In 1913 the occasion had still been blighted by the Redl spy case. This year the young military elite was back with its dash restored.

The grandstands swaggered with hussars and dragoons, with kepis and capes, with slim captains blowing smoke rings at baronesses whose smiles were half-shadowed by their saucy hats. Perhaps Redl had never happened. Perhaps the Empire would last. Perhaps it would not rain.

The day began quite cloudy. But when the future, in the form of the Crown Prince and his consort, entered the Imperial Box, the sun pushed through and the stands burst into applause. Not an overwhelming ovation, it was still a salute livelier than the kind usually tendered to Franz Ferdinand. And who must join it, willy-nilly? Prince Montenuovo in the neighboring box.

Still more satisfying was the press next morning. It revealed a certain burgeoning of the Archduke's image. In the coverage of ladies' fashion at the track, the Duchess of Hohenberg—Franz Ferdinand's Sophie—took up more space than the Archduchesses. Most reports went on and on about Sophie's white voile frock with the black sash, her long black jacket brimming with white lace, her black hat with the white visor, topped by black feathers in—regal!—tiara style . . .

For once, the two left Vienna with pleased faces. Arrived at their Bohemian estate at Konopiste, the Archduke toured his gardens. It was here that he would make a gesture to the populace—his very first. He had decided on it hesitantly some weeks ago. Now he briskly proceeded with its implementation.

For fifteen years he had been developing at Konopiste the greatest rose garden in Central Europe. This spring he would open its gates to the public at the very height of the blossoming. The people had begun to welcome him as their sovereign-to-be. In return he would welcome them into his pleasance on June 15, from morning to night.

First, though, he must do some summit politicking over the weekend of June 12. The Kaiser was coming to Konopiste. With this visit, the display of horticulture mattered less than the cultivation of peace.

Since the occasion centered on Wilhelm, nothing about it was quite calculable, not even his choice in excess of dress.

Expecting something martial, the Archduke appeared at the railroad station in the uniform of a Colonel of the 10th Prussian Uhlan Regiment. However, the Kaiser stepped out of the train in a hunting costume he'd overcoutured himself—brass-buttoned green jacket; shining black leather boots aglitter and ajingle with spurs; and the Order of St. Hubertus, patron saint of the chase, hanging from his neck. In Wilhelm's wake followed Grand Admiral Alfred von Tirpitz, the creator of Germany's huge new navy, as well as Wadl and Hexl, two ferocious dachshunds.

Tirpitz's appearance made Vienna's leading newspaper comment, "How quickly the ravishing floral scent [of the Konopiste garden] can change into the smell of gun powder." As for Wadl and Hexl, they rushed off into the bushes and emerged dragging between them the body of a beautiful golden pheasant. Their kill was the only such bird in the estate, meant to be admired, not hunted.

Franz Ferdinand had to shrug off the loss. The point was to concentrate on bigger game, namely détente in Europe. He resolved not to be deterred by von Tirpitz, bristling braid, forked beard, and all. Fortunately no military retinue accompanied Kaiser or admiral. Indeed Wilhelm said that he had brought along "the sailor boy" because, like Franz Ferdinand, Tirpitz was a breeder of roses. And Franz Ferdinand took Wilhelm very firmly at his word: He sent the rose-loving Grand Admiral away on a walk into the vasts of the garden. Then he led Wilhelm to his automobile.

During long drives through his domain, tête-à-tête in the back seat, Franz Ferdinand presented his case. The argument he'd made in vain three months earlier at Miramare—here he repeated it much more forcibly: that an accommodation was possible, an accommodation was *necessary* between Vienna and the Serbs; but that it was constantly sabotaged by Budapest. He really must correct, he told his guest, the good impression the Hungarian Premier Tisza had managed to make on the Kaiser. Tisza did not want the Kaiser's sharp eyes to see how Magyar chauvinism endangered not only Austria but Germany. After all, the Hungarians were a minority even in the Hungarian half of Austria-Hungary. Yet under Tisza they oppressed the Slav majority there, restricted the voting rights of Serbs and Croats, provided only skimpy schooling in the Serbo-Croat tongue. And through Tisza's influence the Habsburg government refused Serbia access to the Adriatic, refused them even some flea-bitten fishing village of no naval significance. With that, Tisza played right into the hands of the stormy petrels in Belgrade that were always screeching against Austria—and against Germany. Nor was that all. Tisza had begun to tyrannize the Rumanian minority in Hungary. The result? Rumania was being driven away from the Central Powers, away from Austria and Germany, into an alliance with Russia and France. Tisza just kept inflicting absolutely criminal damage. Under normal circumstances he would be disciplined by his King, who was also the Austrian Emperor, Franz Joseph. But there was Franz Joseph's advanced age and his fragile condition. Firmness like that could no longer be expected from Schönbrunn Palace. But it could be hoped for from Europe's most dynamic monarch; it could come from the Kaiser, Austria's trusty ally. Couldn't Wilhelm knock some sense into Tisza's head?

The Archduke signalled to the chauffeur. His car slowed to a stop. It stood surrounded by the thousands of roses Franz Ferdinand had conjured from the earth. Their perfume came down on the Kaiser together with the light-blue stare of Franz Ferdinand's eyes. In sight and smell the Kaiser now bore the full brunt of the Archduke's passion. A daunting experience for a poseur like Wilhelm, able to use an empire as prop for his poses but unable—in contrast to Franz Ferdinand—to command a vision or a cogent policy all his own.

Well, the Kaiser said. Well, he was glad to receive such a . . . such a candid briefing on the difficulty. Yes, the Hungarians did seem to be a bit of a problem, especially when it came to Rumania, which Budapest must not alienate. Yes, he would instruct von Tschirsky (his ambassador to Austria-Hungary) accordingly. He would direct von Tschirsky to tell Tisza, "Sir, be mindful of Rumania!"

As to Serbia, the Kaiser made a less specific commitment, yet couldn't help but voice sympathy with the views the Archduke had so dramatically presented. On the whole Franz Ferdinand's automobile diplomacy at Konopiste appeared to work much better than all his luncheon pleading at Miramare earlier in the spring.

Socially, Wilhelm's visit proved even more auspicious. It ended on Saturday, June 13, with nine courses of a farewell dinner. Franz Ferdinand's Sophie walked into Konopiste Castle's dining hall to sit down at the Kaiser's right. On her head shimmered a tiara of evening feathers. This time the royal connotations came into their own.

At half past eight in the evening the archducal family bade their guest good-bye. Franz Ferdinand accompanied Wilhelm to the train station in a car gliding at slow, stately speed. The military band that had serenaded the diners followed behind with a medley of the Kaiser's favorite marches. As the escutcheoned locomotive of Wilhelm's private train got up steam, he promised to return in the fall; most roses would be gone by then, but the woodcock shooting would be wonderful. Franz Ferdinand applauded the idea, adding that Wilhelm's stay should be coordinated with the hunting visit of the English King, also planned for autumn. "Capital!" roared the Kaiser. Franz Ferdinand smiled: Let German Emperor and British monarch stand side by side, blasting away at game, thereby muzzling the cannons of their armies.

Two days later, at 7 A.M. Monday, June 15, five hundred gendarmes marched by a side entrance into the Konopiste estate. It was the first day of the Archduke's final week at Konopiste, the week before he left on the first leg of his trip to Sarajevo.

The gendarmes distributed themselves according to a prearranged pattern. Soon they were so scattered on the enormous terrain as to be barely noticeable. Yet they could intervene fast when needed.

No need arose. At 9 A.M. the great gates swung open. For the first time ever the public streamed in. Many were peasants in boots and black Sunday suits who had trudged to the castle from neighboring villages. Many were burghers with watch-chained waistcoats, who had arrived by rail or bus or private car. All of them shuffled through this exalted wonderland, hushed, awed, quiet.

They gawked at the endless flamboyance of the roses, at the infinite varieties of their hue from gold to scarlet to white to black, at a horizon brimming with aromas and blossoms. They shook heads over stone vases two stories tall from which cactus flowered or holly sprouted. They admired the obelisks, the marble amoretti, satyrs, and Greek gods, the baroque fountains casting up pillars of water.

The men had removed their hats, as if in church. The women looked for petals dropped to the gravel. Young girls would slip them into their bodices; matrons would press them between pages of Bibles brought for that purpose. Amidst the crowds passing the castle itself, voices were raised here and there.

Long live the Archduke!

Their shouts sounded frail against the massive seventeenth-century turrets. No answer came. Kaiser Wilhelm would have mounted a parapet and strutted in his spurs. Franz Joseph would have appeared and performed his kindly little wave. Not Archduke Franz Ferdinand. He showed himself only during a brief ride down the main path. After that he did not emerge from behind the stone walls.

Though unseen, he saw. He watched from behind a window, holding his Sophie's hand. It is not impossible that he smiled.

On Saturday, June 20, the couple went to Chlumetz, Franz Ferdinand's other, more intimate Bohemian castle. Here they spent a cozy family weekend with their brood, bowling, playing checkers, roaming the woods. And here, on the early morning of Wednesday, June 24, they said good-bye to their daughter and their two sons until a reunion planned for a week later. Then the Archduke and his Duchess began their journey to Sarajevo.

24

THEY TRAVELED TOGETHER ONLY UNTIL VIENNA. THERE SOPHIE TOOK THE express going east to Budapest. Their destination lay south, yet this somewhat indirect path was the only one available by train: rail connections from the Austrian part of the Empire to Bosnia had been constructed as detours via Budapest, at Hungarian insistence. The Archduke refused to let Magyar impudence dictate his route. He'd rather complicate it his own way—by sea. At the same time, being an ever considerate husband, he did not want to subject his Sophie to the extra strain of *his* complication. For himself, of course, thumbing his nose at Budapest would be well worth the discomfort. It would help him keep his cheer.

That he kept it so well seems remarkable in view of his

temper and how it was tested throughout the trip. When he went on alone from Vienna to Trieste, the electric lights of his salon car went out. The Archduke grinned. "How interesting," he said, as footmen scurried to light candles. "Don't we look like a crypt?"

After such a small calamity came a long laboriousness in the summer heat. At Trieste harbor he was piped aboard the Austrian dreadnought *Viribus Unitis,* which carried him down the humid Illyrian coastline to the mouth of the Narenta river, where he was transferred to the yacht *Dalmat,* which in turn sailed upstream to the Hercegovian town of Metkovic, where the archducal party entrained once more, this time heading for Bad Ilidze, a spa just outside the Bosnian capital of Sarajevo.

On the steamy, rainy afternoon of June 25, Franz Ferdinand reached Ilidze at the end of almost forty hours of ceaseless traveling. He bounded out of his rail car and past the honor guard, remarkably unfatigued.

So far the trip had been refreshing hard work. His advisers had primed him on the St. Vitus Day problem. Just during the weekend ahead, Serbs in Serbia as well as on the Austrian side of the border would celebrate their great ethnic holiday. To defuse resentment he had taken a good deal of trouble learning some Serbo-Croat sentences that said how pleased he was to acquaint himself first hand with the history, traditions, and festive occasions of this important region.

He was no linguist. His tongue struggled with those Slavic consonants. A public smile did not come easily to him. Yet he produced the consonants and the smile before any crowd organized for him along the way. Each time, people were surprised by such cordiality from the Archduke notorious for his frown. He, in turn, was exhilarated by their enthusiasm.

He was exhilarated again at Bad Ilidze, a pleasant suburb of Sarajevo. Despite a downpour, a sizable throng awaited him, shouting their "*Zivio!*" ("Long may he live!") and waving their umbrellas. That was nice. Nicer still, the embrace of his wife who had arrived earlier on her much less labyrinthine journey. General Conrad also presented himself, saluting with a grimness that carried, here at least, no power. To avoid the contretemps of previous army exercises, the Chief of Staff had asked to attend this time as a purely passive observer.

Under the Archduke's sole command, then, the simulated war between the "North Camp" (the 15th Austrian Army Corps) and the "South Camp" (the 16th Army Corps) began. For two shower-splattered days it thundered up and down the craggy hills west of Sarajevo, some cautious eighty kilometers away from the Serb border. At the Archduke's order the field pack of each man was ten pounds lighter than the weight set by General Conrad. This prevented exhaustion and enhanced the spirit of the troops. Franz Ferdinand was impressed by the dispatch with which the men handled the most modern equipment. He liked the way the heavy howitzers moved so fast through mud deepening with every squall.

Nothing could dampen the Archduke's uncharacteristic good mood. Usually his aides must try to restore his calm. Now he reversed the process. Once as he observed a "battle" from a hummock, a man suddenly broke out of the underbrush with a black instrument. Nervous bodyguards jumped the suspect. Franz Ferdinand chortled: "Oh, let him shoot me. That's his job! That's just a camera in his hand—he's a court photographer. Let him make a living!"

* * *

On Saturday, June 27, at 10 A.M. the Archduke's signal ended the maneuvers. Shortly thereafter he sent a telegram to Bad Ischl where the Emperor had begun his summer sojourn on the same day.

> I beg to report most humbly that my journey has been excellent despite the unsteady weather; the reception . . . very gratifying and patriotic . . . The condition of the soldiers and their performance were outstanding and really beyond praise. Almost no injured or sick, everybody is healthy and well. Tomorrow I visit Sarajevo, to depart from there at night. In deepest devotion I lay myself at the feet of Your Majesty
>
> Your most humble
> Franz

This, his last report to the Emperor, the Archduke scrawled vigorously in his own hand, using not the Gothic script he preferred but Roman characters as demanded by Army regulation for military cables. And Franz Ferdinand also conformed to another, more hurtful rule. His message said "Tomorrow *I* visit Sarajevo . . ." Morganatic restriction forbade "Tomorrow *we* visit Sarajevo . . ." *We* would include his wife on an equal basis. The long arm of Vienna's protocol reached even into this remote corner of the Empire.

It reached—and struck—the Archduke again, a few hours later, when he showed his First Lord Chamberlain Baron Rumerskirch the toast he had drafted for the evening gala. The

Baron sighed and said he was compelled to suggest that the first three words of the phrase "my wife and I" should be omitted. The toast would not only enter the official minutes but no doubt be widely published in Vienna. It should be framed with care so that the court cabal could not use it against His Imperial Highness.

His Imperial Highness re-framed it with care.

That shadow apart, the day was splendid, ending sumptuously. On the night of June 27 the Archduke hosted a banquet (the very one to which Finance Minister von Bilinski had received no invitation) at his personal headquarters in Ilidze, the Hotel Bosna. General Potiorek attended the dinner together with the region's luminaries. Everybody enjoyed the potage régence, soufflés délicieux, blanquette de truite à la geleé, followed by main entrees of chicken, lamb and beef, followed by crême aux ananas en surprise and cheeses, ice cream, candies. Sommeliers poured an array of wines from Madeiras to Tokays and including, as a bow to local taste, Bosnian Žilavka.

Graciously the Archduke raised a goblet even to General Conrad, then gave a smooth, morganatic, wifeless toast. After all, his Sophie sat quite unmorganatically between two Archbishops. And tomorrow he would make sure that all Imperial obeisance shown him would be hers as well at Sarajevo.

25

MIST SMOTHERED THE BOSNIAN SUNRISE ON SUNDAY, JUNE 28, 1914. THE Archduke and the Duchess began the day on their knees. They prayed at an early Mass in a room specially converted to a chapel at the spa hotel. Afterwards he retired to his bedroom to practice, over and over again, the Serbo-Croation paragraph ending the speech he was to make at Sarajevo's City Hall. Those Slav consonants hadn't gotten any easier, but when he finished work, Sophie rewarded him with a happy bulletin just telephoned from Vienna. Their older son Max had done very well in his examinations at the Schotten Academy. The parents congratulated the boy with a cable anticipating the family reunion set for the day after tomorrow.

By then it was just past 9 A.M. Their train awaited them for the brief ride to Sarajevo. It steamed into the terminal there at 9:20 A.M. On the platform a band of the 15th Army Corps cymballed the Imperial Anthem. Red-carpet formalities over, Franz Ferdinand helped his wife climb into the high, huge Gräf & Stift convertible. That moment the weather changed as dramatically as during their entrance at the Vienna Derby three weeks earlier. The mist lifted like a curtain. Brightness fell on a resplendent pair. The Archduke, tall and rugged, shone in the ceremonial uniform of an Austrian Cavalry General—sky-blue tunic, gold collar with three silver stars, black trousers with red stripes; the green peacock feathers of his helmet bounced above the pale-blue gleam of his eyes, the black spear tips of his upturned hussar's mustache. His Duchess was a stately vision in white: white picture hat with a gossamer white veil, long white silk dress with a red and white bouquet of roses tucked into her red sash, ermine stole draped over her shoulders.

After a long siege of rain, the sun shed on them the radiance of a doubly special day. This Sunday marked not only St. Vitus Day for the Serbs but also the anniversary of a marriage sorely tried yet victorious. Exactly fourteen years ago, on June 28, 1900, Crown Prince Franz Ferdinand and the Countess Sophie Chotek had taken their vows in stealth, in disgrace, in the pointed absence of the Emperor and the entire Imperial clan. For fourteen years the Crown Prince had had to announce his own wife's inferiority of blood. During all court functions of all those years she had had to enter alone after the Emperor; he had had to wait for Sophie to creep in at the tail end of protocol, after the youngest Archduchess toddled by in diapers.

Today would atone for much of that. This morning's dazzle at Sarajevo would be his revenge and her redress.

At the first stop, inspecting the honor guard at Filippovic

Barracks, he undid a good deal of those fourteen years. To Sophie's glory he upended military proprieties. Today the colors dipped for the Duchess no less than for the Archduke. At his instruction she stood not behind him, but at his side. When he walked past the reverence of rifles presented at attention, his hand rested not on the hilt of his saber but on the handle of her parasol as his Sophie strode with him, shoulder to shoulder. Today, instead of denying her existence, he celebrated it. He exalted it. He, Crown Prince of the realm, was her servitor. He carried her parasol at a most public occasion.

And therefore the cannons starting their roar while the Imperial party re-boarded their six automobiles—the cannons booming their twenty-four-fold salute—boomed in her honor as well as his. They boomed while the motorcade rolled along slowly at Franz Ferdinand's orders; he wanted his Sophie to savor her triumph in leisure, and he wanted her to see at least some of Sarajevo's one hundred mosques and ninety churches. The cannons boomed from the hilltop fortress specially repainted for the occasion—its Habsburg yellow matched the black-yellow flag fluttering from Franz Ferdinand's car. The cannons boomed as the procession passed Cemaszula Street just renamed Franz Ferdinand Boulevard. They boomed as the huge cars turned into Appel Quay along the Miljacka river. They boomed across spires, domes, minarets, whitewashed houses on one side of the street; they boomed across poplars and cypresses greening the hills against the sky on the other. They boomed above gold-crested police helmets behind whose thin line stood a somewhat thicker crowd of people crying "*Zivio!*" They boomed over portraits of the Archduke placed on many window sills—hundreds of stern Franz Ferdinands glaring down from picture frames at the Prince's now more amiable live face, gliding by in the seat next to his wife.

The last boom reverberated away. A peculiar echo followed

it. One of the cars behind the Archduke's seemed to have blown a tire. The Duchess reached for the back of her neck where she thought a gnat had stung her. At the same time, confused shouting spread along the quay. Gendarmes started running toward some sort of scuffle that was tumbling down the river embankment.

The Archduke's raised hand signaled the procession to a halt. A member of his retinue, Count Franz von Harrach, jumped out to reconnoiter.

Two minutes later he was back, breathless: A bomb had been thrown at the car behind them. It had injured some bystanders as well as Lieutenant Colonel Erich von Merizzi of the Archduke's escort. But Merizzi had only been hit in the hand, by a splinter. The perpetrator had just been arrested as he'd tried to escape across the river.

Pale but composed, the Duchess said that a splinter must have touched her, too, in the back of her neck. Instantly the Archduke examined her. He found the barest evidence of a tiny scratch; the skin had not been broken.

"Madness!" the Archduke said. "But let's go on."

They went on. Count von Harrach did not resume his seat by the chauffeur. He stood on the running board to shield the Archduke. Shortly after 10 A.M. the motorcade reached City Hall. It was just a few minutes late, as though nothing had happened.

And nobody at City Hall thought anything had. Under the red-gold moorish loggias, on top of a white staircase, bowed an array of Bosnian notables. Turbaned mullahs, bishops in miters and gilt vestments, rabbis in kaftans, municipal personages with sash and decorations. The mayor Fehim Effendi

Curćić, in fez and tailcoat, had heard a bang; to him and to the others it had sounded like some additional salute from a smaller cannon. Blithely the mayor launched into his own fulsome greeting: "Your Imperial and Royal Highness, our exalted Crown Prince! Your Serene Highness, our Crown Prince's most esteemed wife! At this most happy moment our hearts are overflowing with gratitude for the most gracious visit bestowed—"

"*Mr. Mayor!*" The Archduke's gravel voice cut through the air. "*What kind of gratitude! A bomb has been thrown at us! Outrageous!*"

The mayor gagged. Fezzes, turbans, kaftans trembled and huddled. The Duchess whispered briefly into the Archduke's ear. The glare in his eyes softened. "Very well," the Archduke said. "Very well. Mr. Mayor, get on with your speech."

The Duchess's intervention allowed everything to continue with remarkable smoothness. The mayor went through the rest of his oration. For a moment it seemed as if Franz Ferdinand would not be able to answer because the text of his response (with its Slavic finale) had been left in the car disabled by the bomb. Just then an equerry came running with white pages blotched red from the wounded officer.

Franz Ferdinand ripped the script out of the man's hand. The Duchess put one finger on her husband's arm. Once more her touch composed him. Evenly he wiped the blood away with a handkerchief offered by the equerry. Evenly he began to read his speech, improvising only one deft change. "I consider," he said, "the welcome extended to my wife and me as expressions of joy that the attempt on our lives has been foiled."

All dignitaries clapped hands in relief. The Archduke went into his Serbo-Croat peroration: "Standing in this beautiful capital city, I assure you, our Slav and Mohammedan citizens, of our august Emperor's continued interest in your well-being and of my own unchanging friendship."

"*Zivio!*" from the dignitaries. Much applause. A courier roared up on a motorcycle. Good tidings from the garrison hospital to which the injured officer had been brought. Doctors confirmed that he had only a slight flesh wound.

Now the ceremonies resumed their planned course. The Duchess went upstairs to the second floor of City Hall where Muslim ladies wanted to tender their respects to her unveiled. Franz Ferdinand recovered his mordant humor. "Did you hear?" he said to an aide. "The bomb thrower wanted to swallow cyanide? Idiot! Doesn't he know our Austrian criminal justice system? They'll give the man a decoration!" Thin-lipped smiles from the retinue. "And maybe they'll have to give out more than one decoration. Maybe we'll have some more *Kugerln* coming our way." The Archduke was speaking in Viennese dialect, relishing its sardonic diminutives. "*Kugerln*" meant "bulletlets."

More thin-lipped smiles all around. With a mocking bow the Archduke turned to General Potiorek, Bosnia's Military Governor. "What do you think, General? Any more *Kugerln* in your valued judgment?"

"Your Imperial Highness, it was an isolated lunatic," Potiorek said. "I think Your Imperial Highness can go on at ease."

"The program, then, as scheduled," Franz Ferdinand said. "But first I'll visit Merizzi in the hospital."

"Your Imperial Highness, the wound is nothing," Potiorek said. "Merizzi will be released within an hour—"

"This man is my fellow officer," the Archduke broke in. "He is bleeding for me. You'll have the goodness to understand that. You'll have the further goodness to order another car to take my wife back to her hotel—"

Now it was the Archduke who was being interrupted. The Duchess had returned from the upper floor. She stopped his sentence not with words, but with a silent headshake. She stepped closer to her husband. A small step, but irrefutable. She was not going to the hotel in a different car. Not under any circumstances. She was staying by his side.

The Archduke gave a mellowed nod; revoked his order for another automobile. As they walked out of City Hall he took her parasol again. Just outside the entrance, he gripped her hand. They stood in the blinding sunshine on top of the stairs, a clear target for any sharpshooter in the multitude below.

The multitude did nothing but cheer. "*Zivio! . . . Zivio!*"

From Sarajevo's church towers the clocks struck half past ten in the morning. To the notables at City Hall the clangor ended a crisis.

26

THE SAME CHURCH BELLS TOLLED A VERY DIFFERENT MESSAGE TO THE EARS of a teenage schoolboy with a bomb and a pistol under his jacket. "*All is over, all is over,*" they tolled for Gavrilo Princip. It was all over. It had all been for nothing. For nothing, all the training, the planning, the efforts, the hardship of the last four weeks.

Exactly a month ago, on May 28, he had left Belgrade with his two cohorts, Grabež and Cabrinović. Sarajevo lay a little more than a hundred miles away, but it had taken the three youths eight days to cover the distance. Through part of the journey within Serbia they trudged across forest and bush to avoid police checking out transients. Princip didn't mind. He was the youngest, smallest, frailest of the trio. He was also the commander of the mission. With the Black Hand in Belgrade he had mapped out a route, tortuous but safe, called the "Apis Tunnel."

The Tunnel worked. At the town of Sabac, the first station of their trip, Princip found a Serbian Army Captain playing the right exotic card game at the right coffee-house terrace (that of the Café Amerika) at the right time of day. The captain, a Black Hand agent, excused himself "to go for a walk with my nephew." When Princip rejoined his mission-mates half an hour later, he carried in his pocket papers identifying the group as "customs officers" with Princip as "the sergeant in charge."

They were now ready to cross the border into Austria. And just then Princip found himself badly beset by a problem he thought he had eliminated at the outset.

While still in Belgrade he had made his partners take a vow as solemn as their Black Hand oath: to exercise utmost caution and discretion; to avoid all social contacts save those required by common courtesy; to leave politics out of all conversations with outsiders; and, of course, to tell no one the truth of where they were ultimately going or why. The rule applied to all encounters, be they Austrian, Croat or Serb, no matter how friendly. Even a Serb might be an undercover minion of the Serb Prime Minister who was Apis's foe. "What your enemy should not know, you must not tell your friend."

Grabež, a juvenile delinquent until his politicization by Princip, honored this pledge. The unpleasant surprise was Cabrinović. Cabrinović had been an activist even before he'd met Princip. He'd seemed cool and dedicated during target practice in Belgrade. That changed when they embarked on the awesome adventure itself; when they'd marched up the gangplank of the steamer with weaponry and cyanide under their coats, committed to slaughter or suicide or both.

At that point Cabrinović had begun to be nervously garrulous. It was as if he wanted to save his life by "accidentally" giving away the mission. While still on the ship he struck up a prolonged conversation—with a gendarme, of all people. Luckily an impassive, incurious gendarme.

Princip admonished him afterwards, to little effect. In a town close to the Austrian border, Cabrinović ran into an acquaintance, a fellow volunteer for Serbia in the Balkan War of the previous year. With him, Cabrinović's talk became so unnaturally animated that his coat fell open to reveal the bombs. Princip dragged him away just in time.

More folly at Koviljača, a spa near their entry spot into Habsburg terrain. Here Princip decided that they should act like ordinary tourists, engaged in tourist activities like buying postcards. Princip addressed his own card to a cousin in Belgrade, with the message that he was on his way to a monastery where he would prepare himself for high school finals. But Cabrinović? He wrote to friends in Sarajevo and Trieste, inside the Austrian Empire where mail was likely to be monitored at the border. Worse yet, Cabrinović scribbled on one such chancy card the Serb nationalist saying "*A good man and a horse will always find a way to break through.*"

That was too much for Princip, who always reviewed his crew's correspondence. He tore up the card, took Cabrinović to a toilet stall in a café where he confiscated Cabrinović's bombs and pistol. He informed Cabrinović that he must make the rest of the journey alone; alone, he was less likely to endanger his companions or the task they must fulfill. He was to enter Austria separately, at one of the alternate crossing points designated by the Black Hand. If all went well, they would reunite in Sarajevo.

* * *

And reunite they did at the Bosnian capital on June 4, with Cabrinović arriving, obediently, by a different path. Princip had chastised him into prudence, at least for a while. But at Sarajevo Princip met trouble from another source. It was also unexpected: Ilić.

Ilić, the fourth of the quartet of conspirators, had been among Princip's earliest companions in the cause, while Princip had lived in Sarajevo. Ilić had remained there with the Black Hand's knowledge and encouragement. His job: to scout security measures taken in the city, along with other details of the Archduke's coming. Ilić had served as the Sarajevo pillar of the developing plot. Princip found the pillar turning into putty.

Ilić's first words were that he had recruited three more youths "as auxiliaries" in the planned assassination.

"You've tripled the chances of betrayal!" Princip said.

Ilić protested. These three, he said, were all proven idealists. In fact, they would be valuable as part of the core of a new party that might be formed and whose formation might perhaps be a better tactic than the planned action—

Better than the action against the Archduke? Princip couldn't believe his ears.

Well, he had been thinking about it, Ilić said. Better in the sense that—that killing the Archduke at this point might perhaps turn people against the Black Hand, but perhaps if a political party were started first, why, it would give the cause a more legitimate base, make it more widely popular, and then, perhaps, there would be very strong popular support for a radical act later, so that's why he, Ilić, had founded a legal political weekly just three weeks ago, it was called *Zvono*

("The Bell") and it would help create a more revolutionary climate with the ideas of Friedrich Engels, Bakunin, Trotsky buttressing the Serb cause—

"*No,*" Princip said.

The anxiety that had spilled crudely out of Cabrinović was now pouring, more intellectualized, out of Ilić. Nothing but anxiety lay behind all this stuttering.

Princip's small hand came down hard on Ilić's shoulder. *No,* he told Ilić. There was no "perhaps." There was no "better tactic." There was only the deed it was their duty to do. They had not come together in Sarajevo as Socialists or journalists or intellectual politicians. They were warriors for Serb freedom. They had sworn to act. Now they must prepare to perform the action.

Princip's words did not cure Ilić of dread. But Princip's unblinking blue eyes and unrelenting low voice subdued Ilić's resistance. For the next three weeks Ilić kept nursing his misgivings obliquely in the pages of *Zvono*. In the June 15 issue he discussed "Seven Who Were Hanged," a story by the Russian writer Leonid Andreyev, praising it as "a significant contribution to the argument against capital punishment." Ilić printed Andreyev's own comment that " . . . it is my intention with this tale to point out the horror and impermissibility of capital punishment. The death penalty confuses the conscience of even resolute men . . ."

But even as Ilić's essay impugned capital punishment, he himself helped Princip trigger the death sentence to be visited on the Habsburg heir apparent.

Ilić arranged for Princip's lodging at his mother's house. Ilić retrieved the conspirators' arsenal. Princip, ever vigilant, had avoided the risk of entering Sarajevo armed; the bombs and pistols had been deposited with a "safe" cinema proprietor in Tuzla, a town close to Sarajevo. Ilić, who knew the pattern of local police surveillance, brought the weapons into the city. On the day he published his brief against capital punishment, Ilić obediently placed the instruments of execution under Princip's bed.

Together Princip and Ilić combed Sarajevo newspapers for the Archduke's specific whereabouts during his forthcoming visit. The big Jesuit-controlled daily *Hrvatski Dnevnik* spoke the loyalist sympathies of Catholic Bosnia (as opposed to the much more Belgrade-minded Greek Orthodox element). *Hrvatski Dnevnik* looked forward to the Archduke with headlines like HAIL, OUR HOPE! but with no information interesting to people who wanted to get that hope into their gunsights. The German-language *Die Bosnische Post* was more helpful. In Princip's band only Ilić fully had mastered the oppressors' tongue, and on June 18 he found in *Die Bosnische Post* the Archduke's exact itinerary through the city. He mapped it out for Princip long before it appeared on posters calling on the populace to line their Crown Prince's path with cheers.

Every day before the Archduke's arrival, fear and doubt flickered through Ilić. Every day he helped Princip inch closer to the thing he feared and doubted. After a while Princip ran out of the money handed him by the Black Hand in Belgrade. Ilić gave him "a loan" of twenty kronen. When *that* ran out, Princip ordered Ilić to procure gainful employment for himself and Cabrinović. Ilić found Princip office work at a welfare society. He got Cabrinović a job at a printing plant.

Ilić also acted as navigator, evading police patrols, when the band visited Grabež who lived with a girl friend in the village of Pale, 15 miles southeast of Sarajevo. As the band strolled through Pale's remote meadows, Princip would pull out his gun to practice his marksmanship on starlings and finches, then order the others to follow suit.

In Sarajevo itself, Princip drew on Ilić's expertise in devising a surface of innocuous urban adolescence. Princip was a celibate, nonsmoking, nondrinking, murder-intoxicated teenager. He and his friends spent their evenings as normal youths who chased pleasure through the lovely summer nights. They hung about a wine shop popular with the lads and lasses in the street just renamed for Franz Ferdinand. Princip pretended to flirt with girls. For the first and last time in his life he drank Žilavka.

Princip had the plot poised, primed, and camouflaged—when it was threatened once more, again by Ilić. Very early one morning he knocked on Princip's door. The assassination, he breathed, must be postponed—word from the Black Hand in Belgrade, whose emissary he had just met in the nearby town of Bled. Princip said that he, as mission leader, had heard nothing. He demanded proof. Ilić said that written orders were too great a risk, but here was printed evidence of the reason behind the decision—and waved a Bosnian newspaper with reports of turmoil in Serbia between militants of the Black Hand stripe and supporters of the more moderate Prime Minister. Princip read the reports. He dropped the paper and said, "All the more reason to go forward with the plot." The plot went forward.

Two days later Ilić waved newspapers with the bulletin that King Petar of Serbia had retired from active rule; his son Alexander was the Prince Regent. This, Ilić said, might change everything, including their business in Sarajevo. Princip answered that no order about any change had reached him; pistol practice as usual in Grabež's meadow.

These words he said aloud. Silently he determined that

when the time came, Ilić should not be entrusted with a weapon.

The time came. On the late afternoon of June 27, that rainy day before the Archduke's visit, the bombs and pistols were distributed to all conspirators except Ilić. Princip instructed his team to hide the arms. They were to fool and josh the evening away at the usual wine shop—after all, it was Saturday night. But before sleep they were to spend some minutes—always singly, one by one, never together—at the grave of a Black Hand martyr in Kosovo Cemetery. Here they were to meditate; to dedicate and to consecrate themselves for the grim service they would render to Serbia tomorrow.

And at the Kosovo Cemetery they all did just that—one by one, in the misty late-night hours of June 27, 1914.

27

AT 8:15 THE NEXT MORNING, WHILE THE ARCHDUKE AND HIS WIFE PREpared to entrain for Sarajevo, Princip summoned his band for the last time. They met in the back room of the Vlajnic Pastry Shop, near the scene of the day's action. Suddenly it was Cabrinović—not Ilić—who created a last-minute difficulty.

Since his return to Sarajevo, Cabrinović had lived in his parents' house, telling them he'd come home to leave behind his life as a hobo radical. He'd behaved himself accordingly, working in his father's café, acting "nicely"—until now; until the imminence of the climax became too much. That morning the elder Cabrinović decided to hoist the Imperial colors from his establishment. He was a Habsburg loyalist and wished to show respect for the Crown Prince. Suddenly his son broke into protests against "the odious flag." An argument erupted. The father told the boy to leave the house if he didn't like its banner. The boy stalked off, shouting that soon the Austrian Crown Prince would be a joke—the Serbian King would rule Bosnia!

When Cabrinović joined the other confederates in the pastry shop, he was still shaking with an anger all the angrier for its admixture of fear. He came into the back room spouting about his father. Princip restricted him to a whisper. Hissing furiously, Cabrinović not only reported his fight at home but announced yet another indiscretion. He would have himself photographed right now; if he should die for Serbia this morning, at least a picture of him would survive—the world would have a photograph of him just before his sacrifice—a memento for his father!

Princip remained calm. One must be calm at the brink. Coming down hard on Cabrinović now would only have upset the fellow still more. The thing to do was to factor Cabrinović's instability into his, Princip's, final dispositions.

He told Cabrinović to post himself at 9 A.M. sharp with the unarmed Ilić and the three armed auxiliaries near the corner of Cumunja Bridge and Appel Quay. Princip's own station as well as Grabež's would be some three hundred yards farther down the Archduke's route along Appel Quay, closer to City Hall.

With this deployment, the unreliables (Cabrinović, Ilić, the auxiliaries) would be tested first because they would see the target first. If they failed, the serious core of the squad, namely Princip backed by Grabež, could still bring the enterprise to the desired end.

Still calm, Princip dismissed his group. They bade each other farewell since they might never see each other alive again. Princip told them to leave the pastry shop one by one and to arrive at their respective posts a few minutes apart along different paths. Cabrinović was allowed to go to a photographer's studio on condition that he appear at the exact spot at the exact time, as ordered.

Cabrinović swore to his leader that he would. During that brief huddle in the back room, Princip had managed to invest Cabrinović with some of his own self-control. Cabrinović proved that a few minutes later in the street. He stumbled on an old crony (with whom he presently had his picture taken), and then on two girls of their acquaintance. Crony and girls wore their Sunday clothes; they were on the town for the gala morning that featured an Archduke's visit. Crony and girls joked with Cabrinović. None of them noticed anything amiss.

Neither did Maxim Svara, son of the Attorney General of Sarajevo and a former schoolmate of Princip's. Princip happened to run into him on the way to what no one must know was his battle station. Princip casually small-talked with Maxim, pistol and bomb arranged so as not to bulge his jacket even slightly. For six blocks they strolled together on Appel Quay. All along they watched flags being run up on poles and people assembling to watch the Habsburg prince ride by. Then the two youths wished each other good day. Maxim turned left to the Cathedral where the bishop was offering High Mass in honor of the dynasty. Princip continued walking along the Quay until he reached Latin Bridge.

From 9 A.M. on he stood there. He waited in the gathering crowd. His ear was cocked for the motorcade. His hand was ready for the trigger of his pistol, for the cap of his bomb, for his capsule of cyanide.

Just after 10 A.M. he heard cries of *"Zivio! . . . Zivio! . . ."* followed by a powerful growl of car engines and then, suddenly, a detonation. The bang faded into shouts. At once Princip pressed forward fiercely through the throng and saw, at last, the bomb-smashed wooden shutter of a store front with the Habsburg flag waving above, a big car with gesticulating generals and blown-out tires, some people sitting on the curb bloodying their Sunday best—and Cabrinović held in a rough grip by two gendarmes . . . Cabrinović retching from the cyanide, dripping from the river across which he'd obviously tried to escape. No sign of the Archduke, but Princip assumed his body had been spirited away.

So Cabrinović, the unstable, had come through after all. Yet obviously he had been prevented from swallowing the cyanide and might not be able to remain silent under tough interrogation. He would give away the Black Hand. Princip's fingers tightened around the Browning. He must kill first Cabrinović, then himself. That moment a whole new stampede of gendarmes came down on Cabrinović with their gold-crested helmets and whisked him off. Princip heard the sputter of car engines being cranked up. The motorcade sped off much faster than it had come. And everywhere people who had been closer to the lead car were saying how calm the Archduke had acted, how crazy these fanatics must be with their bombs, how lucky the Archduke had not been hurt.

The Archduke had not been hurt.

It had all been for nothing—at least so far. Desperately Princip looked for his confederates in order to regroup. But they were hard to find in the excitement everywhere and the rapid influx of new spectators. The bomb had made the high visit dramatic. Now the Archduke was much more than an interesting sight. He had become a sensation. Very soon this sensation was due to drive back from City Hall, again along Appel Quay. More and more people brimmed on the sidewalk. Nobody of Princip's team was among them, no matter where he looked. They had all fled. They had scattered. They had deserted. Princip was alone. Alone with his bomb, his pistol, and the knowledge of how unlikely he was to use either because of the precautions the enemy would now take.

But, having driven himself so far without mercy, he decided to go on without much hope. He crossed over to the other side of the Quay. That way he would be closer to the automobiles, just in case the Archduke really did return along Appel Quay, as called for by the original schedule. Once more, he waited, this time at the corner of the quay and a side street. He heard the church clocks strike 10:30 A.M., tolling *all is over, all is over,* into his ears. He heard the motorcade return at 10:32, and all would have been over indeed—the very spot on which Princip stood would not be memorialized today by two footprints sunk in concrete, the house at his back would not have become a museum enshrining Princip's heroism, the bridge to his left would not now be named Princip Bridge—*if* . . .

If two mistakes had not been made by the entourage of the Austrian Crown Prince. The first was nearly logical. Since Cabrinović had thrown the bomb from the river side of the quay, an officer of the escort stood on the running board on the same side—not on Princip's side—to protect the Archduke with his body. The second mistake was as mysterious as fate itself. The chauffeur of the lead car, filled with police, had been clearly instructed on what route to take to the garrison hospital where the Archduke wished to visit his wounded aide. Nonetheless the chauffeur made the wrong turn on Appel Quay into the side street off Latin Bridge.

This mistake did not escape General Potiorek, who sat in the front seat of the second car, that of the Archduke. The General cupped his hands to shout to the first car, *"Turn back! Back to the Quay!"* The chauffeur obeyed. To obey he must make a U-turn. To make a U-turn in the narrower side street he must come to a halt. Since *he* came to a halt, so must the drivers of the motorcade behind him. An inevitability decreed that the second car must stop at the corner, directly in front of a thin, small youth who was reaching inside his coat.

The many days Princip had spent on target practice, the weeks of training and rehearsal, the months of waiting, planning, of steeling himself and disciplining his crew, of patience, cunning, and perseverance—they all converged on this one moment, at 10:34 A.M., on this sunlit corner of the Appel Quay and Rudolf Street, in front of the Schiller Delicatessen Store.

The chauffeur had just begun to work the wheel for the U-turn. Count Harrach of the Archduke's escort stood on the running board, on the river side of the quay. There was nothing between Franz Ferdinand von Habsburg and Gavrilo Princip except five feet of translucent summer air. For this one moment the pale blue eyes of the son of a postman looked into the pale blue eyes of a lord descended from thirteen European dynasties. The next second the son of the postman realized he could not throw the bomb he was already gripping inside his coat: the Archduke was too close and the crowd too dense around him for hauling out his arm. Therefore he pulled out his Browning. He turned his head away (later he would say he had been confounded by the sight of the Duchess, a woman) and, perhaps to compensate for this lapse, pressed the trigger twice.

And then all was really over. After the two bangs Princip saw the car pull away fast, the Archduke still sitting upright, unaffected, unscathed, even after this final effort.

Princip put the pistol to his own head, but someone wrested it from his hand. He reached for the cyanide capsule, managed to get it between his teeth, bit it open, already felt a taste of bitter almonds, but a policeman's stick came down on his head and knocked the thing out of his mouth. From everywhere arms reached for him, gripped him and punished him, yet nothing punished him more in this nightmare tumult than the fact that he was still alive and so was the Archduke.

General Potiorek, the Military Governor of Bosnia, was under that same impression, but only for about five more seconds. After the explosions he looked back instantly at the august pair; the two sat erect and unruffled. But just as the car turned back onto the Quay, the Duchess began leaning oddly against the Archduke. The Archduke's mouth began to dribble red. Count Harrach on the running board, appalled, fumbled for his handkerchief and leaned over to wipe the blood from the Archduke's lips. The Duchess, leaning, cried at her husband, "For heaven's sake, what has happened to you?" The Archduke, who usually roared at any irritation, sat stiffly and silently as he bled. The General shouted at the driver to proceed at top speed to his residence. The Archduchess's head had drooped onto her husband's knees. Blood from the wound in her abdomen soaked through her white silk dress and stained the red and white bouquet of roses clenched in her hand. The Archduke, still sitting stiffly, whispered with his blood-filled mouth: "*Sopherl, Sopherl, stirb nicht! . . . Bleib am Leben für unsere Kinder!*" ("Little Sophie, little Sophie, don't die! . . . Stay alive for our children!") Then he, too, began to droop forward. Count Harrach tried to hold him up as the car hurtled and veered. He asked, "Is Your Highness in great pain?" The Archduke's head had slumped down onto the head of his wife resting on his knees. "It's nothing," he said, quite clearly even above the car engine's roar. "It's nothing," he said again. He kept saying it, more softly, seven more times, the last time just before the car stopped at the Governor's residence. When the two were lifted out of the automobile, her blood had mingled with his on the leather seat.

In the residence a doctor tore open the Archduke's collar to reach his smashed jugular. The gold collar had turned scarlet. Inside the collar seven amulets against seven evils became visible, all wrought of silver and gold. They, too, were dripping scarlet. By the time the church clocks of Sarajevo struck 11 A.M. Franz Ferdinand and Sophie had both stopped breathing, she less than ten minutes before him. They died as they had lived, in unison.

History's will was done.

THAT SUNDAY VIENNA'S SKIES WERE AS BRIGHT AND JOVIAL AS SARAJEVO'S. So were those of nearby Baden, a cozy Biedermeier spa where, on a bench under an oak tree, the writer Stefan Zweig was reading a biography of Tolstoy. Shortly after half past two in the afternoon, something made him look up from the page. Something had stopped happening. It took him a moment to realize just what: a few hundred feet away, in the band shell of the Spa Park, the musicians had broken off in the middle of a waltz.

At Aspern Airfield on Vienna's southern edge, a young summer-happy crowd under straw hats and flowered bonnets craned necks at an aeronautical display. At half past two the smartly kepi'd brass band launched into "The Airmen's March." They never finished it.

In Vienna itself all green spaces were teeming vivaciously. Everybody was outdoors, celebrating Peter and Paul, a favorite Saint Day of the town. The poor basked and munched bacon rind on the "free" park benches. The less poor sliced cervelat on more comfortable chairs costing one heller each. The rich nibbled chocolate cake served prettily doilied on café terraces. All enjoyed the jasmine-scented air, the violins undulating in pergolas. Sometime before 3 P.M., policemen seemed to shoot out of the ground to whisper into the ears of orchestra conductors everywhere. Everywhere bows dropped away from strings. Flutes fell silent. The music stopped.

Never since the suicide of Crown Prince Rudolf twenty-five years earlier had so much music stopped so suddenly in Vienna.

There was a difference, though. Back in 1889, Rudolf had been Austria's gracious and graceful young promise. His death had anguished the Empire, seeming to sever it from its future. Now, in 1914, Vienna was startled but not stricken. Franz Ferdinand's arctic image had thawed a bit lately, yet for most citizens he evoked neither hope nor youth nor grace. His public face was lined too grimly, his mustaches were too much like fixed bayonets. He augured oppression at home, abrasiveness abroad.

"If that Archduke had lived to sit on the throne," Freud said the day after the assassination to his patient the Wolf Man, "war with Russia would have been inevitable." The truth was precisely the reverse. Yet most Viennese shared Freud's breezy misjudgment and his mistaken relief. This included the realm's highest councillors, who knew the Archduke well. They absorbed his death rather briskly. Many had been offended by his un-Austrian, unmannerly directness, by his uncouth insights. The journal of Foreign Minister Count von Berchtold confides that during the first cabinet meeting after the outrage ". . . one noted, yes, consternation and indignation but also a certain easing of mood."

One noted it in Franz Joseph, too, at his Alpine villa in Bad Ischl. The All-Highest summer holiday had started earlier than usual in order to elude an encounter with Franz Ferdinand. By going on vacation the Emperor avoided official business like the Archduke's personal report on the Bosnian maneuvers. No more danger of that now. Franz Joseph promptly returned to his capital to deal with the enormity that freed him from all further vexations by his nephew.

"Certainly Papa was shocked," his daughter the Archduchess Valerie records in her diary, "but I found him amazingly fresh. When I said that Karl [The Archduke Karl, Franz Ferdinand's nephew, just become the new Crown Prince] would acquit himself well, Papa said 'For me it is a great worry less.' "

Throughout the Empire headlines screamed from front pages framed in black. But to his adjutant, the Emperor was candid about his composure. "God will not be mocked," he said. "A higher power has put back the order I couldn't maintain." Crown Prince Franz Ferdinand had disordered the hierarchy by inflating his wife's place in it. Now she had lost her life, and soon she would lose her inflated place.

At first, however, the Duchess's status seemed unchanged by her slaying. Cannons from the great fortress of Sarajevo had boomed to greet the live Crown Prince and his wife at their entry into the city on the morning of June 28. The cannons boomed again, twenty-one times, on the evening of June 29, to bid farewell to their embalmed remains. Though the funeral train puffed through the Bosnian night without halting, army regiments stood at attention at every station it passed. The train rolled on to the Adriatic coast where the foremost dreadnought of the Imperial fleet was waiting, the *Viribus Unitis,* on which the breathing Archduke has sailed toward Sarajevo just five days earlier. Now marines in dress uniforms sheltered the two caskets under a baldachin on the quarter deck and draped them with flags and flowers. Early on June 30, the huge man-of-war began to stream northward at a speed solemnly slow, under a hot sun, under black pennants and a flag at half-mast, followed by other battleships, cruisers, destroyers, civilian yachts, motorboats, fishing boats, even ferries, all with flags half-mast and flying black ensigns. This giant, wave-borne cortege moved close to the shore, where more cannons rumbled their mourning from the hills and priests stood in full vestments on the beaches, swung thuribles censing the corpses, and called out blessings for the souls of the faithful departed.

On the evening of July 1, the dolorous armada steamed into the harbor waters of Trieste. More cannons boomed, more regiments presented arms and lowered colors as the caskets were transferred from the black-garlanded ship to a black-garlanded special train. Twenty-four hours later, on the night of July 2, it came to a halt in Vienna's South Terminal.

Here the responsibilities of the military ended. Here began the jurisdiction of Prince Montenuovo, First Lord Chamberlain of His Majesty, foe of Archduke Franz Ferdinand for life and beyond.

* * *

Neither Franz Joseph nor any member of the dynasty met the funeral train. There was just one exception. Only the new Crown Prince, the Archduke Karl, escorted his predecessor through the dark and empty streets.

Next morning the dead couple lay in state at the Palace Chapel from 8 A.M. to noon. Not one second longer. Some 50,000 people converged from every district of the town onto the Inner City. It was not so much affection that drew them as awe and curiosity. Most were turned away because of the absurd briefness of the viewing period. Those who managed to pass the chapel portals found something curious indeed.

The two coffins stood side by side, but their closeness only emphasized their inequality. Franz Ferdinand's was larger, much more ornate, and placed twenty inches higher than Sophie's. His bore the many insignia of his rank—the Archducal crown, the General's plumed helmet, the admiral's hat, his ceremonial sword, and all his principal decorations including the Order of the Golden Fleece. Her coffin was bare except for a pair of white gloves and a black fan. These were the emblems of a lady-in-waiting.

She had been a lady-in-waiting before her marriage. Her subsequent elevations to Princess and then to Duchess were now cancelled. Only a little over 100 hours earlier Franz Ferdinand had committed for her sake yet another disorderliness against the privileges of genealogy. He had carried her parasol before the honor guard at Sarajevo in order to lift her to his level before the world. Now his caparisoned coffin was used to push her down again, to exhibit her inferiority by contrast. The First Lord Chamberlain and the Serb schoolboy assassin, working in tandem, had put the woman back in her place.

There were many wreaths that morning, sent to the chapel from great notables like the American President Wilson down to humble folk like the Shoemakers' Guild of Lower Austria.

There was no wreath from the Emperor or any other Habsburg.

At the stroke of noon the public was turned away. At 4 P.M. Franz Joseph appeared, accompanied by Archdukes and Archduchesses but not by any of Franz Ferdinand's children. Their mother was a morganatic corpse. They were morganatic orphans, hence not members of the Highest Family. No foreign dignitaries attended. Every monarch and president in Europe had wired his intention to come. By return cable the First Lord Chamberlain had advised them to "kindly have your ambassador act as representative to avoid straining His Majesty's delicate health with the demands of protocol." (The King and Queen of Rumania were politely stopped at the border.)

So the ambassadors came—and departed again almost immediately together with the Emperor. Vienna's Cardinal Piffl ran through the funeral services in less than fifteen minutes. At 4:15 P.M. the bodies were locked away. They had been brought to the chapel in the dark of the previous night. They were not taken out again until the new night was very dark again.

Vienna of the *schöne Leiche,* of the corpse beautiful, where paupers scrimped and schemed to be buried like princes, now had a prince reduced to an impoverished and furtive funeral. None of the nobility had been invited to pay their final respects to the Heir Apparent or to accompany him on his last journey through the streets of the capital. But as the remains of Franz Ferdinand and Sophie were rolled out of the chapel, a band of aristocrats pushed past the police. Led by the Archduke Karl and by Count Chotek, Sophie's brother, they made less lonely the scant procession behind the coffins moving to the West Terminal.

Near midnight a car coupled to a milk train took the dead sixty miles west along the Danube to the small town of Pöchlarn. There only a delegation of local veterans saluted, in old uniforms wetted down by a sudden squall.

Two plain black hearses of the Vienna Municipal Undertaking Service transported the coffins onto a ferry. In midstream a thunderbolt frightened the horses into a panic that almost pitched the caskets into the Danube.

At 1 A.M. on July 4, the hearses gained the other shore. A few minutes later they stopped before the castle of Artstetten,* Franz Ferdinand's family manor. In its crypt the pair found the peace that now began to drain away from the world outside.

* Today the town of Artstetten, like thousands of others all over Europe, has a memorial to the local fallen of the Great War. But only in Artstetten does the list begin with a Crown Prince and his wife: The Archduke Franz Ferdinand von Habsburg-Este and Sophie, Duchess von Hohenberg.

29

THE NEXT DAY ALL OF VIENNA WAS ABUZZ WITH THAT MIDNIGHT IN ARTstetten. Some deplored its meanness. No one saw it as overture to vast, lethal chaos. On the contrary. The court considered that funeral a fitting end to dissonance. It recovered a harmony disturbed by the slain Crown Prince himself.

His very testament assaulted tradition. For centuries Habsburgs had been buried beneath the nave of Vienna's Capuchin Church. Franz Ferdinand, however, had anticipated that his Sophie would not be allowed to enter eternity among them. Since they would exclude her, he would exclude himself. His Last Will defied the custom of the house he had come so close to heading: He was to lie not with his kinsmen but with Sophie in the vault he had had built for them both in Artstetten.

As a result—in Palace eyes—their remains were inevitably subject to the consequences of his wilfulness. Since Franz Ferdinand and Sophie had died together, his final journey must share not only the destination but the limits of hers. Their funeral must not take on the grandeur his would have shown had he married suitably. The aberration he had visited on Habsburg while alive must not be ratified by *their* state funeral after his death. No: The ceremonies of his death must atone for the irregularity of his life. And the fact that a teenage zealot had killed him made not a scintilla of difference. The madness of a schoolboy must not change dynastic principle. That principle must override assassin and assassinated. In sum, the funeral was essential to Franz Joseph's "restoration of order."

Of course another source of disorder remained: Serbia. It was more dangerous than the man it had killed. Sarajevo proved that Serbia had been eating away far too long at the Empire's security, dignity, tranquillity. The First Lord Chamberlain's etiquette had disciplined the late Archduke. Next, Serbia must be punished. And for that purpose etiquette was not enough.

Within twenty-four hours of the murder, the Belgrade government wired condolences to Vienna, vowing that Serbia would ". . . certainly, most loyally do everything to prove that it would not tolerate within its borders the fostering of any agitation . . . calculated to disturb our already delicate relations with Austria-Hungary." These sentiments came too late. They were not enough.

Belgrade's Prime Minister made a further gesture of appeasement that at the same time rebuked the ideology of

Colonel Apis's Black Hand. The Prime Minister ordered all places of entertainment closed in Belgrade on the day of Franz Ferdinand's funeral. He also cancelled the rest of the week-long celebrations of St. Vitus, the Saint's Day so sacred to the Serb national soul. It was not enough.

Throughout Bosnia, Habsburg-loyal Croats and Muslims smashed shops and inns and hotels owned by Serbs. In Bosnian schools, Serb students were beaten up. In Vienna, mobs kept attacking the Serb Embassy, barely stayed by police. It was not enough.

Not after Sarajevo. Not when Princip's initial interrogations established the fact that he had done the deed after a stay at Belgrade, probably with Belgrade's help. None of it was enough.

Order in Franz Joseph's sense could be restored only by a decisive act of the Habsburg government against Serbia. But an act of what kind? Of what force? Franz Joseph instructed his ministers to submit options.

At a cabinet meeting hastily called on June 29, four days before the funeral, Foreign Minister von Berchtold showed himself still guided by the pacifism of the late Crown Prince. He proposed relatively temperate demands: that Serbia dismiss its Minister of Police, jail all suspected terrorists, and dissolve extremist groups.

Prime Minister Tisza of Hungary sided with Berchtold for reasons of his own. Tisza could not be very furious with the Serbs for removing his worst enemy, the Crown Prince; nor did Tisza relish a war in which a victorious Austria would swallow Serbia, thereby increasing the Empire's Slav population and reducing the Magyars to an even smaller minority. Still, neither Berchtold (whose main resource in a debate was a small, fine flourish of his cigarette-holder) nor the Calvinist Tisza (who kept quoting I Kings 2:33 on the dangers of bloody vengeance) were a match for General Conrad. For now Conrad's anti-Serb wrath was triumphant. His one tamer, the Crown Prince, lay dead. And the Crown Prince's very death by a Serb documented that Conrad had been right all along. There was a deadly snake hissing at Austria's heels, he now said; it would not do to slap at this serpent. Its skull must be crushed.

Conrad's argument would have overridden all others, had it not been for the German envoy in Vienna, Count von Tschirsky. Von Tschirsky acted in the spirit of his monarch's prudence vis-à-vis the Serbs, the prudence so laboriously inspired in the Kaiser by the late Crown Prince. On June 30, two days after Sarajevo, the German ambassador called on the Austrian Foreign Minister to warn ". . . with great emphasis and seriousness against hasty measures in settling accounts with Serbia."

Berchtold made the most of these cautions when he went to his Emperor. Austria, he argued, could not afford to define its stance against Serbia without Berlin's backing. After all, Russia was Serbia's protector; Austria needed the weight of the German army—the world's most powerful—as counterpoise to the Tsar's endless regiments. Only Germany's full support would keep St. Petersburg from meddling. But, as the German ambassador had just shown, only a temperate Austria would earn such support.

The Emperor agreed: Conrad was not to do any Serb skull-crushing, at least not yet. Any decision of the kind must be made shoulder to shoulder with Berlin. Franz Joseph himself would elicit Kaiser Wilhelm's sympathies in a handwritten letter.

Of course Berchtold wanted the sympathies to be low-key rather than inflammatory. He knew that the Kaiser had lost a boon companion at Sarajevo—but that going to war over this loss would mean cancelling the Kaiser's delightful summer cruise to Scandinavia. Berchtold knew that the Kaiser was much better at attitudinizing gorgeously than at thinking cogently or feeling deeply. Being a bit like the Kaiser himself, Berchtold knew that His Majesty's emotions were unsteady, unsure, manipulable. In addressing such a man, Franz Joseph's letter must manipulate accurately.

Berchtold saw to it that in writing the Kaiser, Franz Joseph modulated his phrases a shade closer to restraint than to firmness. Franz Joseph's letter spoke of "the terrible events at Sarajevo" and of the need to "neutralize Serbia as a political power factor"; it did not, however, mention military action nor did it preclude purely diplomatic means.

The letter was a discreet invitation to answer circumspectly. All-Highest circumspection from Berlin would reinforce similar circumspection in Vienna; it would work toward an honorable peace rather than an onerous war; it would improve the chances for the Kaiser's Scandinavian cruise and, for Franz Joseph, the prospect of a cloudless sojourn at Bad Ischl.

Foreign Minister Count von Berchtold schemed well. His own chef du cabinet, Count Alexander Hoyos, outschemed him. Hoyos performed no echoing deeds before or after July 1914. But during that one month his intrigues were historic.

Berchtold had chosen Hoyos as his chief assistant because, as an aristocrat, he habitually preferred mode over matter. To the Foreign Minister, Hoyos's politics—as rabidly anti-Serb as General Conrad's—signified less than the Hoyos cachet: Originally of Spanish origin, the Hoyos clan had long been prominent in the inner sanctum of the Court. Indeed the name

Hoyos runs scarlet through the final Habsburg decades. In 1889 Count Josef von Hoyos had been invited to Crown Prince Rudolf's hunting lodge at Mayerling on the morning of Rudolf's suicide; he had brought the news to Vienna. Twenty-five years later his young cousin Alexander Hoyos also became a messenger after an Archducal death. The later Hoyos, however, did more than report calamity. He sped it on its way.

On the afternoon of July 4, 1914, twelve hours after Franz Ferdinand's burial, a courier was about to carry Franz Joseph's letter to Berlin. Suddenly Alexander Hoyos volunteered to take it himself. Why? Because, Hoyos claimed, His Majesty's words (and their nuances) would be amplified by the fact that they traveled to Germany with a senior official of the Austrian Foreign Minister's office.

Such reasoning made sense to the Foreign Minister. He thought he was finessing General Conrad through his Emperor's letter to the Kaiser. Actually he was being finessed by General Conrad through Count Hoyos.

Hoyos arrived in Berlin on July 5, just after the German Foreign Minister Gottlieb von Jagow had left for his honeymoon in Lucerne. The timing, while accidental, served Hoyos well. As mere chef du cabinet he would have had no easy access to von Jagow, a personage of full ministerial rank in Berlin. But the German Under Secretary for Foreign Affairs who acted for the Minister in his absence was a different matter.

While the "Wrinkled Gypsy" (the Kaiser's name for Szögyény-Marich, Austria's aged ambassador to Germany) was at Potsdam Palace, presenting Franz Joseph's letter to the Kaiser, Hoyos sat in the Under Secretary's office "interpreting the letter's unofficial essence." He explained that Franz Joseph's phrase "neutralizing Serbia as a political power factor" meant nothing less than the detoxification of Serbia by full force. Hoyos also "interpreted" an implication that, he said, Franz Joseph was too diplomatic to spell out, namely, that the time had come for Germany to prove herself a full-blooded and reliable ally at long last, and that furthermore, only Germany's outspoken willingness to place its unique might behind Austria's action would prevent reprisals by other powers. Berlin's courage would do more than buttress the brother-Empire; it would ensure the peace of Europe.

The German Under Secretary listened and took fire. He telephoned the Kaiser's Chancellery at Potsdam Palace to ask, urgently, for an audience.

Next morning the Kaiser strolled the Palace gardens with his Chancellor and the Under Secretary. Theobald von Bethmann-Hollweg, the German Chancellor, "Lanky Theo" (in the Kaiser's badinage), was eager to return to his country estate, wary of Balkan complications yet also too weary to interrogate the Under Secretary who was aflame with Hoyos's "oral elaboration" of the letter from Vienna. The Chancellor let the Under Secretary spout.

And the Kaiser lent his ear. His stroll became a strut. He heard that between the lines Franz Joseph was appealing to his, Wilhelm's, valor as Germany's first soldier, to Wilhelm's chivalry as a Prussian knight who would not fail his venerable fellow-sovereign in Vienna. Then and there Wilhelm swore not to fail him. And since, by not failing him, Wilhelm at the same time was ensuring the peace of Europe, he could take off safely for his Scandinavian cruise.

On July 6, at 9:15 A.M., Wilhelm's train steamed for the port of Kiel where his yacht *Hohenzollern* rode anchor. "This time," he told the industrialist Gustav von Krupp at an on-board dinner that night, "this time I haven't chickened out."

Austria-Hungary saw proof of that the following day. Berchtold in Vienna and Tisza in Budapest received telegrams from Berlin. They were identical and both were signed by the Wrinkled Gypsy, the Habsburg ambassador to Germany. However, both had been drafted by the victorious Hoyos. "His [German] Majesty," the cable read, "authorized me to convey to our august sovereign . . . that we may count on the full support of the German Reich. He quite understands that His Imperial and Royal Apostolic Majesty [Franz Joseph], with his well-known love for peace, would find it hard to march into Serbia, but if we [Austrians] really recognize the necessity of military measures against Serbia, he [Kaiser Wilhelm] would deplore our not taking advantage of the present moment which is so favorable to us."

This, of course, was drastically different from previous German advice on the subject. It almost mandated the occupation of Serbia. An astonished Berchtold began to telephone long distance. He discovered the turn of events in Berlin. In vain he reported to the Vienna cabinet that Hoyos had overstepped his authority. That Hoyos had not been empowered to meet substantively with the German Under Secretary. That Hoyos had expressed his personal opinions, not those of the Emperor or the Austrian government. That Hoyos's distorted account of the Habsburg position had distorted the Kaiser's response.

All in vain. All too late. Hoyos had maneuvered irrevocably well. The Kaiser himself had been recruited in General Conrad's cause. Who dared unrecruit the Kaiser—especially a

Kaiser away on his Norse cruise? Who dared resist Conrad's imperative to crush the Serb skull, now that Prussia's spiked helmets were massing behind the General?

No one in Vienna. Wafflers in the cabinet, like Finance Minister Bilinski, came around to General Conrad's side. After a while even Tisza relented. And Berchtold? Berchtold caved in quickly, easily, even lithely. No deep convictions encumbered the Count. The wind had veered and he veered with it, making the movement into ballet.

The new Berchtold proposed that Serbia should be invaded, yes; but only after it had rejected Austrian demands that were diplomatically impeccable as well as absolutely unacceptable.

The cabinet nodded. General Conrad agreed, too. A diplomatic showdown would condition the populace for a call to arms. And it would give him time to mobilize fully for the crushing of the Serb skull for the total extirpation of Serb power.

Now the cabinet's collective sense must receive All-Highest approval. On the night of July 8, Berchtold entrained for Bad Ischl where Franz Joseph had returned after the Archduke's funeral. It is a measure of Berchtold's spinelessness that he invited Hoyos along, to brief His Majesty on the strength of the new German support. It was as though Hoyos had never tricked Berchtold in Berlin.

Berchtold smoothly submitted the cabinet's position. The early morning sun shone on this crucial encounter. Outside the windows of the Imperial villa, thrushes and larks were in sweet voice. Franz Joseph pondered. Yes, the restoration of order, the redemption of Austria as a major power that couldn't limply suffer the gunning-down of its Crown Prince—yes, that did require a settling of accounts with Serbia. But a settling so dangerous? Causing what repercussions? International war was a supreme disorder Franz Joseph had no wish to face at his age. Berchtold, however, spoke only of a police action deftly justified, well prepared in advance, and executed fast enough to render pointless any aid Serbia's friends might want to extend.

How decide on such a sun-dappled day? Frau Schratt was waiting to be taken for a stroll through lilies in full flower. As a lover, Franz Joseph was an ascetic, but an ascetic with style. As a Foreign Minister, Count von Berchtold lacked policy, consistency, vision. But he wore his lacks with style. Nothing but style underpinned the Empire—style and an army with the world's smartest uniforms. That's why the Emperor held on to his stylish Berchtold. Perhaps Berchtold's proposal carried some risks. But it was not raw. It was steeped in style. The Emperor nodded at the Count. The Count bowed from the waist. An hour later he and Hoyos boarded his salon car at Ischl station and rode back to Vienna. The ultimatum was on its way.

30

On July 9, then, the decision fell to crush the Serb skull. General Conrad's agenda would be honored. But it would be implemented à la Count von Berchtold. It would be much more civilized than the murder it avenged. It would be sophisticated theater of the sort only Vienna could devise.

This skull-crushing would come as a fine third-act surprise. Until then the secret would be nursed backstage, refined and rehearsed behind shuttered blinds in Count von Berchtold's offices at the Ballhausplatz. Like a cunning playwright, Berchtold planned his plot. He would mislead his audience—Serbia's patrons like Russia, France, and France's ally, Britain. He would lull them all into mid-summer drowsiness. For the next few weeks he would play down *diminuendo* the

Austrian hue and cry over Sarajevo. He would encourage the holiday mood of the season. At the same time, unbeknownst to all, the Ballhausplatz would craft its diplomatic time bomb; the Ministry of War would hone its mobilization plans. Then, out of nowhere, Berchtold would spring the ultimatum. But, as in a drama of hidden identities, it would go by another name; only a "note" would be thrust at Serbia, yet a note charged with conditions much tougher, with a deadline much shorter, than most ultimatums. This nonultimatum super-ultimatum would be abruptly posed, inevitably refused—and followed instantly by the lethal pounce of Conrad's troops. Before the audience could catch its breath, before Europe's torpid chancelleries could stir, it would be over. The curtain would fall on Serbia conquered. Austria would take bows, having performed as a still vital and puissant great power.

All in all, an excellent Habsburg libretto. Act I called for marshalling, discreetly, the evidence to be used later against Serbia. Here the best source was testimony from the conspirators, now in police custody.

Princip and Cabrinović had been quickly apprehended. Within four days of the deed, police sweeps of possible suspects happened to net Ilić and Grabež. Arrests continued and spread all over Serbia. Many hundreds with no connection at all to the crime were jailed and grilled. Princip knew that because he was allowed to read newspapers. Therefore he became more responsive at interrogations. He talked (as he put it) "to prevent more innocent people from coming to harm." He also talked for propaganda reasons "to educate the new generation with our martyrdom." But he talked selectively; he named only Grabež and Ilić as well as the band's "auxiliaries," who, already on the list of the potentially seditious, would have been rounded up in any case. He did not breathe a syllable about Colonel Apis or the Black Hand. Grabež and Ilić talked a bit more. Ilić was most anxious to save his life; therefore he talked the most, but even he did not give away the Apis group.

On July 10, Berchtold dispatched an aide to Sarajevo to evaluate the information. On July 13, an analysis arrived by top-secret cable from the Bosnian capital:

> Statements by accused show practically beyond doubt that accused decided to perpetrate the outrage while in Belgrade, and that outrage was prepared . . . with help of Serb officials . . . who also procured bombs, Brownings, ammunition and cyanide. Bombs definitely proven to be from Serb Army stores, but nothing to show they had been taken out for this express purpose . . . Hardly any room for doubt that Princip, Grabež, Cabrinović smuggled across frontier with help from Serb customs . . . However, no evidence of complicity of Serb government ministers in directly ordering assassination or in supplying weapons . . .

All this fell a bit short of Berchtold's hope. It failed to implicate Belgrade's highest authorities. However, it did taint them for condoning, if not encouraging, a terrorist climate and the willingness on the part of lesser officials to cooperate in the outrage. And that was enough to activate Berchtold's scenario. It started to go forward on tip-toe, while Europe dozed.

* * *

The groundwork for deceiving the continent had already been laid on July 8, in a conference between the Foreign Minister and the Chief of Staff. "I recommend," Count von Berchtold had said to General Conrad, "that you and the Minister of War leave Vienna for your vacation so as to keep an appearance that nothing is going on."

On July 14, the Army announced that General Conrad had started his holiday at Innichen, a remote hamlet in the Dolomites, 3,500 feet high. War Minister Krobatin, the official *Wiener Zeitung* said a day earlier, had gone to take the waters at Bad Gastein. All along Franz Joseph remained in Bad Ischl, apparently with little on his mind save sniffing blossoms with Frau Schratt.

As for Berlin, it played along. Chancellor von Bethmann-Hollweg was charmed by Berchtold's dramaturgy; Berchtold's denouement would prove that Austria was not a baroque carcass but suprisingly alive, doughty, adept, decisive—a worthy confederate of Germany.

And so the Germans acted on Habsburg's cue. On the yacht *Hohenzollern* the Kaiser sported innocent through the North Sea. The German Chancellor holed up in his country place where he communed with Beethoven on the grand piano and read Plato in the original Greek. The German Foreign Minister continued to honeymoon at Lake Lucerne in Switzerland. The German Minister of the Navy, Grand Admiral von Tirpitz, promenaded with wife and children through the greenery at Bad Tarasp in the Engadine. The Chief of the German Admiralty also went on holiday, and so did the German Minister of War. General von Moltke took the cure at Carlsbad, again.

The sun shone. The days passed. The jolt of Sarajevo subsided. The world discovered that Austria, instead of rounding on the Serbs, rusticated placidly along with its German ally. Belgrade relaxed. So did St. Petersburg, Paris, London. The feeling grew that Habsburg's response to the assassination would be as reasonable as it was tardy.

And since so many leaders jaunted away from Vienna and Berlin, why should their counterparts elsewhere stick to their desks? One by one the dramatis personae of the opposing camp began to play their parts in Count von Berchtold's script.

Together with his daughter, the Chief of Staff of the Serbian Army went on vacation—in Austria, of all countries, at Bad Gleichenberg. On July 15, Raymond Poincaré, President of France, that is, of Serbia's closest Western ally, embarked on a cruise as cheery as the Kaiser's. With his Prime Minister he sailed on a summit junket to Norway and Russia. Tsar Nicholas II, Serbia's eastern protector, awaited his French guests at Tsarskoe Selo, a pleasure dome of multi-hued marble overlooking the Gulf of Finland that served as his summer castle. "Every day," he noted in his diary, "we play tennis or swim in the fjords."

In England, the Foreign Secretary Sir Edward Grey, a childless widower and lover of leafy solitude, indulged himself in leafy solitude. Near Winchester, by the banks of the river Itchen stood his cottage, brushed by willows and embraced by ivy. During much of that July, Sir Edward could be found here. He spent the days leaning against the rail of a footbridge, lowering his rod down to the stippled trout.

The First Lord of the British Admiralty pursued a more ebullient pastime at Overstrand on the Norfolk coast: There Mr. Winston Churchill had his holiday house. On its beachfront he worked away with spade and bucket, assisted by his children. The Churchill family was building sand castles that featured deep moats to trap the tide.

At almost the same time the British Prime Minister Sir Herbert Asquith sent his daughter off to Holland "so that the girl can have some fun." Sir Herbert himself did not stray too far from No. 10 Downing Street. After all, he had to tend to something of a crisis. More fuss was afoot about the Irish Home Rule Bill.

The sunny, stable high over Europe was of double benefit to Vienna. Politically, it painted just the right trompe l'oeil backdrop for Count von Berchtold's stage. But the fine summer also met the personal needs of the Viennese. Perhaps more than other cities, theirs had been an incubator of the treacheries of the human soul. Perhaps more than others, it cultivated the therapy of the meadow.

After many rainless weeks, a nocturnal downpour on July 9 washed away the dust. At dawn the west wind scented the streets with the pine of Alpine pastures. (It was the day Berchtold's team began to draft in secret the nonultimatum super-ultimatum.) By noon the sun had re-burnished the foliage of the Vienna Woods. And since only a few streetcar stops separated the Viennese from their Woods, the weather drew them outdoors in unprecedented numbers. They might stoop the work day away in dank factories or behind cramped desks. But on Sunday the lagoons of the Danube splashed with swimmers. At night, the vineyard inns sounded with more song than ever. "*Wien . . . Wien . . .*" they sang, turned toward the heart of the city, namely its past. They still sang about its dreamy courtyards, its gothic alleys, its Biedermeier gardens—all dear and cozy and going, going, gone. Who would suspect that, hidden away at the Ballhausplatz, Count von Berchtold was preparing a giant grenade? In July 1914, Vienna presented itself as a spectacle of nature and nostalgia—the very opposite of imminence and war.

31

NATURE AND NOSTALGIA. THEIR TWIN LURE WAS FELT BY MANY DURING JUST those weeks. On July 12, Sigmund and Martha Freud left Vienna for Carlsbad. They arrived there at almost the same time as the Chief of the German General Staff, General von Moltke. The Freuds, though, lived just outside the spa. They took rooms at the Villa Fasolt on the Schlossberg, a hummock among wooded knolls. This landscape resembled the environs of Fribor, a small Moravian town where Freud had lived during his first four years. In Fribor, by the foothills of the Carpathians, he had been ". . . the happy child who received his first indelible impressions from this air . . . from this soil." Even as an adult ". . . I never felt really comfortable in the city. I believe now that I was never free from a longing for the beautiful woods near our home."

During this summer Freud began to develop thoughts for a paper (never published) called "Philogenetic Fantasy," about mankind's infancy—a pre-Ice Age, pre-Angst, pre-Jung Eden with food and space aplenty, succeeded by much rawer and more crowded times in which paranoia became a survival instinct.

In contrast to Freud, Leon Trotsky could not afford an expensive resort. He spent July of 1914 in his sparse apartment near the flowering edge of the Vienna Woods. Longingly, no doubt. His autobiography shows that for all his sophistication, Trotsky retained the yearnings of a country boy born in the Southern Ukraine ". . . a kingdom of wheat and sheep . . . The village would flare up in my consciousness and draw me on like a lost paradise . . . In my years as commander of the Red Army . . . I was greatly pleased to see each new [rural] fence constructed of freshly cut pine boards. Lenin, who knew this passion of mine, often twitted me about it."

Yet this same summer saw Lenin sharing this same passion. His headquarters at Cracow near the Austro-Russian border had been chosen for reasons beyond revolutionary expediency. "Illyich likes Cracow so much," his wife would write, "because it reminded him of Russia." But Lenin, born in a Volga backwater many miles from the nearest railroad, liked better yet a nook in his Habsburg exile that was smaller and greener than Cracow.

"Autumn is magnificent in the Tatra range," he'd written his sister Maria in April 1914. "If we have a fine autumn we shall probably live in the country." The summer of 1914 was too seductive. Lenin didn't wait for fall. In July he and his wife Krupskaya moved to Poronin in the Tatras. Krupskaya suffered from a goiter and couldn't walk far from their cottage. But Lenin took off with knapsack, walking stick, and notebook "clambering up the steeps like a mountain goat." Sometimes he stopped to make notes on the contentious Socialist Congress scheduled in Vienna for the following month. But for most of July (while the Ballhausplatz hatched the nonultimatum super-ultimatum) Lenin hiked the glorious days away.

Lenin was an occasional visitor in Vienna. Hitler, like Trotsky, had lived there for years. Unlike Trotsky he'd never been drawn to the city's green precincts. He had painted, brooded, ranted, on pavement only; in fact he'd meticulously kept away from the Vienna Woods as if their fragrance might compromise his bitterness. But in this balmy summer he seemed to be haunted by leaf and tree. In July Hitler meandered through Munich's sub-Alpine outskirts, those pointing toward Salzburg and his native Upper Austria. He sketched river shores and villas, often with a garden motif.

That summer the idea of the garden, of nature and nostalgia, also haunted another demon. A virtuous demon, this one, obsessed with morality as others are obsessed with hate. Karl Kraus was the most merciless critic in Austria of Austria. About three times a month he published *Die Fackel* (The Torch), a magazine of inexhaustible indignation and surgical brilliance. At first it had printed polemics from a variety of writers. But by 1914 no other Jeremiah even approached Kraus's eloquence; by then every syllable in *Die Fackel* hissed from his pen. His wit seared Vienna's operetta Machiavellis, its hand-kissing nastiness, its whipped-cream ethics. *Die Fackel* lit up the ways in which the city debased manners and debauched language.

But the summer of 1914 proved that Kraus, Austria's scourge, shared certain sympathies with the late Austrian Crown Prince. Of course both were dedicated haters—the Archduke forever frowning and the torch-hurling Jew. But there was another affinity. Both men were drawn to nature and nostalgia, the dual hallmark of the season. Both loved the garden because it sustained virtue that had withered elsewhere. For the Archduke, the garden—particularly his great garden in Bohemia—was a haven of divine grace; it sheltered him and his Sophie against the godless and malevolent artifice of Vienna's court. For Kraus, the garden was a sanctuary from civilization, which had "betrayed God to the machine."

The Crown Prince loved the garden lavishly, naively, as evidenced by the vast rose beds of Konopiste. Kraus loved the garden mystically. Show him a border of violets, and his acid genius would pulse in an orphic vein. To Kraus, nature occasioned a transfiguring nostalgia. Nature and nostalgia were part of a trinity whose third member was the Maker Himself.

Not long before the summer of 1914, Karl Kraus wrote "The Dying Man," a poem that spies a beacon glimmering from the garden of Creation. It glimmers on through the Fall to guide the fallen toward Redemption; a Redemption whose flowers are the same as those of Genesis.

In the poem God, the Gardener, addresses man, the moribund:

Im Dunkel gehend, wusstest Du ums Licht.
Nun bist Du da und siehst mir ins Gesicht.
Sahst hinter Dich und suchtest meinen Garten.
Du bliebst am Ursprung. Ursprung ist das Ziel.

(Walking through darkness you surmised the light.
Now you are here, you are standing in my sight.
Looking back, you sought the garden gate.
Source is your destination. Source, your anchorage.)

But the garden did more than furnish Kraus with apocalyptic metaphor. During July of 1914, he experienced the garden as a very personal, real, blooming, and twittering haven. In the park of Janowitz, the Bohemian estate of his mistress, Baroness Sidonie von Nadherny, he could lean back under chestnut boughs. He could breathe deeply and release himself from his angers. In public he was the mordant aphorist capable of defining a woman as "an occasionally acceptable substitute for masturbation." In private, among Janowitz's groves, he kissed his baroness's slim fingers as they intertwined with his own. In Janowitz Park he relished his rare moments of repose and affection.

Less than fifteen miles away from Janowitz lay Franz Ferdinand's Konopiste. On June 15, when the archducal gardens had opened to the public, Kraus and his baroness had been among the dazzled visitors. This was the ultimate garden. Therefore it was the ultimate antithesis to what Kraus hated most: Vienna's artificiality, especially the kind perfected by the Viennese press with its deliciously concocted slanders, the bribed bias of its reportage, the slick charm of its feuilletonists. Through sheer organic honesty of stalk and leaf and petal, the garden rebuked all such ink-stained turpitude.

Shortly after visiting Konopiste, Kraus fired off a philippic culminating in the declaration

> that the preservation of the wall of a manor park, where between a five-hundred-year-old poplar and a bluebell flowering today, all the miracles of creation are salvaged from the wreck of the world—that such a thing is more important in the name of the spirit than the pursuit of intellectual infamy which takes God's breath away!

These words in *Die Fackel,* vibrating on the rim of "the wreck of the world," were the last Kraus wrote before the shots of Sarajevo.

After Sarajevo (while Berchtold was hatching the nonultimatum super-ultimatum), *Die Fackel* of July 10, 1914, ran a eulogy of the late Crown Prince that was also a hymn to nature's naturalness as well as the indictment of a culture. "In this era so deplorable for humanity," wrote Kraus,

> which in our Austrian laboratory of the apocalypse is expressed by the grimace of gemütlich sickliness—in such an era the Archduke had the measure of a man. Only now, as Vienna mimics mourning, do we realize . . . how much he disdained that indispensable affability used by the powerful to promote their careers . . . He was no greeter. He had no winning ways to charm the people past their grievances. He did show character through his radical championship of the commonplace against a fake modernity.
>
> He proved himself by his taste. At his estate he opened to the people a floral landscape intelligible on the most popular level, a park with few rarefied pretensions . . . He was not part of the fancy dynamics of Austrian decay . . . he wanted to rouse our era from its sickness so that it would not sleep past its own death. Now it sleeps past his.

Even as Kraus wrote that passage, Europe drowsed on toward a great death. In fact, some of his admirers had a hand in both the drowsing and the dying. Many bright young diplomats read him with awe. This included the group under Count von Berchtold laboring on the composition of the missive Berchtold was to unveil exquisitely, explosively, during the second act of his scenario—the nonultimatum superultimatum to be served on Serbia.

"We were all devotees of Karl Kraus," one of the group would later reminisce in a memoir. "We all devoured, fascinated, every issue of *Die Fackel.* From Kraus we had learned to believe in the magic of the word as the womb of thought . . . We were the last generation [of Habsburg Foreign Office officials], and our highest aim was to crystallize language into utter perfection. For four weeks we worked on the phrasing of the ultimatum as if we were polishing a jewel."

To Kraus, had he known of it, such adulation would have been abomination. For him "the magic of the word" lay in quarrying the truth, not in tricking it out. *Die Fackel* aimed to expose, as he once put it, the "difference between an urn and a chamber pot." In July of 1914 his fans on the Ballhausplatz manipulated the word in order to blur just this distinction. They were festooning the chamber-pot crassness of an ultimatum with the adornments of an urn, to be passed on a silver server from Excellency to Excellency.

32

MEANWHILE EXCELLENCIES ALL OVER EUROPE CONTINUED IN THE ROLES assigned to them by Count von Berchtold's Act I. The weather continued as the Count's obedient stagehand. A slumbrous tropical sun made the continent a lotus land. Belgrade announced that the Serbian King would shortly travel to a spa abroad. In London, the Chancellor of the Exchequer, Lloyd George, took a languid view of international relations; speaking at a banquet, he said that while some clouds always hovered on the horizon, there were fewer this year than last, and that His Majesty's Government would help to dissipate even those . . . In Vienna itself, a skeptical journal like the Socialist *Arbeiter Zeitung* relaxed its suspicions of the government. "The quiet and slow pace of events," it wrote, "suggests that no drastic action will be taken against Serbia."

Just past the midpoint of July, rumors skittered along the Ringstrasse. What was happening behind those drawn blinds at the Ballhausplatz? The stock market registered a sudden, though not major decline.

But Count von Berchtold knew how to restore the blandness required by his scenario. On July 18, he visited British Ambassador Sir Maurice de Bunsen at the ambassador's summer residence Schloss Stixstein. The Foreign Minister "was unusually chatty and agreeable," Sir Maurice would later report, ". . . not a word was let drop that a crisis impended."

To the Italian ambassador, who seemed a bit unnerved by Austria's impassivity after Sarajevo, the Foreign Minister said that the situation was not grave—"it just needs to be cleared up." And the French ambassador, who did not find much clarification in *that* statement, was assured by Berchtold that Vienna's note to Belgrade would be "reasonable."

The French ambassador duly relayed this news to his government. Paris, not overly alarmed in the first place, let its attention wander. Just then a magnificent scandal was engulfing France. On July 20, a judge's gavel at the Court de Seine started a trial mesmerizing the Gallic imagination. Mme. Henriette Caillaux, wife of the Finance Minister (widely touted to be the next Prime Minister), had pumped six bullets into the body of France's most powerful journalist, the editor in chief of *Le Figaro,* Gaston Calmette. That had been back in March. But now, in mid-July, fireworks between prosecutor and defense counsel lit up the erotic glamor behind this charismatic homicide. Much of the trial revolved around the love letters Caillaux had written Henriette during the extramarital affair that preceded their wedding—letters whose imminent publication in *Le Figaro* had driven Mme. Caillaux to murder.

The shots at Sarajevo faded rapidly as those from the *Figaro* office resounded once more in newspaper columns. This was the stuff of prime gossip, made even tangier by a courtroom duel. It enlivened millions of French vacations. Certainly it piqued President Poincaré on his summer cruise. About to land in St. Petersburg, he asked to be apprised of every moist detail by cable.

Britain also had an absorbing domestic concern—apart from holiday-making, of course. The Irish Home Rule Bill was roiling tempers very badly. On July 20—on the morning the Caillaux judges assembled in scarlet robes at the Seine Tribunal—His Britannic Majesty summoned the contending parties to Buckingham Palace, taking a very rare step beyond his constitutional role as a reigning, not a ruling, monarch. And King George did manage to postpone the crisis—until a superior urgency submerged it. But who would have expected such an urgency? Where would it come from? The Henley Regatta?

British King and Paris murderess were spear-carriers for Count von Berchtold's stagecraft. They both diverted attention as he readied the surprise climax. Vienna itself remained quiet, basking its way through July. It did generate some official news—though of a literally festive character. The City Fathers were planning the First International Vienna Music Festival, scheduled for June 1915. Newspapers reported a spirited debate on the subject in the Municipal Council. Among the main points discussed were (1) should the program consist of concerts only? and (2) if operas were included, would this be aping Salzburg, whose own first large-scale festival was slotted for August of *this* year and which would feature the great Felix Weingartner conducting Lotte Lehmann in *Don Giovanni*?

Vienna, then, looked preoccupied with matters either esthetic or bucolic and at all events harmless. As late as July 20, the Russian ambassador saw no reason for not leaving town on a two-week holiday. He left. From St. Petersburg came an even more conclusive signal of détente. On July 21, the Tsar and his guest, French President Poincaré, exchanged toasts that dwelled on the international picture: The Serb-Austrian problem wasn't even mentioned.

But forty-eight hours earlier, while Europe sunned and napped, Count von Berchtold had tiptoed toward the last scene of his first act. On the afternoon of July 19, a number of taxis and private automobiles drew up before his Palais overlooking the Strudlhof Steps. The cars arrived at intervals, avoiding a dramatic convergence. It was Sunday. The scene seemed to point to some weekend social gathering. A passerby, had he cared to notice, would not have spotted a single official limousine.

Yet this was an official occasion, as crucial as it was covert: a cabinet meeting of the Joint Ministers of the Austro-Hungarian Empire. Berchtold had summoned them to review the text of the note to the Serbian government. On the morning of that day the "jewel" had finally been polished to perfection.

Next morning, on Monday July 20, a courier left the Ballhausplatz for the Emperor's villa at Bad Ischl. He made this trip routinely, every weekday, carrying state papers. On the twentieth he carried "the jewel" for Franz Joseph's inspection. On Tuesday the twenty-first, a brief, laconic item in the official *Wiener Zeitung* reported that Foreign Minister Count von Berchtold had gone to Bad Ischl "to discuss current business with His Majesty." And that morning, at 9 A.M., he was received by the Emperor.

Berchtold's diary records a Franz Joseph braced, tart, taut, not at all octogenarian.

"Well, Berchtold, ever on the go?"

"Yes, Your Majesty, one has to be. These are fast-moving times."

"Exactly, as never before. The note is pretty sharp."

"It has to be, Your Majesty."

"It has to be indeed. You will join us for lunch."

"With humble pleasure, Your Majesty."

Hoyos, whom Berchtold had brought along to the audience, took the official copy of the demarche from his briefcase. Franz Joseph initialed it. "The Jewel," already endorsed by the Joint Ministers, now bore the Imperial imprimatur.

Actually this was only the formal ratification of action taken twenty-four hours earlier. On Monday the Emperor had read and approved the note handed him by the courier. On that same Monday it had been wired to the Austrian Embassy in Belgrade. It was ready to be thrust at Serbia by the time a white-gloved footman set down a tureen before Franz Joseph, Berchtold, and Hoyos at midday of July 21.

In summary, the note said

> 1. that preliminary investigations prove that the assassination of the Austrian Crown Prince was planned in Belgrade; that Serbian officials and members of the government-sponsored *Naradna Obrana** had provided the culprits with arms and training; that chiefs of the Serbian frontier service had organized and effectuated passage of the culprits into Austrian territory. . . .

* The cultural society promoting Serb nationalism. Since neither Princip nor his accomplices gave away the Black Hand during their interrogations, it is not mentioned in the Austrian note.

2. that even before the outrage, Belgrade had encouraged for years terrorist societies and criminal actions aiming to detach Bosnia-Hercegovina from the Habsburg realm. . . .

3. that in view of the above, and in order to end this intolerable, long-standing, and ongoing threat to its territories and to its tranquillity, the Imperial and Royal Government of the Austro-Hungarian Empire sees itself obliged to demand from the Royal Serbian government

(a) the publication on the front page of Belgrade's Official Journal of July 26, 1914, of a declaration by the Serbian Government which regrets, condemns, and repudiates all Serbian acts, official or nonofficial, against Austria, and all Serbian violations of rules governing the comity of nations—and that such a declaration be also published as "Order of the Day" by the King of Serbia to the Serbian Army.

The Austrian Government further demands

(b) a guarantee from the Serbian Government that it will henceforth suppress any publication inciting hatred against Austria or menacing Austria's territorial integrity; that it will dissolve any and all societies engaged in propaganda, subversion, or terrorism against Austria, and that it will prevent such societies from continuing their activities under another name or form . . .

The Austrian Government further demands

(c) that the Serbian Government will eliminate instantly any and all educational materials in Serbian schools that are anti-Austrian in character . . .

> The Austrian Government further demands
> (d) that the Serbian Government will remove from the Serbian Army and the Serbian administration all officials guilty of anti-Austrian acts, including specific individuals whose names and activities will be detailed to the Serbian Government by the Austrian Government; and that the Serbian Government will accept the participation of Austrian Police in the suppression and apprehension of anti-Austrian subversive groups, particularly those involved in the Sarajevo crime . . .
> Finally, the Austrian Government demands
> (e) that the Serbian Government will notify the Austrian Government without delay of the execution of these measures . . . and to convey unconditional agreement to all of the foregoing at the latest by Saturday, July 25, 1914, at 6 P.M.

This was the super-ultimatum. In the words of the British Foreign Secretary, it constituted "the most formidable document ever addressed by one state to another." It was also the nonultimatum. Though its tone left no doubt over the consequences of noncompliance, it did not mention the possibility of war, and therefore arrived at the Austrian Embassy in Belgrade labeled as a mere "demarche with a time limit."

And there were other fine aspects to Berchtold's game. The sledgehammer message came phrased in fastidious diplomatic French, the last such "final notice" to be written in that language. Last but not least, Berchtold used precision timing, always important in a theatrical enterprise. Belgrade relied on two principal protectors, Russia and France. Just then the French Head of State was finishing his visit with the Tsar. Berchtold did not want the two to react jointly when the "demarche with a time limit" struck. Through German diplomatic sources, Berchtold had learned that President Poincaré would end his stay at the Russian capital in the early afternoon of Thursday, July 23. By 5 P.M. he would be floating away on the cruiser *France.* Berchtold instructed the Austrian Ambassador in Belgrade to deliver the "demarche" at 6 P.M. sharp.

As ordered, so done. Berchtold had successfully achieved the end of Act I.

Act II opened well, or so it seemed. Abruptly, out of the blue of yet another lovely day, the Austrian Ambassador Baron von Giesl placed a telephone call "of utmost urgency" to the Ministry of Foreign Affairs in Belgrade. It was 4:30 P.M. on July 23, and the Ambassador said that he must deliver "an extremely important communication" to the Prime Minister—who was also the Foreign Minister—that very afternoon at 6 P.M.

Prime Minister Pašić was not even in town. He had no reason to stay close to his office. True, at the beginning of the month, Serbian diplomats abroad had reported rumors that something "strong" might be brewing in Vienna. Yet week followed week after Sarajevo, and nothing "strong" materialized. Serbia began to turn to internal matters. An electoral campaign engrossed the country in mid-July. Pašić left the capital for a political tour, speaking against Apis's extremist party. It was at this point that the Austrian ambassador placed his peremptory call.

Since the Prime Minister was away on the hustings in the Southern provinces, the Finance Minister substituted for him. The Finance Minister received that astounding note from the ambassador at 6 P.M. of July 23. It did not reach Pašić until

8 P.M. that night, when he heard over the telephone details of the suddenness, the severity, the smooth murderousness of Vienna's demands. He had less than forty-eight hours to answer them.

Pašić cancelled all further election speeches. He returned to Belgrade at five o'clock the next morning and immediately called a cabinet meeting. Sessions continued throughout the day, through most of the night that followed, and through most of the day after.

Shortly after 6 P.M. of Saturday July 25, a tall rotund man with a seignorial white beard and a black formal frock coat hurried on foot from the Foreign Ministry to the Austrian Embassy a few blocks off. It was Prime Minister Pašić, holding in his hand an envelope with his government's reply.

When he was admitted to the Ambassador's office it was 6:15 P.M., a quarter of an hour after the deadline set by Vienna. Therefore Ambassador von Giesl did not ask the Prime Minister to sit down. He himself read the note standing. It was a messy document, revised and re-typed many times, after frenzied debates and febrile consultations with the Russian and French embassies. The final version in Baron von Giesl's hands had an inked-out passage and a number of corrections made by pen. That did not interest the Austrian ambassador, nor did the reply's conciliatory and mournful prose, nor did its acceptance of all points of the demarche except those demanding the participation of Austrian police in pursuit of Serbian subjects on Serbian soil. Such requests, the note said, Belgrade "must reject, being a violation of the Serbian constitution and of the law of criminal procedure."

It was this rejection that mattered to the Ambassador. It was the necessary next event in Austria's scenario. The Ambassador had counted on it. He had anticipated it. That was why he stood before the Serbian Prime Minister in his traveling clothes. That was why his code-book had already gone up the chimney, why his secret papers had been shredded, his luggage packed, and his motor-car readied at the front door. That was why he only needed to sign a statement prepared in advance: It said that "due to the unsatisfactory nature" of the Serbian response, the Austro-Hungarian Empire saw itself forced to break off relations with the Kingdom of Serbia.

At 6:20 P.M. a messenger took the statement from Baron von Giesl's desk for delivery to the Serbian Prime Minister's office. As the messenger left, Giesl repeated the statement orally to the Prime Minister who still stood before him. Then the Austrian ambassador bowed, wished the Prime Minister good day, walked to his car. At half past six he boarded a train that crossed the Austrian frontier ten minutes later.

33

THAT SAME EVENING OF JULY 25, THE AUSTRIAN FOREIGN MINISTER Count von Berchtold sat in the Ischl office of Emperor Franz Joseph's military aide-de-camp. They were waiting for a call from the War Ministry in Vienna, which in turn waited for a telephone call from the Embassy in Belgrade. When the clock struck 6:30 P.M., the Foreign Minister, white-faced, said he had to leave, he must get some fresh air. Two minutes after he had gone, the telephone rang with the staccato news. *Serbia rejects essential demand.* The aide ran to have himself announced at the Emperor's villa.

Franz Joseph received his message (as the aide would remember) "hollow-eyed" and "hoarse of voice." "*Also doch* . . ." he said. ("So, after all . . ."). Then, after a long silence, he added, "But the rupture of relations needn't necessarily mean war! . . ."

What sudden change. Barely two days earlier, in the same idyllic Alpine setting, with the same beneficent weather, the same Emperor and the same Foreign Minister had looked forward to just this news: Serbia's rejection of the demarche, which now justified its military punishment. Why, then, was the Emperor shaken? Why the Foreign Minister's ashen cheeks?

Because the play had begun to fail.

In Belgrade Berchtold's libretto had proceeded on cue, but elsewhere the second act was suddenly unravelling. The trouble began with Austria's chief supporting actor, namely Germany.

On the surface nothing seemed wrong. Vienna had sent the text of the "jewel" demarche to Berlin on July 22. Within a day the Austrian ambassador cabled from the German capital that the Kaiser's Foreign Minister "thanks for the communication and assures me that the government here is entirely in agreement with the contents of the demarche."

Actually the Wilhelmstrasse was only imitating the attitude struck by its overlord, the absentee Kaiser (still away on his cruise) before he had boarded his yacht. Aping their master, German ministers stepped before the footlights to stiffen their upper lips at Europe: On July 27, Berlin officially and publicly advised its ally not to accept an offer of mediation from Britain.

But Berlin performed only the external mechanics of the Austrian script, as Vienna was soon to know. Internally things were rather different. A cable sent by the German Foreign Ministry to its principal diplomats abroad said ". . . we have had no influence of any kind on the wording of Austria's note to Serbia, and no more opportunity than other powers to take sides in any way before its publication . . ." The tart implication here was made plain to the Austrian ambassador by the German Foreign Minister von Jagow shortly after he had read Vienna's demarche. "I at once gave my opinion to His Excellency [Jagow's memoirs would state] that the contents of the Austrian note to Serbia seemed pretty stiff and going beyond its purpose . . . I expressed my pained surprise . . . that the decisions of the Austrian government had been communicated to us so tardily that we were deprived of the possibility of giving our views on it. The Chancellor, too, to whom I at once submitted the text of the ultimatum, thought it was too harsh."

If Berlin thought so, in its heart of hearts, what about capitals less friendly?

On July 24, the British Foreign Secretary Sir Edward Grey returned to London from trout fishing on the river Itchen, and the First Lord of the Admiralty Mr. Winston Churchill from his beach idyll near Norfolk. They met in Parliament, which was still in something of a dither over the Irish Home Rule Bill. But the debate suddenly gave way to Sir Edward's voice. He was reading from a paper just handed to him—the Austrian note to Serbia, ". . . an ultimatum [this is Churchill describing the scene] such as had never been penned in modern times before. The parishes of Fermanagh and Tyrone [i.e., the Irish issue] faded back into the mists . . . and a strange new light fell on the map of Europe."

Little more than forty-eight hours later the Admiralty announced that new orders had been issued to the First and Second Fleets of the British Navy. They were the most powerful units of the world's most powerful marine force, and they happened to be concentrated in the English Channel for maneuvers just finished. Now, contrary to previous plans, they were not to disperse. All shore leaves were cancelled.

In Paris, a hastily called Ministerial Council cabled the text of the Austrian "jewel" to President Poincaré on the battle cruiser *France*. Poincaré was about to visit some Scandinavian ports. He cancelled all further travels. The *France* headed straight for Dunkirk.

At his summer residence on the Gulf of Finland, the Tsar stopped playing tennis. The Russian General Staff *Gazette* proclaimed a "State of Pre-Mobilization." It involved, among other measures, preparations to deploy troops quickly at "any threatened frontier" (in this case the Austrian) and the recall of reservists to bring border divisions to full strength.

Overnight Berchtold's libretto had gone to pieces. He had miscalculated entirely its effects on its intended audience.

The pause he had spun out so cunningly after Sarajevo; the lethargy so studiously orchestrated through four weeks; the dolce far niente put on by the Ballhausplatz that was to have gentled Europe into a summer sleep so sweet that, by the time it woke and rubbed its eyes, it would see Serbia crushed—all that artfulness had produced a very different outcome and an altogether unwanted mood.

During the long month, Sarajevo had dimmed into a trivializing distance. By the end of July, Vienna's abrupt growl at Serbia sounded—even in diplomatic French—like a savage vendetta over a remote cause. Huge Habsburg looked like a brute seizing a stale pretext to exterminate little Serbia. Now it was the ultimatum that looked like an outrage, not the Archduke's assassination.

And that wasn't all. Vienna's month-long "peace" act produced yet another unpleasant result. During the many days the Ballhausplatz had spent styling the nonultimatum super-ultimatum, General Conrad on his nonholiday holiday had seethed and scribbled and cabled in his Dolomite village, perfecting the mobilization schedules of his army. Of course he had put none of them in effect as yet—that would have rattled the fair-weather scenery. But with the demarche delivered, this backstage phase of his effort was over. On July 26, the General charged into Berchtold's office saying that the martial moves made by Serbia's friends in the last twenty-four hours had revised his plans. To prepare for all contingencies, Austria's forces must now be at absolutely maximum strength and in optimum condition before striking Belgrade—a goal he, Conrad, would need at least three weeks to reach; the army could not start its offensive until then.

Count von Berchtold took all this like a true Viennese. Yes, he had lost his poise temporarily in Ischl. But he recovered it fast, together with his instinct for make-believe. So the fiction that was to beguile Europe had misfired. Very well, he would produce another fiction.

This one he believed in himself. Cleverly it turned Conrad's bleak news of the Army's unreadiness into the semblance of an advantage. Now (as one of the Foreign Minister's lieutenants would later recall)

> Berchtold regarded even the declaration of war as not more than an extreme form of pressure to obtain a diplomatic surrender from Serbia which still had almost twenty days for reflection, seeing that military operations would not commence before August 15th . . .

How induce the proper "reflection" in Serbia and her allies? Again by theatrical means, naturally. The Foreign Minister decided that Habsburg would put on a face that was absolutely resolute *and* charmingly patient at the same time.

To show absolute resolve, Austria declared war on Serbia at 1 P.M. of July 28, by cable. For the first time in history a telegram opened hostilities between two countries (a first time balancing the last time of Austria's ultimatum in diplomatic French). Austria also trumpeted its determination with thousands of mobilization posters materializing overnight, black print on gold background, from one end of the Empire to the other; by patriotic fireworks in newspapers amenable to government influence; by the announcement that His Majesty was about to issue a ringing manifesto calling his subjects to arms.

At the same time the mask of charming patience spoke. Austrian ambassadors—especially those accredited with Serbia's friends—pointed to Habsburg restraint. Here was a great power at war. Yet so far Austria had not taken advantage of its enemy's smallness but only of the fact that the Serb capital lay just across from the Austrian border. Austria had done no more than shell that capital from its own territory. There was still no invasion of Serbia. Furthermore, despite the enormity of Sarajevo, the Austrian government asked only justice from Belgrade and not one square inch of Serbian land.

Surely this demonstrated Vienna's patience? As for Vienna's charm, consider her treatment of General Radomir Putnik, Chief of Staff of the Serbian Armed Forces. When Vienna had surprised Belgrade with the ultimatum, the General was still sipping the waters of the Austrian spa Bad Gleichenberg. Of course he departed instantly. On his way home via Budapest, he was hauled off the train and held as a potential prisoner of war—the war Austria would declare within hours.

However, "orders from an All-Highest level" had the General released. An Austrian army physician was detailed to attend the General's asthma while he remained on Austrian soil. An honor guard escorted him to the personal train of General Conrad; and it was in the luxury of Conrad's salon car that he was allowed to proceed to the Serbian border to assume command against the troops of his host.

Shouldn't such Viennese gallantry sway Belgrade's heart, even as Austria's might should soften Belgrade's impertinence? And wouldn't Belgrade's allies be wise to help Belgrade practice moderation? Shouldn't they join Berchtold's effort to prevent the deepening and widening, indeed the very continuance, of the conflict? Shouldn't they make Belgrade see reason on the one sticking point in the Austrian demarche (participation of Austrian police in the pursuit of Sarajevo accomplices on Serbian soil)—the one point whose settlement on Austrian terms would stop the war before it had really begun? This was the outline of Berchtold's new plot. But Libretto B fared no better than Libretto A. And once more Germany chimed in with the wrong note.

Not that Berlin had changed its—public—willingness to sing along. This time, though, the Heldentenor himself, the Kaiser, insisted on making an entrance. When the crisis broke, he was still away on his Nordic cruise. His ministers tried to keep him there. They knew too well His Majesty's impulsiveness, unevenness, hollowness—the thunder of his tongue, the shaking of his knees. During Libretto A they had encouraged the blithe continuation of his voyage. The Wilhelmstrasse had radioed the Imperial yacht *Hohenzollern* as little of the tension as late as possible. In fact, the Kaiser first learned of the

Austrian ultimatum not from his Berlin Chancellery but from his yacht's radio officer who had listened to news agency reports on July 24.

This irritated Wilhelm, but not enough to abandon his sail along the glitter of the fjords. He did ask Berlin to keep him abreast of developments in detail. In return he received a long, ingeniously murky telegram from his Chancellor, climaxing in the sentence "the diplomatic situation is not entirely clear." By then it was early in the morning of July 27. Libretto B was on. The Kaiser wired Berlin that he proposed to head home. Back came a telegram saying "Your Majesty's sudden reappearance might cause undue alarm." And just that alarmed His Majesty at last.

Never mind that Berlin had just announced that he would not return until August 2. He not only decided to turn his yacht around, he transferred to the swiftest of his escorting cruisers, the *Rostock*, to speed his homecoming.

On the afternoon of July 27, he hastened down the gangplank at Swinnemünde to be greeted by his pale, hand-kissing ministers as well as by the news that stock markets were quaking all over Europe. En route to Berlin he realized that a major crisis had matured rapidly in his absence. He faced it in character, by blurting out epithets. At this point he still blurted grandiosely, hand on sword hilt, repeating some exclamations he had made on board. He called Berchtold "a donkey" for pledging to let Serbia keep all its territory. He accused his naval chief of "incredible presumption" for advising against drastic fleet movements at this precarious juncture. He said that the Balkan countries were mostly contemptible scum.

Still exclamatory, he entered Potsdam Palace on the evening of July 27. The text of Serbia's response to the ultimatum had reached Berlin rather tardily only that afternoon.

But the German Foreign Minister delayed its transmission to Potsdam yet further. He waited until late at night after the Kaiser had retired: better to let His Majesty calm down first with a good rest.

Next morning Wilhelm was shown the Serbian note. Again he began to exclaim—but in the opposite direction. "A brilliant achievement in a time limit of only twenty-four hours!" he annotated Belgrade's reply. "More than one could have expected! A great moral success for Vienna! All reason for war is gone! After that I should never have ordered mobilization!"

As he scribbled this, he had no idea that Vienna had done much more than mobilize. A few minutes later, an aide handed him a bulletin: Austria had declared war. It staggered the Kaiser. Within an hour the German Chancellor von Bethmann-Hollweg stood before him, peremptorily summoned, "very humble, with a pale and wretched face."

"How did all this happen?" the Kaiser demanded.

Bethmann tried to explain the purpose and hope of Libretto A, as devised by Vienna: true, the nonultimatum that was an ultimatum had not worked out right, but perhaps this war just declared would yet turn into a nonwar, maybe the Serbs would give in after all, maybe—

Wilhelm, blurting epithets, cut him off. The Chancellor, "utterly cowed, admitted that he had been deceived all along by Vienna and submitted his resignation." Wilhelm refused him.

"You have cooked this broth," said His Majesty. "Now you are going to eat it."

The Kaiser knew that it was beyond his ability to eat it himself. According to Prince Bernard von Bülow—eye-witness of the scene above—Wilhelm was "well aware that he was a neurasthenic. His exaggerations were mainly meant to ring in the ears of the Foreign Office . . . His jingo speeches intended to give the impression that here was another Frederick the Great. But he did not trust his nerves under the strain of any really critical situation. The moment there was danger His Majesty became uncomfortably conscious that he would never lead an army in the field. Wilhelm did not want war."

Quite simply the Kaiser did not feel up to the nervy part demanded of him by Vienna's script. Therefore the Chancellor must renounce all participation in Libretto B, claiming that Germany had been lured into it by Vienna's seductive bad faith. Almost immediately after the Kaiser had dressed him down, the German Chancellor wired his ambassador at the Habsburg Court:

> I regard the attitude of Austria with increasing astonishment . . . Austria is entertaining plans which it finds advisable to keep secret from us in order to ensure herself of our support in any event . . . Pray speak to Count von Berchtold with great emphasis . . .

With great emphasis the Ambassador spoke to Count von Berchtold about Berlin's new position. In effect this position constituted Libretto C, authored posthaste by the Kaiser himself: Vienna should forgo the total knuckling-under of Serbia; instead it should proceed with a temporary and token occupation of Belgrade, just across the frontier, avoiding any further substantial penetration of territory. After this punishment Austria should declare its honor satisfied and withdraw.

* * *

But Libretto C failed much faster than Librettos A or B. It could not go far without Franz Joseph's approval. However, by the time Wilhelm proposed it to him on July 28, the old Emperor had passed the point of authorizing alternatives to the inevitable. He was now the prisoner of quite another, invincible dramaturgy.

On July 25, his Minister of War had appeared in audience at Ischl to receive permission to mobilize. Franz Joseph gave it, not like a monarch commanding a general but like a puppet controlled by a ghost. "Go . . ." he had whispered to the Minister. "Go. . . . I can do no other." A few hours later he walked on foot, as usual, to the villa of Frau Schratt. From the way he stooped his way across the little bridge before her gate, she knew what turn history had taken. "I have done my best," he said to her. "But now it is the end."

"Very quickly," the Tsar of Russia cabled a few days later to his cousin and soon foe, the Kaiser, "I shall be overwhelmed by the pressure brought on me." Not only had Franz Joseph I and Nicholas II been disenfranchised but so had all their august peers.

Their ministers thrashed about impotently. They had been yanked from their vacations, out of their hunting boots, their fishing waders, their beach wear. The crisis had slammed them back into their striped trousers. Now they were pacing around telegraph keys that kept clattering adjurations and avowals from chancellery to chancellery. Vienna cabled St. Petersburg that the Austrian Army had mobilized solely against Serbia. St. Petersburg cabled Vienna that the Russian mobilization was only partial and wholly defensive. Berlin cabled Paris about the dangerous consequences of French mobilization. Paris cabled that it mobilized only to protect French security. Berlin cabled London, urging Britain to stop the mobilization of its allies. London cabled Berlin, asking

Germany to ask Austria to use mediation, not mobilization, in the Serbian matter. Austria cabled London its willingness to negotiate but without delaying its "operations against Serbia." London cabled Vienna that it could not remain neutral in a European war. All cables invoked the sacredness of peace. All countries involved kept thrusting bayonets into the hands of their young men.

Power had drained from thrones and chancelleries into the offices of Chiefs of Staff. Clumsily, diplomats tried to bluff their counterparts into peace. Efficiently, each Chief of Staff activated his mobilizing apparatus. Inevitably, the mobilizations accelerated each other.

Now the subordination of Chiefs of Staff to heads of state was only nominal. Now the Chiefs drew their true prerogative from an unofficial but tremendous power. Overnight this power had become visible. It was surging through the streets all over the continent.

34

THE NEW POWER DID NOT WAIT FOR PROCLAMATIONS FROM GOVERNMENTS. It needed no galvanizing by propaganda, no goading from the press (which was by no means uniformly militant in the principal countries). The new power had already divided the world into Allies-until-Victory and Enemies-unto-Death. This new power had gathered thousands along the shores of the Danube where they sang, fervently, "The Watch on the Rhine" against France. The new power burned German flags in Paris while café orchestras along the Champs Elysées played "God Save the King." The new power raised a sea of fists against the Russian Embassy in Vienna, against the German Embassy in Paris, and its stones shattered eleven windows of the British Embassy in Berlin. Even restaurants felt the fingers of the new power. "Menu cards here in Vienna," Karl Kraus wrote to his beloved Sidonie, "now have their English and French translations crossed out. Things are getting more and more idiotic . . ."

But Kraus himself knew better. It wasn't mere idiocy that was governing things now. It was something far more formidable. Sarajevo had only been a flash point of its strength.

> Our politicians [Kraus said in *Die Fackel* of July 1914] are unconsciously right in their suspicion that "behind this schoolboy . . . who killed the Archduke and his wife stand others who cannot be apprehended and who are responsible for the weapon used." No less a force than progress stands behind this deed—progress and education unmoored from God . . .

A key sentence on the century's key moment as nations were turning themselves into regiments. Kraus did not amplify here on the God from whom progress had severed mankind so fatally. He had done that earlier elsewhere, in his poem "The Dying Man." There God meant the Presence in the pristine garden that was both "source and destination." But now men had paved over His soil and their souls. Concrete had strangled the "source." They had lost their sense of origin and of final purpose. Therefore they must claw from the barrenness a new "destination"—an angrier destiny. Under the oppressiveness of a loss, the new power had been forged.

It had forged the life of Gavrilo Princip, modernity's foremost assassin, who had triggered the crisis. The family of "this schoolboy" had lived for centuries in an approximation, however imperfect, of Kraus's garden. As a *zadruga,* that is, as a tight-knit, farm-based Bosnian clan, the Princips had raised their own corn, milled their own flour, baked their own loaves, and worshipped a God close enough to their roof to be their very own protector.

Progress had broken all that apart. Princip's father could no longer create bread from his earth. He could no longer live his livelihood. He must earn it with the estranged, endless trudgings of a postman. His son Gavrilo, more educated than his father, more sensitive, more starved for the wholeness that is holiness and thus more resentful of the ruins all about him, had to seek another garden. He sought something that would satisfy his disorientation and his anger; something which, as his readings of Nietzsche suggested, would restore the valor of the vital principle that his race had lost. He found it in the Black Hand. It conjured "the earth that nourishes . . . the sun that warms." It was part of the new power. It offered him the cohesion, the communal fortitude and faith of the shattered *zadruga.*

Progress had shattered numberless *zadrugas* by hundreds of other ethnic names, from the hamlet of Predappio in Italy's Romagna where a blacksmith named Mussolini had a son named Benito, to the village of Didi-Lilo in Russia's Transcaucasia where a cobbler named Dzhugashvili sired a boy later called Stalin. The Stalins, Mussolinis, Hitlers, Princips were the monsters of progress. Progress had abused and bruised them, but they could turn the sting outward and avenge the injury. There were many millions like them with less fury in their bafflement, less steel in their deprivation: the *lumpenproletariat* on whose backs Europe rode toward the marvels of the new century. Their anonymous pain fermented the new power.

A year before Sarajevo, Vienna's *Arbeiter Zeitung* published a survey documenting that it was always the most rapidly industrializing areas which produced among the poor the highest rate of alcoholism, of syphillis and tuberculosis, of emotional pathology, and by far the highest rate of suicide. Their sickbeds and their graves marked the trail of "progress unmoored from God." But now Princip's deed was inspiriting its live and able-bodied victims. With two shots he had set in motion a firestorm that was to burn meaning into the numbest slums.

Instead of beating their heads against the prison of their class, instead of deadening themselves with toil or liquor, the masses now had something to kill for. Before Sarajevo, hundreds of thousands had been on strike in Russia. Not long afterwards the factories hummed again all day. At night, toilers massed before the Winter Palace in St. Petersburg with torches and holy ensigns, acclaiming the Tsar as their defender. "Wonderful times . . ." said a British diplomat who saw the spectacle. "Russia seems to have been completely transformed."

In Vienna the transformation was just as wonderful. On May Day 1914, workers had marched on the Ringstrasse with the chant *"Frieden, Brot, und Freiheit!"* ("Peace, Bread, and Freedom!"). On August 1, many of the same crowd marched again with *"Alle Serben müssen sterben!"* ("All Serbs must die!"). "The patriotic enthusiasm of the masses in Austria-Hungary seemed especially surprising," Trotsky wrote in his autobiography. "I strode along the main street of the familiar Vienna and watched the most amazing crowd fill the fashionable Ring, a crowd in which hopes had been awakened . . .

What was it that drew them to the square in front of the War Ministry? . . . Would it have been possible at any other time for porters, laundresses, shoemakers, apprentices to feel themselves masters of the Ring? . . . In their demonstrations for the glory of Habsburg arms, I detected something familiar to me from the October days of 1905 [when Trotsky had led a short-lived insurrection]. No wonder that in history war has so often been the mother of revolution."

In Paris workers had sung the "Internationale" on May Day before returning to their tenements. Now their throats rang with the "Marseillaise" while the Kaiser's effigy went up in flames. Everywhere life leaped from lonely gray grind to grand national adventure. Hurrah!

But the poor weren't the only ones grateful for the zest provided by the crisis. The middle classes, too, felt exhausted and baffled. Progress had fed them well. Yet the more meat on their table, the less tang was there to each morsel, the more intolerable the superior cut of somebody else's steak. No doubt they were dining well. Were they still eating together? They consumed as they produced: aggressively against each other. When worshipping, they knelt on velvet in churches unmoored from a common God. Their mansions brimmed, but they did not feel sheltered. They promenaded in spats and top hats—where from? To what end?

Germany's most popular almanac for 1913 featured a poem by the writer Alfred Walter Heymel. It was called *"Eine Sehnsucht aus der Zeit"* ("A Longing in Our Times").

Im Friedensreichtum wird uns tödlich bang.
Wir kennen Müssen nicht noch Können oder Sollen
Und sehnen uns und schreien nach dem Kriege.

(In the wealth of peace we feel the deadliest dread.
We are bereft of prowess, mission, or direction,
And long and cry for war.)

Hurrah!

The cry came, as the British poet Rupert Brooke phrased it, from "a world grown old and cold and weary." It came from "this foul peace which drags on and on . . ." as General Conrad wrote to his mistress Gina von Reininghaus. For worker or burgher or poet or Chief of Staff, Mars was the God of Liberation. "A crisis had entered Western culture," a high Habsburg official would write later, "and many of its representative citizens had been oversaturated into desperation. Like men longing for a thunderstorm to relieve them of the summer's sultriness, so the generation of 1914 believed in the relief that war might bring." Their longing for thunder was the new power.

The thunderstorm with its mortal flash—this image shivers ubiquitously through the whole period. In the summer of 1914, Europe's musical sensation was still Stravinsky's *Rite of Spring* premiered a year earlier in Paris, where Nijinsky's "lightning leaps" celebrated the theme of the ballet, namely the enchantments of death.

In painting, a dominant mode was Futurism, which anticipated the lightning-like strokes of stroboscopic photography; the Futurist manifesto exalted war because it would blast away the stultification of present concepts and structures; as though defining lightning's lethal beauty, the manifesto proclaimed that "movement and light must destroy the substance of objects."

"The sense of approaching catastrophe," wrote a Futurist who didn't know he was one, in his book *Mein Kampf*, "turned at last to longing: Let heaven finally give reign to the fate that could no longer be thwarted. And then the first mighty lightning flash struck the earth; the storm was unleashed, and with the thunder of heaven there mingled the roar of the World War batteries."

"The war," said German Chancellor von Bethmann-Hollweg in his book on the subject, "would be a thunderstorm to clear the air."

"The palpable beginnings of the European crisis reach back a number of years," wrote Count Ottokar Czernin who would succeed Count von Berchtold as Habsburg Foreign Minister, ". . . certain dynamics must take their course before a thunderstorm discharges its lightning and thunder."

"I am convinced the storm is coming," French President Raymond Poincaré remarked to a friend in July of 1914. "Where and when the storm will break I cannot say."

"There is a crisis in the air," Freud had written Lou Andreas-Salomé as 1913 turned to 1914, referring to Jung yet articulating much more than psychoanalytic weather. "May it soon explode so that the air is cleared!"

The shots of Sarajevo sounded like an answer to many prayers in many nations. Afterwards some tried in vain to push back the bolt that came down from the blue—for example, in Paris on the sudden death of Jean Jaurès, the French Socialist leader and Europe's most eloquent voice against war. On July 31, as he sat in the Café du Croissant, a nationalist zealot gunned him down. His comrades organized a pacifist parade around his body. They were swamped by a mob of conscripts. Brand-new lieutenants graduated from St. Cyr led the warriors, shouting, "We'll go into battle with white plumes on our kepis and with white gloves on our hands!" Behind them young men roared by the happy thousands. The French General Staff planned for 87 percent of called-up reservists to appear at induction centers; 98.5 percent did. Hurrah!

In Austria, where Viktor Adler had groomed the worker to be a thinker and a doer, the proletariat accomplished not a single thoughtful act to halt disaster. Adler himself, though, did intervene in history without knowing it. During the anti-Russian hysteria in Austria, Habsburg constables in Galicia arrested Lenin "as a Tsarist spy" on August 8. In response to an appeal from Lenin's wife, Adler went to the headquarters of the political police in Vienna, cited their own sponsorship of this useful Bolshevik as an enemy of the Tsar and thus as a friend of Austria (Hurrah!), and obtained Lenin's release and safe passage first to Vienna, then to Switzerland. A few days later he helped usher Trotsky across the Swiss border. In other words, Adler put into place the preliminaries of the Russian Revolution three years later.

He also couldn't help collaborating in the genesis of its most important preliminary, namely that of the Great War. No matter that his *Arbeiter Zeitung* had published many warnings against the threat of international slaughter. On August 5, the day before Austria issued its first declaration of war against a major power—Russia—this same *Arbeiter Zeitung* intoned, "However the fates decide, we hope they will decide for the holy cause of the German people." Hurrah! Two days earlier Adler's paper had reported that his German comrades, the Socialist deputies to the Reichstag in Berlin, had joined the other parties in voting the government the war credits it needed. This action marked, said the *Arbeiter Zeitung*, ". . . the proudest and loftiest exaltation of the German spirit." Hurrah!

Two men made dogged, last-ditch attempts against that inexorable hurrah. They were Nicky and Willy. That was how the two Emperors signed their respective cables, which started jittering, on the night of July 29, between the palace of Tsar Nicholas II in St. Petersburg and the palace of Kaiser Wilhelm II in Potsdam. Nicky "in the name of our old friendship" begged Willy to stop his Austrian ally from going too far. Willy, in turn, declaring himself to be Nicky's "sincere and devoted friend and cousin," said he was sure that Nicky as a fellow monarch wanted to see the murder of the Austrian Crown Prince duly punished. Nicky thanked Willy for "the conciliatory and fraternal" message but in view of it voiced astonishment at the ominous tone of the note just delivered by Willy's ambassador to his, Nicky's, Foreign Minister. Willy answered that just because Nicky shared so cordially the wish for peace, he hoped Nicky would agree to remain "in a spectator role" in the Vienna-Belgrade conflict, for only by localizing the matter and by not taking Russian military measures could Nicky avoid "involving Europe in the most horrible war ever witnessed." In reply, Nicky, "grateful for the speed of your answer," assured Willy that all Russian military measures were purely precautionary with no offensive intent and should therefore not interfere with Willy's "much-valued role as mediator with Vienna." Willy's response regretted that he could not mediate in Vienna while Russia persisted in mobilizing. To which Nicky answered that it was "technically impossible" to stop Russian military preparations but that since, like Willy, he was very far from wishing war, he gave Willy his solemn words that "my troops shall not commit any provocative action." Whereupon Willy thanked Nicky for his telegram but said that "only immediate, clear, unmistakable, and affirmative answer from your government can avoid endless misery." And he begged Nicky to order his troops "on no account to commit the slightest act of trespassing over our frontiers."

This cable, ending the series, leaped from Berlin to St.

Petersburg on August 1, at 10:30 P.M. Three and a half hours earlier, at 7 P.M., the Kaiser's ambassador had presented the German Government's declaration of war to the Russian Foreign Minister.

It was no longer important what Willy said to Nicky when. Quite aptly the two Emperors had reduced themselves to diminutives: two sashed little figurines raising toy scepters against the storm. The storm paid little attention. All over the continent young men filed into barracks in clockwork fulfillment of mobilization plans. Troop trains kept hurtling toward frontiers.

The martial *hurrah* of multitudes kept echoing on the square before Wilhelm's palace. Through his Lord Chamberlain the Kaiser thanked his subjects for this show of loyalty but asked them to disperse "so that His Majesty can attend undisturbed to the challenges of leadership." The hurrahs continued.

Less than twenty-four hours after Willy's final telegram to Nicky, Willy rose from his desk in the Star Room of his palace. It was a desk made from the wood of Lord Nelson's flagship *Victory*—a gift from Willy's grandmother Queen Victoria. On this desk he had just signed the order that let his soldiers flood across the borders of Luxembourg and then of Belgium. "Gentlemen," he said hoarsely to the military dignitaries assembled around him, "you will live to regret this."

Shortly afterward he sent a note to the British ambassador: Let King George of England be informed that he, Wilhelm, would never ever, as long as he lived, wear again the uniform of a British Field Marshal. Coming from the Kaiser, this signified ultimate bitterness. As usual, his statesmanship became a matter of epaulettes. From now on his role would be to gesticulate. Others commanded.

In these commanders the new power now began to manifest itself quite nakedly. They were the ones who controlled the final libretto, Libretto D, the libretto of Kraus's progress crescendoing toward a titanic fusillade. The spotlight, after shifting from the futility of Excellencies to the helplessness of Majesties, now came to rest on the supremacy of generals.

On July 31, German Chief of Staff von Moltke sent his Austrian counterpart a cable whose imperatives bluntly bypassed the Ministers of War in Vienna and in Berlin; a telegram which ignored both Emperors, theoretically the All-Highest decision-makers. "Stand firm!" von Moltke cabled Conrad. "Austria must fully mobilize at once!"

"How odd," Foreign Minister von Berchtold said when Conrad showed him the message. It contradicted the tenor of two other cables, one from the German Chancellor to himself, the other from Wilhelm to Franz Joseph. "Who rules in Berlin?"

He might just as well have asked: "Who rules in Vienna?" By then his own cables were following almost verbatim General Conrad's proposals.

Who ruled in Russia? "I shall smash my telephone," the Russian Chief of Staff General Janushkevich told the Russian Foreign Minister. By which he meant that he would refuse to do again what he had done the day before, namely to rescind mobilization on telephoned orders from the Tsar. His pressure forced the Tsar to renew the order. "Now you can smash your telephone," said the Foreign Minister meekly.

Who ruled in France? Not René Viviani, though he was Prime Minister as well as Foreign Minister. His problem: He was a Socialist and peace-seeker. He had wept at the bier of the great pacifist Jean Jaurès slain on July 31. He had given his arm to the widow walking behind the coffin on the way to the grave. Therefore it didn't matter that he was the Chief Executive of the Republic while Raymond Poincaré as President was only the symbol of state. It did matter that Poincaré had been born in Lorraine, the province lost by France to Germany in the War of 1870 and which must be won back again. It mattered that Poincaré had a stake in the war to come. Hurrah!

Under Poincaré's secret manipulation, the French Embassy in St. Petersburg stopped being an instrument of Foreign Minister Viviani and became a tool of General Joseph Joffre, Chief of the French General Staff. The French ambassador withheld from his Foreign Minister news of the martial intentions of the Russian General Staff. But he did convey General Joffre's encouragement to his Russian colleagues "to commence an offensive against East Prussia soonest." The ambassador deliberately delayed Viviani's very different, moderating words to St. Petersburg until it was too late.

"Russian troops," Poincaré announced to the French cabinet on August 2, "will be in Berlin by All Saints' Day." Hurrah! The Zeitgeist vested in him the power withheld by the French constitution.

Who ruled in Britain? On July 29, First Lord of the Admiralty Winston Churchill wrote his wife that he would "do my best for peace and nothing would induce me to wrongfully strike the first blow." Yet the same letter confessed that "war preparations have a hideous fascination for me. I pray to God to forgive me for such fearful moods of levity." Two days later he mobilized the fleet, against the explicit decision of the British cabinet. "Winston," said Prime Minister Asquith indulgently, "has his war paint on." "The lamps are going out all over Europe," said Foreign Secretary Sir Edward Grey. "We shall not see them lit again in our lifetime." The shores darkened. Churchill's dreadnoughts fanned out across the North Sea. Hurrah!

* * *

Who ruled the world? In Habsburg's Prague, the insurance official Franz Kafka was just developing some notions on the subject. At another time he was to refer to himself ruefully as "the nerve end of humanity." Right now, on July 29, 1914, the day after Austria's declaration of War on Serbia, two days before Germany's ultimatum to Russia, the name "Josef K" appears for the first time in Kafka's journal. That week he began to sketch out ideas for *The Trial*[*]—the novel registering in a personal compass an evil erupting internationally: some incalculable force, insidious, inexorable, operating beyond all normal jurisdictions, closing in on its victims.

With what phrases did such power enter history? This was the time when ambassador after ambassador appeared before Foreign Minister after Foreign Minister to declare that he had the honor to inform His Excellency that his government, in order to protect the security and integrity of its realm, was forced to consider itself at war.

Honor? Security? Integrity? Excellency?

On August 9, 1914, while such words were still being intoned, Ludwig Wittgenstein began to ruminate systematically about the disjunction between language and truth. On that day he began the notebook that led to his *Tractatus Logico-philosophicus*. The *Tractatus*, purging language of its routine shams, was born on the grandest proscenium of such shams, Imperial Habsburg. Flourish, not fact, held the realm together; flourish painted the mirage of dynastic communality between crown and people. Progress was

[*] The other cornerstone of modernist fiction also saw birth on Habsburg soil: in March 1914, in Trieste, James Joyce started to write *Ulysses*.

corroding all things communal, but flourish painted over the corrosion. In the Empire of the flourish, Wittgenstein developed the philosophy that punctured, on the deepest modernist level, the theatrics of style. And here Kafka wrote the paradigmatic modernist novel, steeped in the angst underlying our daily charades.

Meanwhile great charades of state lit up the horizon. On August 4, the Kaiser stood on the balcony of his Berlin palace. He had not wept, like the Tsar, when the declaration of war had been published. But his face (in Grand Admiral von Tirpitz's description) "looked ravaged and tragic." The thousands who had come to hear him didn't notice. They only saw that their sovereign wore a spiked helmet under which his mouth shouted its mustachioed duty from the speech text handed him: *"We draw the sword with a clean conscience and clean hands . . . from now on I no longer know parties. I only know Germans!"*

Hurrah!

The masses cheered. They cheered him and their own relief. Hurrah! Here in Berlin as well as in Paris, in London, in Vienna, in St. Petersburg, war had freed them from politics, from partisanship, from all apartness. Until now they had been mutually separated. Competition had driven them against each other. Or poverty had marooned them. Or they had been isolated in their cocoon of envy and alienation. Now it was all marvelously different. Now the worn-down unemployed, the trodden-under scullion, the unfulfilled genius, the bored coupon-clipper, the jaded boulevadier—they could all link arms and walk forward together in the same electrifying adventure, against the enemy. Now they were Germans together, Frenchmen together, Englishmen together, Russians together and—most astounding—ethnically motley Habsburg subjects together. The enemy made it possible for them to break through to one another. Now the same patriot warmth embosomed them all. "Hurrah!" they all cried with one voice. "Hurrah!"

The most inveterate outsiders joined this surge. In Munich, Adolf Hitler had been living without a friend, without a lover, without even the bleak commonalty of Vienna's *Männherheim.* "The war," he says in *Mein Kampf,* "liberated me from the painful feelings of my youth . . . I fell down on my knees and thanked heaven with an overflowing heart for granting me the good fortune to be alive at that time." Hurrah!

Dr. Sigmund Freud, outcast from his city's medical establishment, grim practitioner of the Viennese affectation of despising Vienna—this same Freud now said, "for the first time in thirty years I feel myself to be an Austrian"; that England (hitherto his favorite country) was "a hypocrite" for supporting "Serbia's impudence"; that "all my libido goes to Austria-Hungary." Now the war with Jung fell away. Freud hurried from Carlsbad back to Vienna, where his sons Martin and Ernst joined the colors "for the noble cause" to which the over-age Freud himself made a contribution: He refused to give male patients of conscription age Certificates of Nervous Disability; he would not help them evade service to their country. Hurrah!

Ludwig Wittgenstein *was* medically exempt from war service, having undergone a double hernia operation in July. He should have been immune to the war spirit since he was a recluse, a maverick, a deviant from norms sexual, semantic, or financial (he had just given away most of the vast fortune left him by his industrialist father). On August 9, he started his notebook exploring the deceptions of language. On August 7, he showed that he was at one with the deceived crowd. He enlisted. Hurrah!

Years earlier Arnold Schönberg had gone abroad because the Austrian capital grated on him as much as his music grated on it. In the summer of 1914, he returned and joined Vienna's own regiment, the Deutschmeister. The atonal heretic began to compose military marches for Austria's glory. Hurrah!

Oskar Kokoschka made the same fast transition from enfant terrible to waver of flag. Before Savajevo he had spoken of "the personal misery of living in Vienna, utterly alone, without a friend," and sought opportunities as distant as possible from the Danube, ". . . perhaps a commission for a fresco in America." After Sarajevo he sold his most valuable painting, *The Tempest* (showing him with Alma Mahler), to a Hamburg pharmacist. With the proceeds he bought a horse and a cavalry uniform—a light blue tunic with white facings, bright red breeches, and a brass helmet. Now he could volunteer for the 15th Imperial Dragoons who prized war so much that they shaved before each battle. Now Kokoschka's fellow rebel, the architect Adolf Loos, could print a photograph of the helmeted painter as a postcard publicizing Kokoschka's hurrah!

What about the poet Rainer Maria Rilke? Born in Habsburg Bohemia, he was an itinerant solitary, a free-floating mystic who considered Austria and Germany countries to which he was attached "only by language." In the summer of 1914, he reattached himself with a vengeance. He rhapsodized along with the throngs in German and Austrian streets. His *Five Cantos / August 1914* celebrate the War God:

> . . . the Lord of Battle has suddenly seized us
> Hurling the torch: and over a heart filled with homeland
> His reddened sky, where He reigns in His rage, is
> now screaming.

Hurrah!

"To be torn out of a dull capitalistic peace was good for many Germans," said Hermann Hesse. "I esteem the moral values of war on the whole rather highly." For Thomas Mann, war was "a purification, a liberation, an enormous hope. The victory of Germany will be a victory of soul over numbers." Hurrah!

It was a clamorous, resonant, exultant summer, this summer of "progress unmoored from God." It was a summer catapulting men from their separate vacations into a much higher, gallant, and collective holiday. "We saw war," Freud would write some months later "as an opportunity for demonstrating the progress of mankind in communal feeling . . . a chivalrous crusade."

"What is progress in my sense?" asked Nietzsche, "I, too, speak of a 'return to nature,' although it is not really a going back but a progress forward—an *ascent* up into the high, free, even terrible nature and naturalness, where great tasks are something one plays with . . . Napoleon was a piece of 'return to nature.' "

Nietzsche had written this twenty-five years earlier, but he was the patron saint of the summer of 1914. That summer millions began to ascend not to Kraus's garden of pristine repose but to Nietzsche's jungled Napoleonic proving ground. It embowered and empowered them. It delivered them from soot, squalor, impotence, loneliness. Here they found what Gavrilo Princip—assassin of the Archduke, disciple of Nietzsche—had invoked when he swore the Black Hand oath: "the sun that warms . . . the earth that nourishes . . ."

* * *

And the sun shone on, over Bad Ischl with its hills and parks but no longer with its Emperor Franz Joseph. On July 27 he settled down to the last official act he was to perform in his Alpine villa. He revised the "Manifesto to My Peoples" written in his name. From a phrase characterizing Serbia he deleted "blind insolence." He struck the words "inspired by traditions of a glorious past" from a sentence describing the Empire's armed forces. The same day he had said to General Conrad: "If the monarchy goes under, let it go under with dignity." If war must be proclaimed to his peoples, let it be a proclamation without bathos.

Karl Kraus, the scourge of verbiage, was awed by the proclamation. He called it, "An august statement . . . a poem."

To the end Franz Joseph remained the steward of Imperial taste. Now the end was close.

On the morning of July 29, he left Ischl for Vienna, never to return. On August 6, when war was declared between Austria and Russia, he quietly removed from his uniform a decoration he had worn for sixty-five years: the Cross of St. George, Third Class, conferred on him in 1849 by Tsar Nicholas I. For the twenty-six months that were left of his life, he never stirred from Schönbrunn Palace.

The disorder he had sought to cure after Sarajevo had lapsed yet further into an unforeseen disarray, into a derangement whose wild pyrotechnics dazzled Europe. The librettos of his Foreign Minister had been exploded; the populace applauded the glow of the fragments. Machine guns were beginning to perforate the bows and hand-kisses of the stage Franz Joseph had commanded for two thirds of a century. But the bowers of bows and the kissers of hands did not know yet that they were bleeding. All they felt was a thrill and a tingle.

Franz Joseph felt something more final. A change in the Emperor's will detailed how his descendants would receive his fortune, should the family lose the crown. The last principal of the Habsburg drama prepared to retreat into the wings.

His retirement was partial and discreet. Other exits had official character. Sir Maurice de Bunsen, British Ambassador to Austria, turned out to be the last Western diplomat to leave the capital. On August 12, he made this sad statement to Foreign Minister Count von Berchtold: "As of twelve o'clock tonight, Great Britain and Austria will be in a state of war." Berchtold, ever the gentleman, bowed and assured His Excellency that "though Austria must accept this challenge, the two states are still associated politically and morally by tradition and sympathies and common interests."

Two days later, on August 14, the Ambassador and his wife left their residence for the West Railroad Terminal where Berchtold had arranged a private salon train for them, bound for neutral Switzerland.

Much of the town's anti-Allied anger had dissipated, though it had not lost its patriotic exhilaration. The de Bunsens encountered no hostility. They were accompanied by police in dress uniform, resembling an honor guard, and by their own wistful thoughts. It was hard to say good-bye to this city. Eight months ago they had taken up their posts, in December of 1913, during the swirl of the social season. They had leased a castle from Count Hoyos, "a dream of beauty," according to Lady de Bunsen's diary. The whole Danubian ambiance had enchanted them, especially Vienna's carnival, which had begun shortly after their arrival. "The mise-en-scène," Lady de Bunsen had mused of these revels, "was wonderful."

And now, as they departed, the mise-en-scène maintained its wonder. On the way to their train they met an artillery regiment also en route to a railway station. Green sprigs bounced from the kepis of the soldiers, roses garlanded the cannons, a band lilted the "Radetzky March," the march that is more polka than march. Housewives waved kerchiefs from windows, children skipped along, girls popped sweets into the recruits' pockets, all prancing and laughing and never missing a single musical beat. It was an alfresco dance, festive with sun, sporting happy masks.

Of course similar scenes enlivened other capitals as well. They sparkled on the Champs Elysées, at Picadilly Circus, along the Nevsky Prospekt, and up and down the Wilhelmstrasse. But Vienna—origin of this great international midsummer frolic—Vienna out-waltzed friend and foe alike in celebration.

The World War had come to the city by the Danube, dressed as a ball. Tra-la . . . Hurrah! . . .

AFTERWORD

On October 28, 1914, the Sarajevo District Court sentenced Gavrilo Princip to twenty years of hard labor, with a fast once a month; one day a year—June 28, the date of the assassination—he was to spend on a hard bed in a darkened cell. The same sentence was imposed on Trifko Grabež and Nedeljko Cabrinović. These three were under-age for the death penalty. Danilo Ilić, the oldest of the team, was sentenced to be hanged.

Ilić was executed on February 3, 1915. Princip, Grabež, and Cabrinović were removed to the Bohemian fortress at Theresienstadt (later site of the concentration camp under the Third Reich). At Theresienstadt, Cabrinović died on January 23, 1916, of tuberculosis. Grabež died here, also of tuberculosis, on October 21, 1916. Princip died in Theresienstadt of the same disease on April 28, 1918. It is probable that malnutrition and prison conditions contributed to these young deaths.

On a wall of Princip's cell, the following lines were found, written in pencil:

> Our ghosts will walk through Vienna
> And roam through the Palace
> Frightening the Lords.

AFTERWORD TO THE DA CAPO EDITION

WHEN I FINISHED THESE PAGES IN 1989, THE BALKAN MAP REVEALED only half of the devastating truth in Max Weber's observation: "History is a web of unintended circumstances." In response to the assassination of archduke Franz Ferdinand by the Serb Gavrilo Princip in 1914, Austria intended to uphold the honor and integrity of its realm by declaring war on Serbia. Consequence: By 1918, the Hapsburg empire lay shattered into jagged pieces.

Princip's intention, on the other hand, seemed to have prospered. The bullet he put through the archduke's neck did more than punish an Austrian oppressor; it kindled the global conflagration whose aftermath saw the South Slavs unite into one country. Yugoslavia, Princip's dream, emerged from the slaughter as a breathing reality. During World War II the Nazis abrogated it briefly. In 1946 it revived, continued on under communism, and persisted after Tito's death into the late 1980s.

But soon after 1989—the year of this book's publication—history dropped the other shoe. With cannon and sniper it began to disembowel Princip's utopia.

Today, in 2001, Yugoslavia is a minefield rather than a country. It consists of Serbia in turmoil clutching a simmering Montenegro. Slovenia, Croatia, and Macedonia have fought themselves apart into separate states. The province of Kosovo is an explosive U.N. protectorate. Two adversarial entities—one Muslim, one Serb—form Bosnia, each with its own parliament, police, and army. Croat troops ruined much of the Gravoho valley where Princip first brooded over his Pan-Slav ideals.

In the course of the last century, a pageant of the futilities Max Weber had in mind has moved past the corner of Appel Quai and Rudolf Street in Sarajevo. Here on a bright June morning in 1914 the two most fateful pistol shots of all time rang out. After the deed, Austria erected here a column in honor of the slain archduke. This yielded to a memorial to the slayer, put up by postwar Yugoslavia: The spot where Princip had pointed his weapon was marked, Hollywood-fashion, by footprints sunk in concrete. They celebrated Gavrilo Princip as megastar of Serb valor. Then, in 1997, the Muslim-dominated municipality of Sarajevo, hostile to all Serb insignia, used a jackhammer to pulverize Princip's sidewalk immortality.

One irony succeeds another. For what authority will prevent Serbs from avenging this insult to Princip's remembrance? It is the office of the High Representative in Bosnia-Herzegovina, instituted by the international community of fifty-five nations signing the Dayton Peace Accord in 1995. And who enforces the directives of the High Representative to keep the peace among ethnic strains and to establish democracy in Bosnia? A contingent of 25,000 NATO-led troops. Its headquarters are located in Ilidze, near Sarajevo, bristling with barbed wire and sandbag revetments. In 1914 this very building, then known as the Hotel Bosna, was the final lodging of the archduke and his wife before their murder the next morning. The landscape teems with paradoxes.

Not least among them is the background of Wolfgang Petritsch, the High Representative himself, appointed on the eighty-sixth anniversary of Franz Ferdinand's assassination. He has the power to dismiss Bosnian officials high or low and to dissolve parliament. His job before his present position was as Vienna's ambassador to Belgrade. He is, of all things, one of Austria's most brilliant diplomats. Letters threatening his life are often addressed to "His Honor Franz Ferdinand Petritsch."

And so Vienna 1914 ghosts through Sarajevo 2001. The future keeps mocking the past. The past, in eerie resilience, keeps shadowing the present.

—F. M.

ACKNOWLEDGMENTS

WRITING THIS BOOK HAS MEANT INCURRING DEBTS OF GRATITUDE ON TWO continents.

In the United States, my thanks go for vital assistance extended to me to Dr. Wolfgang Petritsch, head of the Austrian Information Service for North America, and his deputy, Dr. Irene Freudenschuss; to Dr. Wolfgang Waldner, Director of the Austrian Institute in New York, and to Friederike Zeitlhofer, the ever-patient, ever-forthcoming librarian of the Institute; to Dr. Walter Klement of the Austrian National Tourist Bureau in New York whose office has been generous with maps and geographical advice. I have also benefited from the tremendous resources of the New York Public Library. Pucek Kleinberger proved a source of comfort. Jonathan Kranz of the Graduate Center of the City University of New York aided this project with significant research. Martin Tanz and Dale Coudert were also helpful, as was David Kahn with his expertise on the history of military intelligence. I am also grateful to Minister Philip Hoyos of the Austrian Embassy in Washington, D.C.; to Roberta Corcoran; Sylvia Gardner-Wittgenstein; Dr. and Mrs. Erwin Chargaff; and my excellent copy editor, Gypsy da Silva.

In Britain, Dr. Edward Timms of Gonville and Caius College, Cambridge, has generously shared his erudition with me.

In Austria, the staff and stacks of the Österreichische Nationalbibliothek have been indispensable to my labors and so has Dr. Brigitta Zessner-Spitzenberg of the Bildarchiv. I am much obliged to the Literarische Verwertungsgesellschaft—and to its President, the novelist Milo Dor—for grants awarded me. I owe Prince Karl von Schwarzenberg many thanks for fine-tuned information on diplomatic and aristocratic aspects of the period covered in this book. Hetti von Bohlen und Halbach provided valuable access to the unpublished memoirs of her father, Prince Alois von Auersperg. I have been the beneficiary of Count Michael von Wolkenstein's advice and of his liberality with *Mohnstriezel.* The editors of the Socialist *Arbeiter Zeitung* furnished photocopied back volumes of their newspaper and thereby gave me the sort of education without which this book could not have been written. Inge Santner-Cyrus and Adolf Holl have been wonderful cultural hosts by the Danube. Further support and ideas have come from Hilde Spiel, Ernst Trost, Peter Marboe, Ernst Wolf Marboe, Alfred Payrleitner, Dr. Kurt Scholz of the office of Mayor Zilk of Vienna, and, at a rough estimate, at least five other people I have left out because of lamentable holes in my memory. Last, and far from least, I want to mention Wolfgang Kraus among my Viennese helpmeets. As President of the Österreichische Gesellschaft für Literatur and as a personal friend, he has been a treasure.

Now I come to a special category of thanks owed. There is my brother, Henry, Professor of Political Science at Queens College, CUNY. I have learned from his acumen and I have profited from the scholarship of his colleague, Professor Keith Eubank (History Dept., Queens College), who has given me crucial advice on researching facets of the genesis of the Great War. Robert Stewart, my editor at Scribners, has been the guardian angel of this book every step of the way. My wife, Marcia, was—as always—of incalculable help in shaping the manuscript.

—F.M.

SOURCE REFERENCES

Periodicals are referred to by the following abbreviations:

AZ	*Arbeiter Zeitung*
Fackel	*Die Fackel*
Fremd.	*Fremdenblatt*
IWE	*Illustrirtes Wiener Extrablatt*
INSJ	*Intelligence and National Security Journal*
NFP	*Neue Freie Presse*
NWT	*Neues Wiener Tagblatt*
WMW	*Wiener Medizinische Wochenschrift*
WZ	*Wiener Zeitung*

Books are referred to by author's last name except where more than one work by that author is cited in the Selected Bibliography, in which case an abbreviation of the title is included. Thus, Tuchman, *Guns*, and Tuchman, *Proud Tower;* Dedijer, *Tito*, and Dedijer, *Sarajevo*.

CHAPTER 1 (*pages 1–14*)

Bankruptcy Ball: *IWE*, Jan. 15, 1913; *AZ*, Jan. 15, 1913.
Parliament vote: *AZ*, Jan. 16, 1913.
Weather: *AZ*, Jan. 15–17, 1913.
Auersperg ball: Auersperg, p. 65.
Greengrocer ball: Schlögl, pp. 40–43.
Trotsky details: *My Life*, pp. 230, 207–9; interviews with Dr. and Mrs. Erwin Chargaff; Wolfe, p. 186; J. Sydney Jones, pp. 164–65.
Stalin details: Deutscher, *Stalin*, p. 210; J. Sydney Jones, p. 249; Delbar, p. 64; I. S. Levin, pp. 96–97.

Archduke Franz Ferdinand details: Kiszling, pp. 192–93.
Tito details: Vinterhalter, p. 44; Auty, p. 29; Dedijer, *Tito*, p. 30.
Auto Mechanics Ball: *IWE*, Jan. 25, 1913.
Freud details: Clark, pp. 352–53.
Hitler details: J. Sydney Jones, pp. 120, 145, 229, and passim; Maser, pp. 33–36.

CHAPTER 2 (*pages 15–23*)
Duties of Minister of Exterior Affairs: *AZ*, June 23, 1913.
Ethnic statistics and details: May, p. 428; A. J. P. Taylor, pp. 221, 263, 265; Kiszling, p. 215; Corti, p. 312; Dedijer, *Sarajevo*, pp. 70, 75, 110.
On nationalities' problem: Possony, p. 149.
Lenin on Stalin: Wolfe, p. 577.
Troyanovsky details: Smith, pp. 279, 284.
Trotsky on Stalin encounter: Deutscher, *The Prophet Armed*, p. 209.
Stalin letter quote: Smith, p. 276.
Stalin's treatise on nationalities: Wolfe, p. 581; Smith, pp. 292–94; Hingley, pp. 71–73.
Stalin's activities in Vienna: Deutscher, *Stalin*, p. 117.

CHAPTER 3 (*pages 24–40*)
Schuhmeier assassination: *NFP* and *AZ*, Feb. 12, 13, 14, 1913.
Schönberg concert riot: Spiel, p. 172.
Student *keller* fights: *AZ*, Mar. 26, 1913.
Attack on Negro: *AZ*, Apr. 8, 1913.
Schuhmeier funeral: Barea, p. 344; J. Sydney Jones, p. 251; Johnston, p. 101; *AZ*, Feb. 17, 1913.
Housemaids' hours: *AZ*, July 24, 1913.
Schuhmeier's Parliament speeches and housing conditions: Barea, pp. 336–37.
Vanderbilt quote on Austrian aristocrats: Barea, p. 356.
Theodore Roosevelt quote on same: Tuchman, *Proud Tower*, p. 327.
Austrian aristocrats, details: Auersperg, pp. 28, 32, 40–45; Friedländer, *Glanz*, p. 194; Fritsche, pp. 265, 363–66.
Princess Metternich sobriquet: Barea, p. 323.
Franz Ferdinand insanity rumors: Steed, *Thirty Years*, p. 367; Auersperg, p. 78.
Franz Ferdinand's courtship and marriage: Brook-Shepherd, pp. 77, 91, 108–10; Kiszling, pp. 39–47.
Franz Ferdinand and General Conrad: Kiszling, pp.160–200 passim.
General Conrad's tic: Redlich, p. 197.
Franz Ferdinand remarks at Duke of Wurtemburg dinner: Kiszling, p. 193.

Franz Ferdinand letter to Berchtold: Kann, pp. 219–20.
Franz Ferdinand's emissary's message to General Conrad: Kiszling, pp. 196–97.
Correspondence between Franz Ferdinand and Kaiser Wilhelm: Kann, p. 80; Kiszling, p. 198.
Emperor Franz Joseph's message to Tsar: Kiszling, pp. 193–94.
Reduction of Austrian forces at Russian border and Franz Ferdinand's travel south: Kiszling, p. 199.

CHAPTER 4 (*pages 41–53*)
March/April mood and weather in Vienna: *IWE* and *Fremd.*, April 1913 issues passim.
Spring suicide statistics and Wärmstuben: *AZ*, Mar. 3, 1913.
Dante's *Inferno* film and Vienna weather: *AZ*, April 1913 issues passim.
German Consul General's dinner party: Redlich, p. 194.
May weather and blossoms in Vienna: *IWE* and *NFP*, early May issues passim.
Spring description by Trotsky's wife: Trotsky, p. 230.
Trotsky quotes on Russia versus the West: Deutscher, *Trotsky*, pp. 180–93 passim.
Stalin's arrest: Deutscher, *Stalin*, p. 122.
Trotsky and art in Vienna: Deutscher, *Trotsky*, 184.
Trotsky and Viennese Socialist café intellectuals: Trotsky, *My Life*, pp. 207–11.
Trotsky and psychoanalysis: Trotsky, *My Life*, p. 220.
Freud-Trotsky analogies: Clark, p. 196; Wolf, p. 254.
Freud conquistador quote: Clark, p. 212.
Freud on Adler: Clark, p. 311.
Freud's patronage of Café Landtmann: based on research by Timms and conveyed to this author in interview in 1988, New York.
Freud's evening habits: Clark, p. 217.
Freud's self-confessed philistinism: Clark, p. 196.
Dr. Starr on Freud's morals: Clark, p. 324.
Freud's comment on Starr's charges: Clark, p. 324.
Jung on Freud's "triangle": *Portable Jung*, p. xviii.
Freud's mushroom hunting: Clark, p. 199; Martin Freud, p. 59.
Psycho-Analytical Society Spring Outing: Ernest Jones, vol. 2, p. 99.

CHAPTER 5 (*pages 54–62*)
On May Day parade conception at Berggasse 19: Clark, p. 112.
May Day weather and workers' march: *AZ*, May 2, 1913.
May 1 as aristocrats' promenade: Groner, p. 446.

Upper class fear of May Day march: Barea, pp. 310–11.
Stefan Zweig on same subject: Barea, p. 312.
Hitler on May Day: *Mein Kampf*, pp. 40–43.
Hitler and prostitutes: J. Sydney Jones, pp. 58–59.
Hitler's philosophy formed in Vienna: Hitler, p. 30.
Hitler's departure for Germany: Bullock, p. 47.
Hitler's last days in Vienna, revisiting old haunts: J. Sydney Jones, p. 243.
Hitler's draft-dodging: J. Sydney Jones, p. 252.
Redlich-Krobatin encounter: Redlich, p. 198.
Montenegro crisis and its end: Redlich, p. 199; May, p. 464; Kiszling, p. 204.
Montenegro, Franz Ferdinand, and Redl: Asprey, p. 263.
Franz Ferdinand at Konopiste: Auersperg, p. 87.
Kaiser's daughter's marriage: Kiszling, p. 204
Franz Ferdinand's Derby plans: Brook-Shepherd, p. 93; Fritsche, p. 371.

CHAPTER 6 (*pages 63–76*)
May weather: *IWE*, May 26, 1913.
Hitler departs Vienna, May 24, 1913: J. Sydney Jones, p. 253.
Detectives' stakeout: Asprey, p. 237.
Why the stakeout: Asprey, p. 236.
Further stakeout background: Asprey, pp. 237–38.
Colonel Redl details: Asprey, p. 269.
Stakeout pays off: Asprey, pp. 243–46.
General Conrad gets Redl news at Grand Hotel: Asprey, pp. 252–53.
Redl instructed to commit suicide at Hotel Klomser: Asprey, pp. 256–58.
Redl news as initially presented in Vienna press: Asprey, pp. 262–63.
Redl fully exposed in press (Kisch story): Asprey, pp. 264–66.
Redl's decorations and honors: Asprey, pp. 194, 222–23, 150.
Redl's corruption: Asprey, pp. 263, 272.
Redl's treason details, information betrayed: *INSJ*, October 1987, p. 187.
Repercussions of Redl case: Asprey, pp. 266, 287–90.
Exclusion of Franz Ferdinand from Imperial wedding in Germany: Kiszling, p. 205.
Franz Ferdinand accuses General Conrad on Redl: Redlich, p. 202; Asprey, p. 280.
Berlin reaction to Redl: Asprey, p. 286.
Franz Joseph's reaction to Redl: Corti, p. 394.

CHAPTER 7 (*pages 77–88*)
Background and description of Corpus Christi procession: Auersperg, p. 63; Friedländer, *Glanz*, pp. 33–38; *IWE*, May 23, 1913.

Derby details: Fritsche, pp. 371–73; *IWE*, June 9, 1913.
Redl's poor childhood: Asprey, pp. 25–26.
Redl's brothers change names: Asprey, p. 289.
Zweig's reaction to Redl: Asprey, p. 267.
Zeppelin over Vienna: *AZ*, June 10, 1913.
Ladies fainting in Berlin: *AZ*, June 15, 1913.
Theater fire: *AZ*, June 18, 1913.
Film watching causes speech regression: *WMW*, July 1913.
Genesis of Second Balkan War: May, p. 465.
Hot summer and police helmets: *AZ*, June 5, 1913.
Postal unemployed: *AZ*, July 2, 1913.
Poor in New York heat: *AZ*, July 5, 1913.
History of Franz Joseph–Schratt relationship: Haslip, pp. 63, 70.
Franz Joseph remark on monarchy going under: Corti, p. 431.

CHAPTER 8 (*pages 89–108*)
Franz Ferdinand's efforts to restrain Austria: Kiszling, p. 210.
Franz Joseph's letter to Schratt: *Briefe*, p. 392.
Franz Joseph's military and diplomatic decisions: *NFP* and *AZ*, Aug. 1–10, 1913, issues; Kiszling, pp. 211–12.
Hitler draft-evasion investigation: Fest, p. 61.
Assassination attempt on Governor of Croatia: Dedijer, *Sarajevo*, pp. 273–75.
Aljinović threatening Franz Ferdinand: Dedijer, *Sarajevo*, p. 276.
Franz Ferdinand's letter to Berchtold: Kann, p. 223.
Franz Ferdinand's sigh about "how" Franz Ferdinand is: Auersperg, p. 89.
Austria sponsoring Lenin: *Lenin*, p. 146; Possony, pp. 134–38.
Bolshevik "summer conference": Possony, pp. 145–46.
Trotsky and 1905 revolution: Wolfe, pp. 285, 333.
Trotsky versus Lenin: Wolfe, p. 253.
Lenin on Trotsky ("absurd, semi-anarchist . . ."): Wolfe, p. 292.
Trotsky on Lenin ("master-squabbler . . ."): Shub, p. 75.
Trotsky off to cover Balkan war: Deutscher, *Trotsky*, pp. 205–6.
Freud off to Marienbad: Jones, vol. 2, p. 99.
Jones on Freud's structuring of International Psycho-Analytical Association: Clark, p. 296.
Freud on Jung as his successor: Clark, pp. 296–97.
Jung on Freud's libido dogma: *Portable Jung*, pp. xviii–xix.
Jung abandoning Freud's libido dogma: Clark, pp. 330–31.
Jung defies Freud in letter to him: Clark, pp. 328–29.
Kaiser anniversary: *NFP*, Jan. 28, 1913.
Tsar newsreels: *AZ*, Aug. 19, 1913.

Rilke on Russian exiles: Leppmann, p. 121.
Freud's reply to Jung: Clark, p. 329.
Totem and Taboo as part of Freud's anti-Jung stance: Clark, p. 352.
Freud's rheumatism: Jones, vol. 2, pp. 99–100.
Freud in the Dolomites: Jones, vol. 2, pp. 100–101.
Psycho-Analytical Congress maneuvering: Jones, vol. 2, pp. 148–52; Clark, p. 331.
Jung to Jones on not voting "Christian": Jones, vol. 2, p. 102.
Freud's "delicious days" quote: Jones, vol. 2, p. 103.
Freud's "lonely weeks" quote: Clark, p. 358; Bakan, p. 123.
Freud's Rome neurosis: Clark, p. 200; Bakan, p. 177.
Freud's first Rome visit in 1901: Clark, p. 202.
Freud's Moses identification: Clark, pp. 12, 358, 360.
Freud as "good hater": Clark, p. 333.
Dreiser on Freud: Clark, p. 421.
Freud quotes on Michelangelo's *Moses:* Bakan, pp. 125–26; Clark, p. 359.
Freud's "nonanalytic child" quote: Clark, p. 358.
Freud on Michelangelo and Pope Julius II: Bakan, p. 127.
Freud's conciliatory intentions vis-à-vis Jung: Jones, vol. 2, p. 149.

CHAPTER 9 (*pages 109–127*)
Bregenz peace meeting details: *AZ*, Aug. 5, 1913.
Vienna's mellow summer scenes: *AZ*, Aug. 7 and 13, 1913.
Schuhmeier widow asks lenience for killer: *AZ*, Sept. 11, 1913.
Zionist Congress: *AZ*, Sept. 19, 1913.
Kafka in Vienna that September: Hayman, p. 168.
Franz Joseph and Kinetophone in Ischl: Corti, p. 394.
Franz Joseph appoints Franz Ferdinand Inspector General: Kiszling, p. 261.
Franz Joseph return to Vienna September 3: *AZ*, Sept. 4, 1913.
Fall fashions: *IWE*, Sept. 29, 1913; *AZ*, Nov. 30, 1913.
Fiacres encouraged: *AZ*, Nov. 10, 1913.
Tangos at Industrialists' Ball: *Fremd.*, Sept. 28, 1913.
Tangos taboo with Kaiser: Cowles, p. 65.
Cotillion at Industrialists' Ball: *IWE*, Nov. 1, 1913.
Austria and Balkan situation: *NFP*, September and October issues passim.
Franz Ferdinand on "Serb horror stories": Kann, p. 231.
Austrian naval build-up: *AZ*, Oct. 1, 1913.
Berchtold peaceable: *AZ*, Oct. 2, 1913.
Pašić communiqué: *Fremd.*, Oct. 4, 1913.
Bolshevik "summer conference" and consequences in Russia: Possony, p. 146; Shub, p. 72.

Lenin on Austria's superior handling of nationalities: Possony, p. 149.
Beilis case: *AZ*, Oct. 7, Nov. 10, 1913.
Pleasant Churchill speech: *AZ*, Oct. 19, 1913.
Woodrow Wilson published in German: *AZ*, Sept. 5, 1913.
William Jennings Bryan peace performance: *AZ*, Sept. 5, 1913.
Jim Brady quote: *IWE*, Sept. 3, 1913.
Franz Ferdinand royal English hunt announced: *WZ*, Oct. 1, 1913.
Sophie incognito luncheon guest at Buckingham Palace: Brook-Shepherd, p. 204.
Franz Ferdinand informs General Conrad on Sarajevo plans via Potiorek: Dedijer, *Sarajevo*, p. 286.
Chicago plans to kill Franz Ferdinand: Dedijer, *Sarajevo*, p. 276.
Bohemian maneuvers: Kiszling, pp. 262–63.
Franz Ferdinand urges modern navy: Brook-Shepherd, p. 142.
Franz Ferdinand barks at Conrad: Kiszling, p. 265.
Conrad to Gina quotes: Gina Conrad von Hötzendorf, pp. 72, 77, 84.
Conrad offers resignation: Kiszling, p. 265.
Franz Ferdinand choice for Conrad successor: Kiszling, p. 266.
Franz Ferdinand summoned to Hofburg: Auersperg, p. 101
Franz Ferdinand's friendly letter to Conrad: Kiszling, p. 266.
Kaiser to Franz Ferdinand on Albania: Corti, p. 391.
Conrad–Franz Joseph exchange on Germany's commitment: Corti, pp. 381–82.
Franz Ferdinand versus Conrad Leipzig scene: Kiszling, pp. 268–69.
Post-Leipzig jockeyings of Conrad and Franz Ferdinand: Kann, p. 232; Auersperg, p. 102.
Austrian and Italian demarches to Serbia: May, p. 468.
Serbia yields: May, p. 468.
Franz Ferdinand letter to Berchtold: Kann, p. 233.
Franz Ferdinand host to Kaiser at Konopiste: Kiszling, pp. 269–70; Brook-Shepherd, pp. 89–90.

CHAPTER 10 (*pages 128–131*)
Franz Ferdinand shooting at Windsor: Brook-Shepherd, pp. 207–10.
London *Times* quote on visit: *AZ*, Nov. 25, 1913.
Russian Prime Minister toast in Berlin: *AZ*, Nov. 20, 1913.
Total of game killed at Windsor: *Fremd.*, Nov. 23, 1913.

CHAPTER 11 (*pages 132–145*)
Trotsky mood: Trotsky, *My Life*, p. 230, and interview with Dr. and Mrs. Erwin Chargaff.

Trotsky "human locust" quote: Trotsky, *My Life*, p. 227.
Trotsky's Bulgaria sympathy: Deutscher, *Trotsky*, p. 205.
Meeting of Bulgarian King and Franz Joseph: *Fremd.*, Nov. 19, 1913.
Schratt soirée for Bulgarian King: Haslip, p. 260.
Vienna celebrates triumph-over-Napoleon centennial: Corti, p. 395; *NFP*, Oct. 17, 1913.
Franz Joseph at celebration: *"Wein 1913: Wartesaal der Geschichte"* (newsreel of event in Austrian State Television documentary).
All Souls' Day: Friedländer, *Glanz*, p. 344; *IWE*, Nov. 3, 1913.
Caruso in Vienna: *AZ*, Sept. 13, 1913.
Maria Jeritza in *Girl of the Golden West: AZ*, Sept. 19, 1913.
Jascha Heifetz: *AZ*, Mar. 1, 1914, referring to earlier appearance.
Pygmalion: AZ and *NFP*, Oct. 16, 1913.
Everyman: AZ, Dec. 20, 1913.
Thomas Mann: *AZ*, Dec. 6, 1913.
Jack Johnson, boxing champion: *AZ*, Sept. 17, 1913.
Chess champ Lasker: *AZ*, Nov. 29, 1913.
John Galsworthy: *AZ*, Oct. 7, 1913.
Zola's *Germinal: AZ*, Sept. 3, 1913.
Austrian economics: Jaszi, pp. 209–12; *AZ*, Dec. 20, 1913.
Slum scenes: *AZ*, Jan. 19, 1914.
Suicide statistics: *AZ*, Jan. 7, 1914.
Funeral habits: Friedländer, *Glanz*, p. 233.
Warm fall and winter weather: *AZ*, Oct. 5, Dec. 5, Dec. 7, and Dec. 30, 1913.
Warm-winter scenes: *AZ*, Dec. 7, 1913; *IWE*, Dec. 27, 1913.
Christmas scenes: Wilhelm, p. 97; Friedländer, *Glanz*, pp. 196–99.
New Year's Eve scene: *AZ* and *IWE*, Jan. 2, 1914.
Pummerin: Groner, p. 450.

CHAPTER 12 (*pages 146–151*)
Molten-lead game: author's interviews.
Archducal baby: *AZ*, Jan. 9, 1914.
Fifty-two suicides: *AZ*, Feb. 26, 1914.
Sudden blizzard: *AZ*, Jan. 9, 1914.
Serb cable on Habsburg baby: *WZ*, Jan. 11, 1914.
Serb Prince on Prime Minister to Russia: May, p. 469.
French-Russian ties against Central Powers: Corti, p. 403.
Conrad pushes for military preparedness: Kiszling, p. 270.
Franz Ferdinand counters Conrad: Brook-Shepherd, p. 211; Auersperg, p. 187.
Conrad's measures: Kiszling, p. 271.
Hitler's arrest and his letter: Maser, pp. 39–42; Bullock, p. 48.

CHAPTER 13 (*pages 152–160*)

Ilić details: Dedijer, *Sarajevo*, pp. 184–85.
Princip details: Dedijer, *Sarajevo*, p. 192.
Young Bosnians: Dedijer, *Sarajevo*, p. 175.
"Only our poets and revolutionaries awake": Dedijer, *Sarajevo*, p. 230.
Young Bosnians' abstinence: Dedijer, *Sarajevo*, p. 208.
Ilić in Second Balkan War: Dedijer, *Sarajevo*, p. 185.
Princip tries to enlist in Second Balkan War: Dedijer, *Sarajevo*, pp. 195–96.
Princip's favorite Nietzsche lines: Dedijer, *Sarajevo*, p. 288.
Princip and Ilić discuss killing Franz Ferdinand, and Princip leaves for Belgrade, via his native village: Dedijer, *Sarajevo*, pp. 283–84.
Kokoschka details: Whitford, pp. 36–37.
Kokoschka and Alma Mahler and the painting *Tempest:* Whitford, pp. 94–95.
Kokoschka on his *Tempest:* Spiel, p. 193.
Haugwitz gala: Fritsche, p. 258.
Bank Employees' Ball: *Fremd.*, Jan. 22, 1914.
Public Bath Attendants' Ball: *AZ*, Jan. 20, 1914.
Laundresses' ball: *NWT*, Feb. 9, 1914.
Ball at Court details: Brook-Shepherd, p. 211; Corti, pp. 407–8; Auersperg, p. 67.
Habsburg family ball: Fritsche, p. 256.
Cumberland Ball: Groner, p. 107; Fritsche, pp. 258–59.
Croy-Sternberg benefit: Fritsche, p. 259.
Vienna weather and mood around Ash Wednesday: *IWE*, Feb. 27, 1914; *NWT*, Feb. 28, 1914.

CHAPTER 14 (*pages 161–171*)

Albanian background: May, pp. 460–67; Corti, p. 407; *AZ*, January and February passim.
Prince of Wied details: *AZ*, February, March, and April 1914, passim; Redlich, pp. 224–28 passim.
Albanian postage stamps: *AZ*, Dec. 29, 1913; *AZ*, Jan. 22, 1914.
Wied's journey to and arrival in Albania: *NFP*, Mar. 8, 9, 10, 1914; Redlich, p. 221.
"Tragic operetta": Redlich, p. 220.
Princip's arrival in Belgrade: Dedijer, *Sarajevo*, p. 287.
Princip commemorations: Brook-Shepherd, p. 271.
Princip's father: Dedijer, *Sarajevo*, p. 189.
Student firebrands in Belgrade: Dedijer, *Sarajevo*, p. 288.

Princip-Cabrinović alliance to kill Franz Ferdinand: Kiszling, p. 285; Dedijer, *Sarajevo,* pp. 289–90.
Franz Ferdinand and Kaiser meeting at Miramare: Brook-Shepherd, p. 212; Kiszling, pp. 273–74; Albertini, p. 508; Duke of Hohenberg on-camera account about his grandfather Franz Ferdinand, in TV documentary made by Ernst Trost for Austrian State Television in the series *Das Bleibe vom Doppel-Adler.*
Mordskerl quote by Franz Ferdinand on Kaiser: Kann, p. 120.
Franz Ferdinand choice of Albanian *mbret:* Kiszling, p. 199.
Hungarian oppression of Serbs in Bosnia: Dedijer, *Sarajevo,* p. 123.
Franz Ferdinand report on Miramare to Franz Joseph: *Franz Ferdinands Lebensroman,* p. 176.

CHAPTER 15 (*pages 172–179*)
Turf gala: *NFP,* Apr. 14, 1914; *IWE,* Apr. 14, 1914.
Aeronautical Parade: Apr. 14, 1914; *IWE,* Apr. 14, 1914.
Unemployed march: *AZ,* Apr. 14, 1914.
Paragraph Fourteen dissolving Parliament: May, pp. 433–34.
"I gave them spring fever": *IWE,* Apr. 15, 1914.
Stürgkh background: May, p. 429.
Conversations with Berchtold at track: *NWT,* Apr. 15, 1914; Redlich, p. 224.
Radoteur wins race: *NFP,* Apr. 14, 1914.
Berchtold meets Italian Foreign Minister in Abbazia: *AZ,* Apr. 15, 1914; Hantsch, pp. 534–36; Fritsche, p. 266.
Russian strikes: *AZ,* Mar. 29, Apr. 7, 1914.
Vienna spring weather: *IWE,* Apr. 23, 1914.
Deliciously traditional questions: *AZ,* Mar. 10, 1914.
Princess Metternich party: Fritsche, p. 78.
Alt Wien exhibit: *AZ,* May 1, 1914.
Franz Joseph's illness announced: Corti, p. 408.

CHAPTER 16 (*pages 180–188*)
Franz Joseph's illness and succession problems and prospects: Kiszling, pp. 252–53; Cormons, p. 154; Redlich, p. 228.
Restaurant Meissl & Schadn: Groner, p. 650.
Franz Ferdinand's plans to change Empire: Kiszling, pp. 81, 252–60, 275–76; Brook-Shepherd, pp. 120, 145–50.
Franz Ferdinand versus Tisza: Dedijer, *Sarajevo,* p. 127; Albertini, vol. 1, p. 509; Kiszling, p. 205.
Franz Ferdinand's prospective appointments: Kiszling, p. 265.

Worriers in vineyard inns: *Fremd.*, Apr. 27, 1914; *IWE*, Apr. 25–May 10, 1914, passim.
"Wien, Wien": Johnston, p. 128.
Grand Hotel restaurant: Fritsche, p. 114.
General Conrad's bleak prospects: Gina Conrad, p. 109.
General Conrad's letter to Gina: Gina Conrad, pp. 29 and 31.

CHAPTER 17 (*pages 189–193*)
Grabež background: Dedijer, *Sarajevo*, p. 212; Brook-Shepherd, p. 217.
Grabež recruited by Princip: Kiszling, p. 285.
Colonel Apis details: Albertini, vol. 2, pp. 26–29; Taylor, pp. 195–96.
Apis assassinates King Alexander: Brook-Shepherd, p. 214.
Black Hand: Dedijer, *Sarajevo*, pp. 371, 376.
Princip contacts Black Hand: Dedijer, *Sarajevo*, pp. 290–93; Albertini, vol. 2, pp. 56–57.
Pistol practice: Dedijer, *Sarajevo*, p. 293.

CHAPTER 18 (*pages 194–202*)
Ilić attacks Socialists of Vienna: Dedijer, *Sarajevo*, pp. 223–24; Brook-Shepherd, p. 226.
Trotsky's impression of Viktor Adler: Trotsky, *My Life*, p. 211.
Young Bosnians' abstinence: Dedijer, *Sarajevo*, pp. 208–9.
Adler's student group: de La Grange, p. 68.
Nietzsche's influence on such groups: McGrath, pp. 69–70.
Hitler gives Mussolini works of Nietzsche: Fermi, p. 433.
Adler's version of new proletarian: McGrath, p. 214.
Socialists' many clubs: Friedländer, *Wolken*, pp. 265–69.
"World's most educated proletarians": McGrath, p. 215.
International situation tense: *NFP*, Apr. 20–May 5, 1914, passim.
Rosa Luxemburg quote: *AZ*, Feb. 21, 1914.
German Reichstag statistics and French election date: *NFP*, Apr. 20–May 5, 1914, passim.
Russian strikes: Possony, p. 154.
Anniversary session of Socialist International: *AZ*, Apr. 14, 1914.
Mahler's Third Symphony, Nietzsche, and May Day: de La Grange, pp. 101, 365–66; McGrath, pp. 222, 244.
May Day march description: *AZ*, May 2, 1914.

CHAPTER 19 (*pages 203–206*)
Freud's symptoms: Jones, vol. 2, p. 105; Schur, p. 91.
Freud's tactics vis-à-vis Jung: Clark, pp. 352–53.

Freud using "Narcissism" paper against Jung: Clark, pp. 336–37.
Jung resignation from *Yearbook:* Clark, p. 332.
Freud's "breach against my will" and "desired rupture" quotes: Clark, pp. 330 and 334, respectively.
Jung is "totally . . . incompatible": Clark, p. 334.
Barrage at Jung and completion of Freud-Jung breach: Jones (abridged), p. 325; Clark, p. 335.
Freud submits to cancer exam: Jones, vol. 2, p. 105.

CHAPTER 20 (*pages 207–215*)
Moltke-Conrad meeting in Carlsbad: Albertini, vol. 1, p. 561.
Moltke character: Thomson, pp. 142–43; Tuchman, *Guns,* pp. 98–99, 513.
Moltke on rigors of next war: Tuchman, *Guns,* p. 38.
Details of Conrad-Moltke meeting: Conrad, vol. 3, pp. 669–73; Tuchman, *Guns,* pp. 93–94.
Colonel House's report: Albertini, vol. 1, p. 550.
Rapid armament growth, statistics: Albertini, vol. 1, pp. 550–51; Kleindel, p. 303; *AZ,* May 29, 1914.
Vienna cold spell and then spring warmth: *AZ,* May 31, 1914.
Franz Joseph's recovery: Corti, p. 408.
Berchtold winner at races: *AZ,* June 3, 1914.
Berchtold speech: Hantsch, p. 538.
Mbret in Albania totters: *AZ,* June 12, 1914.
International situation seems to improve: Albertini, vol. 1, pp. 577–78.
Lenin anticipates no war: Wolfe, pp. 607–8.
Lenin offensive against Mensheviks: Wolfe, pp. 608–9.
Milksop Mensheviks: Wolfe, p. 376.
Lenin solicits financing of Bolsheviks: Possony, pp. 152–53.
Freud's Dresden conference: Clark, p. 365.
Jung resignation: Clark, p. 335.
Freud has no cancer: Jones, vol. 2, p. 105.
Jung speech in Aberdeen: Clark, p. 338.
Freud's Wolf-Man position re Jung: Clark, p. 290.

CHAPTER 21 (*pages 216–222*)
Princess Metternich "mixed dinner": Fritsche, p. 97.
Weather and mood genial in Vienna: *AZ,* June 7, 1914.
Corregidor badly reviewed: *AZ,* June 9, 1914.
Anti-Mahler bias of opera management: Kralik, p. 53.
Salome kept out of opera repertoire: *AZ,* June 17, 1914.
Selma Kurtz curtain calls: *AZ,* May 26, 1914.

Wedekind: *IWE*, May 10, 1914.
Suffragettes in England: *AZ*, June 3, 1914.
French elections: *NWT*, June 2, 1914.
Kerenski: *AZ*, May 20, 1914.
Serbian domestic politics: Reiners, p. 146; Dedijer, *Sarajevo*, pp. 387–89; Thomson, p. 47.
Urbanski sudden retirement: *AZ*, June 7, 1914.
Black Hand initiation ceremony: Dedijer, *Sarajevo*, pp. 292, 294; Albertini, vol. 2, p. 87; Schmitt, pp. 192–94; Brehm, 109–12; Dedijer, *Sarajevo*, p. 375.
Princip and company depart for Sarajevo: Dedijer, *Sarajevo*, p. 295; Auersperg, p. 187.

CHAPTER 22 (*pages 223–229*)
Jovanović calls on Bilinski: Albertini, vol. 2, pp. 102–3.
Pašić information of assassins on the way: Albertini, vol. 2, pp. 90, 98, 100.
Bilinski reasons for not informing Potiorek: Albertini, vol. 2, pp. 21, 112–13; Kiszling, p. 287.
Number of troops at Sarajevo maneuvers: Kiszling, p. 292.
Preparations for Franz Ferdinand visit: Brook-Shepherd, p. 221; Dedijer, *Sarajevo*, pp. 411–12.
Franz Ferdinand discusses Sarajevo visit with Franz Joseph: Conrad, vol. 3, p. 700; Kiszling, p. 290; Corti, p. 408; Auersperg, p. 46.
Sophie's honors at Sarajevo: Dedijer, *Sarajevo*, p. 286.
Franz Ferdinand's fear of tuberculosis: Eisenmenger, p. 174.
Franz Ferdinand's stoicism re assassins: Brook-Shepherd, p. 235.

CHAPTER 23 (*pages 230–236*)
1914 Derby details: *NFP*, June 8, 1914; *Fremd.*, June 8, 1914; *IWE*, June 8, 1914.
Kaiser visits Franz Ferdinand: Brook-Shepherd, pp. 229–32; Kiszling, p. 277.
Newspaper comment on floral scent and gunpowder: *NFP*, June 13, 1914; Brook-Shepherd, pp. 229–30.
Franz Ferdinand argues anti-Tisza case: Albertini, vol. 1, pp. 533–34; Kiszling, pp. 278–79; Hantsch, pp. 544–45; Auersperg, p. 89.
Konopiste dinner and Kaiser departs: Brook-Shepherd, p. 232; Kiszling, p. 279.
Konopiste open to public: Brehm, pp. 155–56.
Franz Ferdinand and wife prepare to leave for Sarajevo: Brook-Shepherd, p. 233; *Fremd.*, June 30, 1914.

CHAPTER 24 (*pages 237–241*)

Rail detour through Budapest: Brehm, p. 190.
Electric lights fail on train: Kiszling, p. 291; Pauli, p. 291.
Franz Ferdinand onward travel to Sarajevo: Brehm, pp.189–91; Albertini, vol. 2, p. 19.
Franz Ferdinand arrives in Ilidze: Kiszling, pp. 291–92.
Maneuver details: Kiszling, pp. 292–93.
Franz Ferdinand's cable to Franz Joseph: Kiszling, pp. 294, 345.
Deletion of "my wife and I": Dedijer, *Sarajevo*, p. 102.
Ilidze dinner: Dedijer, *Sarajevo*, pp. 9–10

CHAPTER 25 (*pages 242–248*)

Franz Ferdinand and wife start last day: Kiszling, pp. 296, 298.
Franz Ferdinand in Sarajevo, details up to first assassination attempt: Dedijer, *Sarajevo*, pp. 11–12; Brook-Shepherd, pp. 244–45; Brehm, p. 235; Kiszling, pp. 296–98.
First assassination attempt: Edmond Taylor, pp. 9, 10; *Fremd.*, June 30, 1914.
City Hall scene: Brehm, p. 241; West, p. 331–32; Kiszling, p. 298; Dedijer, *Sarajevo*, pp. 12–13.
Franz Ferdinand speech at City Hall and City Hall conversations: Dedijer, *Sarajevo*, pp. 14–15; Kiszling, pp. 299–300; Albertini, vol. 2, p. 36.

CHAPTER 26 (*pages 249–256*)

Princip and company start journey from Belgrade to Sarajevo: Dedijer, *Sarajevo*, pp. 291, 294–97; Brook-Shepherd, pp. 223–25.
Princip disciplines Cabrinović: Dedijer, *Sarajevo*, pp. 296–97.
Ilić's doubts: Dedijer, *Sarajevo*, pp. 306–9 passim.
Assassins' days in Sarajevo prior to deed: Dedijer, *Sarajevo*, pp. 305–14; Brook-Shepherd, pp. 226–27, 236–37; Pauli, p. 275.

CHAPTER 27 (*pages 257–264*)

Assassins gather at pastry shop: Dedijer, *Sarajevo*, p. 315.
Cabrinović dispute with his father: Dedijer, *Sarajevo*, p. 315.
Assassins deploy for kill: Dedijer, *Sarajevo*, pp. 316–19; Brook-Shepherd, pp. 242–44.
First attempt to kill: Brook-Shepherd, pp. 245–47; Dedijer, *Sarajevo*, p. 320; Dor, p. 40.
Second, successful attempt at Archduke's life: Dedijer, *Sarajevo*, pp. 15–16, 321–23; Brook-Shepherd, pp. 249–52; Kiszling, pp. 299–301; Dor, pp. 40–41; Pauli, pp. 278–79.

CHAPTER 28 (*pages 265–271*)
Zweig recollection: Zweig, p. 249.
Vienna happy Sunday scene: Cormons, p. 157; *NFP*, June 30, 1914; *Fremd.*, June 30, 1914.
Freud on assassination: Jones, vol. 2, p. 169.
Other responses to assassination: Hantsch, p. 557.
Franz Joseph reacts to assassination: Brehm, pp. 204–5; Corti, pp. 412–13; Crankshaw, p. 390.
Bodies' transport from Sarajevo to Vienna: Brook-Shepherd, p. 260; Kiszling, pp. 301–2; Albertini, vol. 2, p. 117.
Mortuary details in Vienna and Artstetten: Kiszling, pp. 303–5; Brook-Shepherd, pp. 262–69; Albertini, vol. 2, pp. 118–19.

CHAPTER 29 (*pages 272–281*)
Repercussions of Franz Ferdinand's testamentary stipulation to be buried in Artstetten: Kiszling, p. 302.
Serbian government's condolences and mourning: Albertini, vol. 2, p. 273.
Anti-Serb disturbances in Habsburg Empire: *AZ* and *NFP*, June 29–July 3, 1914, passim.
Austrian government deliberations: Albertini, vol. 2, pp. 124–26; Hantsch, pp. 558–60.
Cabinet opinions brought to Emperor by Berchtold: Hantsch, p. 562.
Franz Joseph's letter to Kaiser: Hantsch, p. 562; Albertini, vol. 2, p. 134.
Alexander von Hoyos mission to Berlin: Cormons, pp. 161–63; Albertini, vol. 2, p. 135.
Kaiser's reponse to Hoyos's manipulation: Thomson, p. 44.
Kaiser's words to Krupp: Berghahn, p. 193.
Austrian Ambassador's cable to Habsburg government to take drastic initiative: Albertini, vol. 2, pp. 138–39, 148; Hantsch, p. 571.
Berchtold, too late, on Hoyos's duplicity: Hantsch, pp. 572–73.
Bilinski's waffling: Redlich, p. 236.
Berchtold joins hawks: Hantsch, pp. 583–88; Albertini, vol. 2, pp. 254–55.
Berchtold in Ischl: Hantsch, pp. 589–90; Auersperg, p. 51.

CHAPTER 30 (*pages 282–287*)
Berchtold's game plan for ultimatum: Hantsch, pp. 589–92.
Depositions of caught assassins: Dedijer, *Sarajevo*, pp. 325–28, 329–32.
Cable from Belgrade: Albertini, vol. 2, pp. 173–74.
Berchtold recommends vacation to Conrad: Albertini, vol. 2, pp. 171, 256.

Other such "vacations": *WZ*, July 13, 1914.

In other countries, leaders go on vacation—German Foreign Minister: Thomson, p. 19; Tirpitz: Ludwig, p. 67; Kaiser: Balfour, p. 345, Berghahn, p. 190; Serbian Chief of Staff: Corti, p. 418, *AZ*, July 26, 1914; Poincaré: Thomson, p. 51, Edmond Taylor, p. 211; Tsar: Thomson, p. 52, Auersperg, p. 59; Churchill: Manchester, p. 465; Sir Edward Grey: Thomson, pp. 71–72; Asquith: Thomson, p. 81, Edmond Taylor, p. 210.

Vienna summer scene: *Fremd.*, *AZ*, *IWE*, July issues passim.

CHAPTER 31 (*pages 288–294*)

Freud rusticates in Carlsbad: Jones, vol. 2, p. 172.

Freud's bucolic childhood: Clark, p. 5; Walter, pp. 101–3.

Freud's "Philogenetic Fantasy": *New York Times* Science Section, Feb. 10, 1987.

Trosky's bucolic longings: Wyndham and King, unpaginated quote; Trotsky, *My Life*, pp. xvii, xix, 43.

Lenin's bucolic longings: Wolfe, pp. 40, 566, 613.

Hitler in Munich: Maser, p. 51; J. Sydney Jones, p. 222.

Kraus poem: Timms, pp. 264–65.

Kraus at Janowitz Park: Timms, pp. 255, 265.

Kraus's Manor Park quote: *Fackel* no. 400–403, Summer 1914, p. 95.

Kraus eulogy of Franz Ferdinand: *Fackel* no. 400–403, July 10, 1914, pp. 1–3.

Kraus devotees in Foreign Ministry polish ultimatum: Cormons, pp. 165–66.

Urn and chamberpot distinction: Janik and Toulmin, p. 89.

CHAPTER 32 (*pages 295–304*)

Serbian King plans travel abroad: *AZ*, July 14, 1914.

Pacific Lloyd George speech: *AZ*, July 19, 1914; *Fremd.*, July 20, 1914.

Arbeiter Zeitung placid view: *AZ*, July 10, 1914.

Berchtold's blandness to British ambassador: Dugdale, p. 294.

Berchtold's blandness to Italian ambassador: Beck, p. 35.

Bechtold's blandness to French ambassador: Beck, p. 33.

Caillaux affair: Thomson, pp. 264–67.

Poincaré and Caillaux affair: *NWT*, July 21, 1914.

British King and Irish Home Rule imbroglio: Manchester, p. 463.

Vienna music festival plans: *AZ*, July 21, 1914.

Tsar and Poincaré toasts omit all mention of Serb-Austrian problem: *AZ*, July 22, 1914.

Secret Cabinet session: Albertini, vol. 2, p. 256.

Routine announcement of Berchtold report to Franz Joseph: *WZ*, July 21, 1914.
Berchtold in Ischl re ultimatum: Hantsch, pp. 602–3, 605.
Summary of note to Serbia: Albertini, vol. 2, pp. 286–89.
British Foreign Secretary on note: Albertini, vol. 2, p. 289.
"Demarche with a time limit": Hantsch, p. 604.
Last note in diplomatic French: Crankshaw, p. 399.
Austrian Ambassador phones Serbian Ministry: Albertini, vol. 2, p. 284.
News of Austrian note reaches Serbian Prime Minister: Albertini, vol. 2, pp. 347–49.
Pašić returns to Belgrade: Albertini, p. 348–49.
Pašić at Austrian Embassy: Hantsch, p. 489; Edmond Taylor, pp. 214–15.
Serbian response to note: Albertini, vol. 2, pp. 363–64.
Austrian Ambassador rejects note, leaves Belgrade: Albertini, vol. 2, p. 373; Hantsch, p. 490.

CHAPTER 33 (*pages 305–316*)
Franz Joseph and Berchtold in receipt of Serbian reply: Albertini, vol. 2, pp. 374–75; Hantsch, p. 612.
German government in agreement with demarche: Albertini, vol. 2, pp. 266–67.
German officials stiffen upper lips: Edmond Taylor, p. 218; Albertini, vol. 2, pp. 449–50; Crankshaw, pp. 402–3.
Germans disavow influence on Austria's note: Parkinson, p. 100.
Germans think note too sharp: Albertini, vol. 2, p. 265; Ludwig, p. 92.
Churchill on note's reception in London: Churchill, p. 204.
Churchill's order to fleet: Thomson, p. 91.
Poincaré hurries home: Albertini, vol. 2, pp. 590–91.
Russian Pre-Mobilization: Albertini, vol. 2, pp. 304–5.
Conrad needs two weeks to strike: Conrad, vol. 4, p. 40; Crankshaw, p. 398.
Berchtold on war declaration as not really war: Albertini, vol. 2, pp. 388, 457–58.
War declaration by cable: Albertini, vol. 2, p. 461.
Austrian mobilization posters: Auersperg, p. 153.
Austrian restraint: Albertini, vol. 2, p. 427.
Gallantry vis-à-vis Serbian Chief of Staff: Corti, p. 418; *AZ*, July 26–27, 1914.
Yachting Kaiser kept uninformed: Albertini, vol. 2, p. 439.
"Situation . . . not entirely clear": Albertini, vol. 2, p. 433.
Kaiser hastens home: Balfour, p. 348; *AZ*, July 27, 1914.
Kaiser blusters: Albertini, vol. 2, p. 434.

Delay of transmission of Austrian note text to Kaiser: Albertini, vol. 2, pp. 440–41; Thomson, p. 101.
"Brilliant achievement": Albertini, vol. 2, p. 467.
Kaiser-Bethmann scene: Albertini, vol. 2, p. 437.
Bülow quote: Albertini, vol. 2, p. 436.
Bethmann to German Ambassador in Vienna: Ludwig, p. 223; Thomson, p. 119.
The Kaiser's Libretto C: Albertini, vol. 2, pp. 467–68.
Franz Joseph and his Minister of War: Corti, p. 421.
Franz Joseph and Frau Schratt: Haslip, p. 267.
Tsar's "I shall be overwhelmed": Edmond Taylor, p. 220.
Frenzied international cabling between governments: *NFP* and *AZ*, July 1914 issues; Albertini, vol. 2, pp. 390–651 passim.

CHAPTER 34 (*pages 317–336*)
International pro-war demonstrations: *NFP*, *Times*, July 1914 passim.
British Embassy windows broken: Dugdale, pp. 304–5.
Kraus to Sidonie: Kraus, vol. 1, p. 60.
Fackel quote: *Fackel*, July 10, 1914.
Zadruga's destruction: Dedijer, *Sarajevo*, p. 185.
Mussolini detail: Fermi, pp. 8–9.
Stalin detail: Levine, p. 4.
Pathology of industrialization: *AZ*, Feb. 2, 1913.
Russian rebellion changes to patriotism: Ludwig, p. 373; Trotsky, p. 233.
Austrian masses patriotic: Trotsky, pp. 233–34.
Paris proletariat turns pro-war: *Fremd.*, Aug. 2, 1914.
"Eine Sehnsucht" poem: Cormons, p. 167.
Rupert Brooke quote: Timms, p. 287.
"Foul peace . . . drags on": Gina Conrad, p. 31.
"Crisis . . . entered Western culture": Cormons, p. 167.
Hitler on war: Fest, p. 64.
Bethmann on war: Timms, p. 279.
Czernin on war: Czernin, p. 5.
Poincaré on war: Ludwig, p. 112.
Freud on Jung: Freud, *Freud-Salomé*, Freud letter, Nov. 6, 1913.
Jaurès assassination: Thomson, pp. 148–49.
French reservists: Thomson, p. 155.
Lenin arrested: *Osterreichische Osthefte*, May 1970.
Viktor Adler helps Trotsky as well as Lenin: Trotsky, pp. 235–36.
Arbeiter Zeitung pro-war: *AZ*, Aug. 4, 1914; Ludwig, p. 324.
Nicky-Willy cables: Albertini, vol. 2, pp. 542, 554, 555, 557, 560, 574; Albertini, vol. 3, p. 180.
Germany declares war on Russia: Albertini, vol. 3, p. 182.

Kaiser asks crowd to quiet down: *AZ*, Aug. 4, 1914.
"You will live to regret it": Edmond Taylor, p. 228.
Kaiser on British uniform: Dugdale, p. 305.
Moltke cables Conrad: Albertini, vol. 2, p. 673.
"Who rules in Berlin?" Albertini, vol. 2, p. 674.
Conrad controls Berchtold cables: Hantsch, p. 642.
"Smash my telephone": Albertini, vol. 2, p. 572.
Viviani at Jaurès funeral: Thomson, p. 193.
Poincaré's manipulations: Albertini, vol. 2, pp. 616–19.
"Russians in Berlin by All Saints' Day": Thomson, p. 175.
Churchill letter: Manchester, pp. 968–69.
Churchill mobilizes fleet: Thomson, p. 161.
". . . lamps are going out . . .": Edmond Taylor, p. 229.
"Josef K.": in Kafka's journal: Hayman, p. 183.
Wittgenstein notebook: Shanker, p. 9.
Tsar bursts into tears: Albertini, vol. 3, p. 174.
Kaiser on balcony: Thomson, p. 196; Edmond Taylor, p. 228.
Hitler on war: Hitler, p. 161.
Freud critical of Vienna: Clark, p. 39.
Freud pro-war: Clark, p. 376; Jones, vol. 2, p. 171.
Wittgenstein enlists: Shanker, pp. 8, 9.
Schönberg pro-war: Spiel, pp. 198–99.
Kokoschka's change from outsider to patriot: Whitford, pp. 69, 99–100.
Rilke "attached only by language" to Germany: Leppmann, p. 299.
Rilke's war poems: Leppmann, pp. 296–97.
Herman Hesse pro-war: Eksteins, p. 94.
Thomas Mann pro-war: Tuchman, *Guns*, p. 311.
Freud on war as opportunity for progress: *Major Works*, p. 756.
Nietzsche on progress as ascent: Nietzsche, p. 552.
Franz Joseph edits Manifesto: Hantsch, p. 618.
Franz Joseph on going under: Corti, p. 431.
Karl Kraus on proclamation: *Fackel* no. 404, Dec. 1914, p. 3.
Franz Joseph removes Tsar's decoration: Corti, pp. 430–31.
Franz Joseph changes will: Jaszi, p. 13.
British ambassador declares war: Dugdale, p. 304.
British ambassador and wife loved Vienna: Albertini, vol. 3, p. 534; Dugdale, p. 281.
British ambassador leaving Vienna and street scene: Dugdale, p. 304; *Fremd.* and *NWT*, Aug. 14, 1914.

SELECTED BIBLIOGRAPHY

PERIODICALS

Arbeiter Zeitung, Vienna, 1913–14.

Die Fackel, Vienna, 1913–14.

Fremdenblatt, Vienna, 1913–14.

Illustrirtes Wiener Extrablatt, Vienna, 1913–14.

Intelligence and National Security Journal, London, 1987.

Die Muskete, Vienna, 1913–14.

Neue Freie Presse, Vienna, 1913–14.

Neues Wiener Tagblatt, Vienna, 1913–14.

Österreichische Osthefte, Vienna, 1970.

Reichspost, Vienna, 1913–14.

The Times, London, July 1914.

Wiener Medizinische Wochenschrift, Vienna, 1913.

Wiener Zeitung, Vienna, 1913–14.

GENERAL

Adler, Victor. *Im Spiegel Seiner Zeitgenossen.* Vienna: Verlag der Weiner Volksbuchhandlung, 1968.

Albertini, Luigi. *The Origins of the War of 1914,* 2 vols. London, New York, Toronto: Oxford Univ. Press, 1953.

Asprey, Robert B. *The Panther's Feast.* New York: G. P. Putnam's Sons, 1959.

Asquith, Herbert Henry. *The Genesis of the War.* London, 1923.

Auersperg, Alois Prinz von. *Menschen von Gestern und Heute.* Unpublished Memoir.

Barea, Ilsa. *Vienna.* New York: Alfred A. Knopf, 1966.

Beck, James M. *The Evidence in the Case.* New York and London: G. P. Putnam's Sons, 1914.

Berghahn, V. R. *Germany and the Approach of War in 1914.* New York: St. Martin's Press, 1973.

Bethmann-Hollweg, Theobald von. *Betrachtungen zum Weltkriege.* (2 vol.). Berlin, 1919–1922.

Boyer, John W. *Political Radicalism in Late Imperial Vienna.* Chicago, London: Univ. of Chicago Press, 1981.

Brehm, Bruno. *Die Throne Stürzen.* Munich: R. Piper Verlag, 1951.
Chlumecky, Leopold Freiherr von. *Erzherzog Franz Ferdinand: Wirken und Wollen.* Berlin, 1929.
Churchill, Winston Leonard Spencer. *The World Crisis.* Vol. 1. New York: Charles Scribner's Sons, 1924.
Cormons, Ernest U. *Schicksale und Schatten.* Salzburg: Müller Verlag, 1951.
Cowles, Virginia. *1913, Abschied von einer Epoche.* Frankfurt am Main: S. Fischer, 1969.
Crankshaw, Edward. *The Fall of the House of Hapsburg.* New York: Viking Press, 1963.
Czernin, Ottokar. *Im Weltkriege.* Berlin, Vienna: Ullstein and Co., 1919.
DA Republic Österreich, Staatsamt für Ausseres. *Diplomatische Aktenstücke zur Vorgeschichte des Krieges 1914. Ergänzungen und Nachträge zum Österreichisch-Ungarischen Rotbuch.* 3 vols. Vienna, 1919; London, 1920.
Dedijer, Vladimir. *The Road to Sarajevo.* New York: Simon and Schuster, 1966.
Dor, Milo. *Dor Letzte Sonntag.* Vienna, Munich: Verlag Almathea, 1982.
Eksteins, Modris. *Rites of Spring, the Great War and the Birth of the Modern Age.* Boston: Houghton Mifflin Co., 1989.
Friedländer, Otto. *Letzter Glanz der Märchenstadt.* Vienna: Ring, 1947.
———. *Wolken Drohen Über Wien.* Vienna: Ring, 1949.
Fritsche, Victor von. *Bilder aus dem Österreichischen Hof—und Gesellschaftsleben.* Vienna: Gerlach und Wirdling, 1914.
Groner, Richard. *Wien Wie Es War.* Vienna, Munich: Fritz Molden, 1965.
Hamann, Brigitte. *Die Habsburger.* Vienna: Überreuter, 1988.
Hanak, Harry. *Great Britain and Austria-Hungary During the First World War.* London, New York, Toronto: Oxford Univ. Press, 1962.
Hanak, Jacques. *Im Sturm eines Jahrhunderts.* Vienna: Verlag der Wiener Volksbuchhandlung, 1952.
Hubmann, Franz. *K.u.K. Familienalbum.* Vienna, Munich, Zurich: Verlag Fritz Molden, 1971.
Janik, Allan, and Stephen Toulmin. *Wittgenstein's Vienna.* New York: Simon and Schuster, 1973.
Jaszi, Oscar. *The Dissolution of the Habsburg Monarchy.* Chicago, London: Univ. of Chicago Press, 1929.
Johnston, William M. *The Austrian Mind.* Berkeley, Los Angeles, London: Univ. of California Press, 1972.
Jung, Carl G. *The Portable Jung.* Edited by Joseph Campbell. New York: Penguin, 1976.

Kleindel, Walter. *Österreich—Daten zur Geschichte und Kultur.* Vienna: Ueberreuter Verlag, 1978.
Kralik, Heinrich. *The Vienna Opera House.* Vienna: Rosenbaum Publishers, 1955.
Kraus, Karl. *Briefe an Sidonie von Nadherny.* Frankfurt: Insel Verlag, 1973.
La Grange, Henry Louis de. *Mahler.* Garden City, N.Y.: Doubleday, 1973.
Löwy, A. G. *Die Weltgeschichte Ist das Weltgericht, Bucharin, Vision des Kommunismus.* Vienna, Frankfurt, Zurich: Europa, 1969.
Ludwig, Emil. *July '14.* Translated by C. A. Macartney. New York, London: G. P. Putnam's Sons, 1929.
McGrath, William J. *Dionysian Art and Populist Politics in Austria.* New Haven, London: Yale Univ. Press, 1974.
Massie, Robert K., and Jeffrey Fineston. *The Last Courts of Europe.* New York: Greenwich House, 1983.
May, Arthur J. *The Habsburg Monarchy 1867–1914.* New York: W. W. Norton, 1968.
Moltke, Helmuth von. *Erinnerungen, Briefe, Dokumente 1877–1916.* Edited by Eliza von Moltke. Stuttgart, 1922.
Nietzsche, Friedrich. *The Portable Nietzsche.* Edited by Walter Kaufmann. New York: Penguin Books, 1954.
Parkinson, Roger. *Origins of World War I.* New York: G. P. Putnam's Sons, 1971.
Pauli, Hertha. *The Secret of Sarajevo.* New York: Appleton-Century, 1965.
Redlich, Josef. *Schicksalsjahre Österreich 1908–1919: Das politische Tagebuch Josef Redlichs.* Graz, Cologne: Verlag Hermann Böhlaus Nachf., 1954.
Reiners, Ludwig. *In Europa Gehen die Lichter Aus.* Munich: DTV Verlag, 1952.
Schlögl-Karmel, Friedrich. *Wiener Skizzen.* Vienna: Wiener, 1946.
Shebenko, N. *Souvenirs: Essai historique sur les origines de la guerre de 1914.* Paris: Bibliothèque Diplomatique, 1936.
Spiel, Hilde. *Vienna's Golden Autumn 1866–1938.* London: Weidenfeld and Nicolson, 1987.
Stanojević, Stanoje. *Die Ermordung des Erzherzogs Franz Ferdinand.* Frankfurt, 1923.
Steed, Henry Wickham. *The Hapsburg Monarchy.* London: Constable and Company Ltd., 1914.
———. *Through Thirty Years 1892–1922.* 2 vols. Garden City, NY: Doubleday, Page, 1924.
Stoye, John. *The Siege of Vienna.* New York, Chicago, San Francisco: Holt, Rinehart & Winston, 1965.

Taylor, A. J. P. *The Habsburg Monarchy 1809–1918.* London: Hamish Hamilton, 1957.
Taylor, Edmond. *The Fall of the Dynasties—The Collapse of the Old Order 1905–1922.* Garden City, NY: Doubleday, 1963.
Thomson, George Malcolm. *The Twelve Days, 24 July to 4 August 1914.* New York: G. P. Putnam's Sons, 1964.
Tuchman, Barbara W. *The Guns of August.* New York: Macmillan, 1962, 1988.
———. *The Proud Tower.* New York: Macmillan, 1966.
Vergo, Peter. *Art in Vienna, 1898–1918.* New York: Phaidon Press Ltd., 1975.
Walter, E. V. *Placeways—A Theory of the Human Environment.* Chapel Hill, NC: Univ. of North Carolina Press, 1988.
West, Rebecca. *Black Lamb and Grey Falcon.* New York: Penguin, 1982.
White, Leigh. *Balkan Caesar: Tito versus Stalin.* New York: Charles Scribner's Sons, 1951.
Wilhelm, S. *Wiener Wandelbilder.* Vienna, Leipzig: Brüder Rosenbaum, n.d.
Zweig, Stefan. *Die Welt von Gestern.* Stockholm: Bermann-Fischer, 1944.

Autobiographies, Memoirs, and Biographies

Bülow, Prince Bernard von. *Memoirs (1905–9).* 4 vols. London and New York, 1931.
Conrad von Hötzendorf, Franz Graf. *Aus Meiner Dienstzeit 1906–1918.* 5 vols. Vienna, 1921–1925.
Conrad von Hötzendorf, Gina Gräfin. *Mein Leben mit Conrad von Hötzendorf.* Leipzig: Grethlein & Co., Nachf., 1935.
Dugdale, Edgar T.S. *Maurice de Bunsen: Diplomat and Friend.* London: John Murray, 1934.
Fermi, Laura. *Mussolini.* Chicago: Univ. of Chicago Press, 1961.
Grey, Sir Edward. *Twenty-Five Years 1892–1916.* 2 vols. London, 1925.
Grosse Österreicher: Neue Osterreichische Biographie. Vienna, Munich: Almathea Verlag, 1980.
Hantsch, Hugo. *Leopold Graf Berchtold.* Graz: Verlag Styria, 1963.
Hayman, Ronald. *Kafka: A Biography.* New York: Oxford Univ. Press, 1982.
Karolyi, Michael. *Memoirs of Michael Karolyi.* New York: E. P. Dutton, 1956.
Leppmann, Wolfgang. *Rilke: A Life.* Translated by Russell M. Stockman. New York: Fromm International Publishing, 1984.
Manchester, William. *The Last Lion.* Boston: Little, Brown, 1983.
Österreichisches Biographisches Lexikon 1815–1950. Graz, Cologne: Verlag Hermann Bohlaus, 1957.

Szeps, Berta. *My Life and History*. Translated by John Summerfield. New York: Alfred A. Knopf, 1939.

Timms, Edward. *Karl Kraus—Apocalyptic Satirist: Culture and Catastrophe in Habsburg Vienna*. New Haven: Yale Univ. Press, 1986.

Tirpitz, Alfred von. *My Memoirs*. 2 vols. London, 1919.

Whitford, Frank. *Oscar Kokoschka: A Life*. New York: Atheneum, 1986.

Wolfe, Bertram D. *Three Who Made a Revolution*. New York: Stein and Day, 1984.

On the Archduke Franz Ferdinand

Brook-Shepherd, Gordon. *Archduke of Sarajevo—The Romance and Tragedy of Franz Ferdinand of Austria*. Boston, Toronto: Little, Brown and Co., 1984.

Eisenmenger, Victor. *Erzherzog Franz Ferdinand—Seinem Andenken Gewidmet von Seinem Leibarzt*. Zurich, Leipzig, Vienna, 1930.

Franz Ferdinands Lebensroman: Ein Dokument Unserer Zeit. Stuttgart: Verlag Robert Lutz, 1919.

Kann, Robert A. *Erzherzog Franz Ferdinand Studien*. Vienna: Verlag für Geschichte an Politik, 1976.

Kiszling, Rudolph. *Erherzog Franz Ferdinand von Österreich*. Graz, Cologne: Hermann Bohlaus Nachf., 1953.

On Emperor Franz Joseph

Briefe: Kaiser Franz Josephs an Frau Katherina Schratt. Vienna, Munich, 1964.

Corti, Egon Caesar Conte, and Hans Sokol. *Der Alte Kaiser, Franz Joseph I*. Graz, Vienna, Cologne: Verlag Styria, 1955.

Haslip, Joan. *The Emperor and His Actress*. New York: Dial Press, 1982.

On Freud

Bakan, David, *Sigmund Freud and the Jewish Mystical Tradition*. New York: Schocken, 1965.

Clark, Ronald W. *Freud: The Man and the Cause*. New York: Random House, 1980.

Freud, Martin. *Glory Reflected: Sigmund Freud—Man and Father*. London: Angus & Robertson, 1957.

Freud, Sigmund. *Letters of Sigmund Freud 1873–1939*. Edited by Ernst L. Freud. New York: Basic Books, 1975.

Freud, Sigmund, and Lou Andreas-Salomé. *Sigmund Freud and Lou Andreas-Salomé: Letters*. Edited by Ernst Pfeiffer. New York: W. W. Norton, 1985.

Jones, Ernest. *The Life and Work of Sigmund Freud*. 3 vols. London: Hogarth Press, 1953, 1955, 1957.

———. *The Life and Work of Sigmund Freud.* Abridged Edition Edited by Lionel Trilling and Steven Marcus. New York: Basic Books, 1961.
The Major Works of Sigmund Freud. Chicago: William Benton/Encyclopaedia Britannica, Inc., 1952.

On Hitler

Bullock, Alan. *Hitler: A Study in Tyranny.* Revised Edition. New York: Harper and Row, 1964.
Fest, Joachim. *Hitler.* New York: Harcourt Brace, 1974.
Hitler, Adolf. *Mein Kampf.* Boston: Houghton Mifflin, 1942.
Jenks, William A. *Vienna and the Young Hitler.* New York: Columbia Univ. Press, 1960.
Jones, J. Sydney. *Hitler in Vienna 1907–1913.* New York: Stein and Day, 1983.
Kubizek, August. *The Young Hitler I Knew: The Story of Our Friendship.* London: A. Wingate, 1950.
Maser, Werner. *Hitlers Briefe und Notizen.* Düsseldorf, Vienna: 1973.

On Lenin

Lenin: A Biography. Moscow: Progress Publishers, 1983.
Possony, Stefan T. *Lenin: The Compulsive Revolutionary.* Chicago: Henry Regnery, 1963.
Shub, David. *Lenin.* New York: Mentor, 1948.

On Stalin

Delbars, Yves. *The Real Stalin.* London: George Allen & Unwin Ltd., 1953.
Deutscher, Isaac. *Stalin: A Political Biography.* New York: Oxford Univ. Press, 1949.
Fischer, Louis. *The Life and Death of Stalin.* New York: Harper Brothers, 1952.
Hingley, Ronald. *Joseph Stalin: Man and Legend.* New York: McGraw-Hill, 1974.
Levine, Isaac Don. *Stalin.* New York: Cornwall Press, 1931.
Lyons, Eugene. *Stalin: Czar of All the Russias.* Philadelphia: J. B. Lippincott, 1940.
MacNeal, Robert H. "Trotsky's Interpretation of Stalin." In Rigby, T. H., ed. *Stalin.* Englewood Cliffs, N.J.: Prentice-Hall, 1966.
Murphy, J. T. *Stalin.* London: 1945.
Smith, Edward Ellis. *The Young Stalin.* New York: Farrar, Straus and Giroux, 1967.
Souvanine, Boris. *Stalin: A Critical Study of Bolshevism.* New York: Longmans, Green and Co., 1939.

Trotsky, Leon. *Stalin: An Appraisal of the Man and His Influence.* Translated by Charles Malamuth. New York: Harper and Brothers, 1946.

On Tito

Archer, Jules. *Red Rebel: Tito of Yugoslavia.* New York: Julian Messner, 1968.

Auty, Phyllis. *Tito: A Biography.* London: Longman, 1970.

Bilainkin, George. *Tito.* London: Williams & Northgate Ltd., 1949.

Dedijer, Vladimir. *Tito.* New York: Simon and Schuster, 1953.

Vinterhalter, Vilko. *Der Weg des Joseph Broz.* Vienna: Europa Verlag, 1969.

On Trotsky

Carmichael, Joel. *Trotsky: An Appreciation of His Life.* New York: St. Martin's Press, 1975.

Deutscher, Isaac. *The Prophet Armed: Trotsky: 1879–1921.* New York: Oxford Univ. Press, 1954.

Howe, Irving. *Leon Trotsky.* New York: Penguin, 1978.

Serge, Victor. *Vie et Mort de Trotsky.* Paris: Le Livre Contemporain, 1951.

Trotsky, Leon. *My Life.* Gloucester, MA.: P. Smith, 1970.

———. *Our Revolution.* New York: Henry Holt, 1918.

Wyndham, Francis, and David King. *Trotsky, A Documentary.* London: Penguin, 1972.

On Wilhelm II

Balfour, Michael. *The Kaiser and His Times.* Boston: Houghton Mifflin, 1964.

On Wittgenstein

Shanker, Stuart, ed. *Ludwig Wittgenstein: Critical Assessments.* London: Croom Helm, 1986.

INDEX

THUNDER AT TWILIGHT VIENNA 1913 / 1914

THUNDER AT TWILIGHT is a landmark of historical vision, drawing on hitherto untapped sources to illuminate two crucial years in the life of the extraordinary city of Vienna—and in the life of the twentieth century.

It was during the carnival of 1913 that a young Stalin arrived in Vienna on a mission that would launch him into the upper echelon of Russian revolutionaries, and it was here that he first collided with Trotsky. It was in Vienna that the failed artist Adolf Hitler kept daubing watercolors and spouting tirades at fellow drifters in a flophouse. Here Archduke Franz Ferdinand had a troubled audience with Emperor Franz Joseph—and soon the bullet that killed the Archduke would set off the Great War that would kill ten million more.

With luminous prose that has twice made him a finalist for the National Book Award, Frederic Morton evokes the opulent, elegant, incomparable sunset metropolis—Vienna on the brink of cataclysm.

FREDERIC MORTON was born in Vienna and lives in New York. His short stories have been chosen for BEST AMERICAN SHORT STORIES, and two of his critically acclaimed nonfiction works, THE ROTHSCHILDS and A NERVOUS SPLENDOR, have been bestsellers.

HISTORY
US $18.95 / $26.95 CAN

Da Capo Press
A Member of the Perseus Books Group
www.dacapopress.com

Cover illustration: Reinhold Volkel, The Cafe Griensteidl